Human-Computer Interaction Series

Human-Computer Interaction is a multidisciplinary field focused on human aspects of the development of computer technology. As computer-based technology becomes increasingly pervasive - not just in developed countries, but worldwide - the need to take a human-centered approach in the design and development of this technology becomes ever more important. For roughly 30 years now, researchers and practitioners in computational and behavioral sciences have worked to identify theory and practice that influences the direction of these technologies, and this diverse work makes up the field of human–computer interaction. Broadly speaking it includes the study of what technology might be able to do for people and how people might interact with the technology. In this series we present work which advances the science and technology of developing systems which are both effective and satisfying for people in a wide variety of contexts. The human–computer interaction series will focus on theoretical perspectives (such as formal approaches drawn from a variety of behavioral sciences), practical approaches (such as the techniques for effectively integrating user needs in system development), and social issues (such as the determinants of utility, usability and acceptability).

For other titles published in this series, go to
www.springer.com/series/6033

David England
Editor

Whole Body Interaction

 Springer

Editor
David England
School of Computing and Maths
Liverpool John Moores University
Byrom St., Liverpool L3 3AF
United Kingdom
D.England@ljmu.ac.uk

ISSN 1571-5035
ISBN 978-1-4471-2651-5   ISBN 978-0-85729-433-3 (eBook)
DOI 10.1007/978-0-85729-433-3
Springer London Dordrecht Heidelberg New York

British Library Cataloguing in Publication Data
A catalogue record for this book is available from the British Library

Springer is part of Springer Science+Business Media (www.springer.com)

Preface

Whole Body Interaction arose from a series of workshops, beginning with the AHRC Methods Network in 2007 entitled Whole Body Interaction: The future of the human body. That title mirrored an art exhibition theme on the Future of the human body at the FACT Centre, Liverpool in that year. My own interest in the area began in the 1990s with work on virtual reality but was rekindled in 2006 when working with new media artists, Josh Nimoy and Caen Botto and their work on physical interaction, as part of the HCI Fun project, http://www.hci-fun.org.uk. More academic workshops followed, firstly at the BCS HCI 2008 conference in Liverpool and then the ACM SIGCHI conferences in 2009 (Boston) and 2010 (Atlanta). The chapters in Whole Body Interaction arise from the 2008 and 2009 workshops.

Whole Body Interaction is aimed at students and researchers who are looking for new project ideas or to extend their existing work with new dimensions of interaction. To show that Whole Body Interaction is not just about Natural User Interfaces we begin with two chapters on interaction in abstract domains. Antle et al. look at balancing justice whilst Holland and colleagues look at teaching musical harmony via whole body interaction. Two contrasting chapters then look at different methods for motion capture. Smit et al. look at a personal network of wearable sensors whilst Krum et al. look at "Holodeck" style interaction by stretching the virtual space available to users. Isbister and her colleagues look at what can be learnt from experiments with the Wii remote and develop some general design patterns for whole body interaction. Johansson and Tholander compare traditional sports with digital interaction to see what lessons can be learnt for whole body interaction. Shoemaker and Booth describe experiments in Body Centred Interaction. Nijholt and colleagues, meanwhile, consider the notions of flow and synchrony as users arrange their own and other people's movements in physical interaction. Moving on to more device-led research Wimmer looks at capacitive sensors for whole body interaction; whereas Fergus et al. examine wearable sensors for use in medical applications. Crane and her colleagues look at the important question of determining the user's emotional state from their motion. The next chapters look at whole body interaction in particular contexts. Vatavu considers the augmentation of desktop applications with body sensing whilst Rico looks at augmenting mobile interaction with physical gestures. Fujisawa looks at head movement as a means for gauging user interest. Finally Diaber and colleagues look at the body as a controller in geographical information systems.

Acknowledgements

Many people have contributed to this area over the years but are not directly represented in Whole Body Interaction. To the staff at FACT: Marta Ruperez, Gill Henderson, Mike Stubbs who supported the HCI Fun project and the first WBI workshop in 2007. The co-organisers of the earlier workshops: Eva Hornecker, Chris Roast, Paul Romero, Paul Fergus, Paul Marshall, Beth Crane and Jennifer Sheridan. Artists who provided inspiration: Josh Nimoy, Caen Botto, Tony Hall and David Rokeby. Also all the previous contributors to the earlier workshops. My colleagues at Liverpool John Moores University who supported my conference attendance, particular Professor Madjid Merabti.

Liverpool, 2011   David England

Contents

Contributors

Kenro Aihara
National Institute of Informatics, The Graduate University for Advanced Studies, Sokendai, 2-1-2 Hitotsubashi, Chiyoda-ku, Tokyo, Japan
kenro.aihara@nii.ac.jp

Alissa N. Antle
School of Interactive Arts and Technology, Simon Fraser University, Surrey, British Columbia, Canada
aantle@sfu.ca

Peter Barrie
School of Engineering and Computing, Glasgow Caledonian University, 70 Cowcaddens Road, Glasgow, UK
peter.barrie@gcal.ac.uk

Allen Bevans
School of Interactive Arts and Technology, Simon Fraser University, Surrey, British Columbia, Canada
alb19@sfu.ca

Mark Bolas
University of Southern California, Institute for Creative Technologies, 12015 Waterfront Drive, Playa Vista, CA 90094–2536, USA
bolas@ict.usc.edu

Kellogg S. Booth
Department of Computer Science, University of British Columbia, 201-2366 Main Mall, Vancouver, British Columbia V6T 1Z4, Canada
ksbooth@cs.ubc.ca

Anders Bouwer
Intelligent Systems Lab, Faculty of Science, Informatics Institute, University of Amsterdam, Amsterdam, The Netherlands
a.j.bouwer@uva.nl

L. Bracegirdle
Newcastle Biomedicine, The Medical School, Newcastle University,
Newcastle Upon Tyne NE2 4HH, UK

Stephen Brewster
Glasgow Interactive Systems Group, School of Computing Science,
University of Glasgow, G12 8QQ Glasgow, UK
stephen@dcs.gla.ac.uk

Greg Corness
School of Interactive Arts and Technology, Simon Fraser University,
Surrey, British Columbia, Canada
gcorness@sfu.ca

Elizabeth A. Crane
Department of Biologic and Materials Sciences, School of Dentistry,
University of Michigan, Ann Arbor, MI 48109, USA
bcrane@umich.edu

Andrew Crossan
Glasgow Interactive Systems Group, School of Computing Science,
University of Glasgow, G12 8QQ Glasgow, UK
ac@dcs.gla.ac.uk

Florian Daiber
German Research Institute for Artificial Intelligence (DFKI),
Innovative Retail Lab, Campus D3_2, Stuhlsatzenhausweg 3,
66123 Saarbrücken, Germany
flowdie@wwu.de

Mat Dalgleish
Department of Music (SPAL), University of Wolverhampton, Gorway Road,
Walsall, UK
m.dalgleish2@wlv.ac.uk

Betsy van Dijk
Human Media Interaction, University of Twente, PO Box 217, 7500 AE
Enschede, The Netherlands
bvdijk@cs.utwente.nl

Christopher DiMauro
NYU-Poly, Six Metrotech Center, Brooklyn, NY 11201, USA
chrisdimauro@gmail.com

David England
School of Computing and Maths, Liverpool John Moores University,
Liverpool L3 3AF, UK
d.england@ljmu.ac.uk

P. Fergus
School of Computing and Mathematical Sciences, Liverpool John Moores
University, Byrom Street, Liverpool L3 3AF, UK
P.Fergus@ljmu.ac.uk

Barbara L. Fredrickson
Department of Psychology, Davie Hall, University of North Carolina
at Chapel Hill, Chapel Hill, NC, USA
blf@email.unc.edu

Kumiko Fujisawa
National Institute of Informatics, The Graduate University for Advanced
Studies, Sokendai, 2-1-2 Hitotsubashi, Chiyoda-ku, Tokyo, Japan
k_fuji@nii.ac.jp

M. Melissa Gross
Department of Movement Science, School of Kinesiology,
University of Michigan, Ann Arbor, MI 48109-2214, USA
mgross@umich.edu

J. Haggerty
School of Computing, Science and Engineering, University of Salford,
Greater Manchester M4 4WT, UK

Dirk Heylen
Human Media Interaction, University of Twente, PO Box 217, 7500 AE
Enschede, The Netherlands

Simon Holland
The Music Computing Lab, Department of Computing, The Open University,
Milton Keynes, UK
s.holland@open.ac.uk

Katherine Isbister
NYU-Poly, Six Metrotech Center, Brooklyn, NY 11201, USA
isbister@poly.edu

Carolina Johansson
MobileLife at Stockholm University, Forum 100, 16440 Kista, Sweden
lina@sics.se

Andreas Komninos
School of Engineering and Computing, Glasgow Caledonian University,
70 Cowcaddens Road, Glasgow, UK
andreas.komninos@gcal.ac.uk

Antonio Krüger
German Research Institute for Artificial Intelligence (DFKI), Innovative Retail
Lab, Campus D3_2, Stuhlsatzenhausweg 3, 66123 Saarbrücken, Germany
kruegera@wwu.de

David M. Krum
University of Southern California, Institute for Creative Technologies,
12015 Waterfront Drive, Playa Vista, CA 90094–2536, USA
krum@ict.usc.edu

Oleksii Mandrychenko
School of Engineering and Computing, Glasgow Caledonian University,
70 Cowcaddens Road, Glasgow, UK
oleksii.mandrychenko@gcal.ac.uk

Paul Mulholland
The Music Computing Lab, Department of Computing, The Open University,
Milton Keynes, UK
p.mulholland@open.ac.uk

Anton Nijholt
Human Media Interaction, University of Twente, PO Box 217,
7500 AE Enschede, The Netherlands
anijholt@cs.utwente.nl

Marco Pasch
Faculty of Informatics, University of Lugano, Via Buffi 13, 6900
Lugano, Switzerland
marco.pasch@usi.ch

Stefan-Gheorghe Pentiuc
University Stefan cel Mare of Suceava, 720229 Suceava, Romania
pentiuc@eed.usv.ro

Dennis Reidsma
Human Media Interaction, University of Twente, PO Box 217, 7500 AE
Enschede, The Netherlands
dennisr@cs.utwente.nl

Julie Rico
Glasgow Interactive Systems Group, School of Computing Science,
University of Glasgow, G12 8QQ Glasgow, UK
julie@dcs.gla.ac.uk

Johannes Schöning
German Research Institute for Artificial Intelligence (DFKI), Innovative Retail
Lab, Campus D3_2, Stuhlsatzenhausweg 3, 66123 Saarbrücken, Germany
j.schoening@wwu.de

Garth Shoemaker
Department of Computer Science, University of British Columbia,
201-2366 Main Mall, Vancouver, British Columbia, V6T 1Z4 Canada
garths@cs.ubc.ca

Philip Smit
School of Engineering and Computing, Glasgow Caledonian University,
70 Cowcaddens Road, Glasgow, UK
philip.smit@gcal.ac.uk

Evan A. Suma
University of Southern California, Institute for Creative Technologies,
12015 Waterfront Drive, Playa Vista, CA 90094–2536, USA
suma@ict.usc.edu

M. Taylor
School of Computing and Mathematical Sciences, Liverpool John Moores
University, Byrom Street, Liverpool L3 3AF, UK

Jakob Tholander
MobileLife at Stockholm University, Forum 100, 16440 Kista, Sweden
jakobth@dsv.su.se

Ovidiu-Ciprian Ungurean
University Stefan cel Mare of Suceava, 720229 Suceava, Romania
ungurean.ovidiu@gmail.com

Radu-Daniel Vatavu
University Stefan cel Mare of Suceava, 720229 Suceava, Romania
vatavu@eed.usv.ro

Katie Wilkie
The Music Computing Lab, Department of Computing, The Open University,
Milton Keynes, UK
k.l.wilkie@open.ac.uk

Raphael Wimmer
University of Munich, Amalienstr. 17, 80333 Munich, Germany
raphael.wimmer@ifi.lmu.de

Chapter 1
Whole Body Interaction: An Introduction

David England

Bill Buxton speculated [1] that if some future archaeologist dug up a current personal computer, he might imagine that the user had two hands, with one dominant hand to control the mouse, one eye for mono-vision, limited hearing and no legs, nor mouth. His point of course was that current personal computers make limit use of the full range of human capabilities. As a musician use to using two hands and his mouth to play instruments he wondered why this was so?

Until very recently this picture of computer use, criticised by Buxton, was the norm for most people. Fuller, physical interaction was restricted to expensive virtual reality labs, devoted to special studies in medicine, sports or military training. Even these uses are normally restricted to capturing data and post-session analysis rather than true interaction with their environment. However, as sensors, camera vision and associated software become more available designers and researchers are exploring richer ways of interacting. These new methods also bring with them new challenges of design approaches, engineering of interactive systems and, indeed, research philosophy.

We explore Whole Body Interaction that is

The integrated capture and processing of human signals from physical, physiological, cognitive and emotional sources to generate feedback to those sources for interaction in a digital environment. [England [6]]

Which involves input from and feedback via

- Physical Motion capture via new methods
- Physiological inputs such as breathing rate, pulse rate and skin resistivity
- The normal five senses plus the sense of balance and proprioception
- Cognitive State
- Emotional State
- Social Context

D. England (✉)
School of Computing and Maths, Liverpool John Moores University,
Liverpool L3 3AF, UK
e-mail: d.england@ljmu.ac.uk

D. England (ed.), *Whole Body Interaction*, Human-Computer Interaction Series,
DOI 10.1007/978-0-85729-433-3_1, © Springer-Verlag London Limited 2011

The key word here is *integration*. We wish to use two or more of these input categories in combination so that we can, if necessary, triangulate the event input data to get a richer picture of what the user intends when they move their body in a whole body interaction setting.

Development of Technology

The ability to capture whole body interaction, as defined above, has arisen due to the developments in technology. So we have miniature sensors for motion sensing and advances in wireless networking so people can move unimpeded. In addition algorithms have been developed to model human kinematics and also perform real-time motion capture via video, such as [3].

In the mid 1990s there was a great deal of hype about Virtual Reality and expensive Motion Capture Labs where set up. Mostly these were relegated to capturing movement that was then used in post-processing, be it in cinema or games, or in the scientific analysis of movement for sports and medical uses. Only rarely did such environments consider the person interacting with a digital environment, and then due to the cost and complexity of the systems, only limited and experimental user actions were possible. Such systems were usually restricted to situations where the costs of the simulation could be justified.

Now, however, we have a range of lower cost commercial sensors coupled with a growing knowledge base in Computer Games technology. However if we wish expand our interactions beyond games into everyday life we need to learn more about how people make meaningful movements and express themselves more fully in a digital environment. Here we can think of examples such as

- The monitoring of elderly people to prevent potentially fatal falls
- The assessment of people with disabilities outside a lab environment
- Providing people with special needs with new ways of developing hidden skills
- Supporting digital artists with new means of expression and audience participation

We can already see some small-scale examples of this kind of work. For example, Josh Nimoy, drawing on the pioneering artwork of from Myron Krueger, developed his Mixed Hello Computer-Vision artwork, which uses his own edge-detection software with a standard PC, webcam and projector to provide an interactive, camera-vision installation [5].

Similarly Johnny Chung Lee [7] has experimented with the Nintendo Wii Remote to provide, finger tracking, an electronic whiteboard and head tracking.

These two small-scale examples so what can be done with comparatively little expensive. At the other end of the spectrum the work of the Stanford Markerless Motion Capture project [Corazza [3]] begins to answer another of the challenges of whole body interaction, which is to capture human motion without the impediment of wearing sensors or standing in a particular location. Their approach also demonstrates a need for the understanding of human biomechanics as part of the knowledge base for Whole Body Interaction.

Moving away from motion capture alone Beth Crane's work [4] looks at identifying emotional states from motion. Here we are moving towards a more integrated approach to Whole Body Interaction. Once we can identify an emotional state we can put a physical movement or gesture into context. Does a slow movement of the arm in a sad state indicate dismissal? Or is it a quick movement in a contented state indicating celebration?

Challenges for Whole Body Interaction

As we said above there are three main areas of challenge before we can move towards true whole body interaction. These are in the design approach, the engineering of the interaction and research philosophy.

Design for Whole Body Interaction

Design for Whole Body Interaction must start with the premise that all aspects of the human user are involved in interaction and only later are elements removed that are not required. The next stage is to specify the how those elements are integrated. Then the interaction design with the individual elements will be expanded. The design process would be iterative as we discover more information about the users and their context of use.

As an example let us consider the design of a multi-user air guitar. For the sake of the example we will assume that certain technologies of camera vision and motion sensing are available to us. In this scenario the users are stood in front of a screen and camera. There are pressure pads on the floor in front of the screen. The screen displays "strings" and as the users move their hands in front of the camera, optical flow is used to measure the speed of hands across the string to produce musical notes. The users can use the floor pads to produce effects by changing the pressure of the pads. As we experiment with the systems we find that the users have difficult associating their hand movements with the strength of the effect on the "strings" so we add piezoelectric transducers to their hands that vibrate as their hands cross the "strings". We also find that users have difficulty using the strings and floor pads at the same time but multiple users can coordinate their use of strings and pads so we decouple the strings and pad interaction from individual users. So having formed our initial frame of

- Visual strings
- Optical flow interaction
- Piezoelectric transducer feedback
- Floor pad controls

We can work on refining the interactions with each element, bearing in mind the interaction and integration with the other elements. The greater challenge is to discover the general design principles of Whole Body Interaction that would help us make good design choices as early as possible in the design process.

Engineering of Interaction

Many of the interaction scenarios describe in subsequent chapters of Whole Body Interaction are only possible because of recent developments in interaction technologies. Thus researchers have appropriated the Wiimote from Nintendo or the Microsoft Kinect to use in non-gaming domains. Or they have used publically available toolkits like OpenCV on which to base their experiments. However, each of these has their limitations, from the inaccuracy of the Wiimote, the time lag of the Kinect or the limitations in algorithms supported by OpenCV. For true whole body interaction we need at least four points of reference on the body whether from sensors or cameras. We also require the processing and feedback of signals to be in real time. Thus true whole body markerless motion *interaction* is not currently feasible. No doubt in time processing power will improve to deal with real time markerless interaction but even then we have to ask about the recognition of the patterns we receive. Gesture recognition is still advancing but gesture recognition thresholds are still not suitably high enough, in all domains, for it to proving a usable experience. Thus there will need to be further advances in machine learning techniques, so that the blobs from camera vision, or the sensor patterns from inertial devices, can be used to support fluid, continuous gesture recognition. Then we can start to ask Human-Computer Interaction questions about what gestures mean in a given context, how users learn gestures and how machines learn about the users' behaviour.

Research Philosophy

Human Computer Interaction is a multidisciplinary subject. Much of the work in Whole Body Interaction takes place in cross-disciplinary contexts. However, HCI research has begun to fragment with topics such as mobile HCI, ubiquitous computing, location awareness, tangible computing, physical interaction, embodied interaction and virtual/augmented/mixed realities, for example, all having their particular perspective on interaction. Whole Body Interaction is in one sense a reaction to that fragmentation and attempts to bring us back to the user as central in our design and research thinking. We need to raise questions about our research philosophy and methods. Psychology is one of the underpinning disciplines of Human Computer Interaction and it has undergone changes in perspective in thinking which are reflect in HCI research. So early on Freud's psychology was inward and introspective. Skinner rejected this view with his external-view, Behaviourist approach. Cognitive Psychologists, looking to model thought processes, in turn rejected behaviourism. Cognitive Psychology and its methods became one of the founding approaches to modern HCI. Now as we think about embodied interaction researchers (e.g. [8]) take a more external view, informed by Phenomenology and *knowledge-in-the-world*. However, this perspective does not help us deal such factors as

- Abstraction – especially in the visual sense
- The role of emotion in interaction
- Physiology in interaction
- And the interplay between these and other factors

For Whole Body Interaction we need to be flexible about integrating knowledge-in-the-head with knowledge-in the world.

The same flexibility in perspective is needed in evaluating Whole Body Interaction scenarios. Buxton and Greenberg [2] point out the dangers of doing evaluation too early or using inappropriate methods in evaluation. We would echo their call and ask researchers to look at a range of methods of evaluation, which allow for experimentation in design and which cover the breadth of the user experience.

We trust the reader will find the following chapters useful and motivating in their own explorations of Whole Body Interaction.

References

1. Buxton, W., Myers, B.: A study in two-handed input. Proceedings of CHI '86, pp. 321–326. ACM, New York (1986)
2. Buxton, W., Greenberg, S.: Usability evaluation considered harmful (some of the time), Proceedings of CHI '08. Proceeding of the Twenty-Sixth Annual SIGCHI Conference on Human Factors in Computing Systems, ACM, New York (2008)
3. Corazza, S., Muendermann, L., Chaudhari, A., Demattio, T., Cobelli, C., Andriacchi, T.: A markerless motion capture system to study musculoskeletal biomechanics: visual hull and simulated annealing approach. Ann. Biomed. Eng. **34**(6), 1019–1029 (2006)
4. Crane, E., Gross, M., Rothman, Ed.: Methods for quantifying emotion-related gait kinematics. In: Proceedings of 3rd International Conference on Virtual and Mixed Reality, Springer Verlag, Berlin (2009)
5. England, D., Ruperez, M., Botto, C., Nimoy, J., Poulter, S.: Creative technology and HCI. In: Proceedings of HCI Ed 2007, Aveiro (2007)
6. England, D., Randles, M., Fergus, P., Taleb-Bendiab, A.: Towards an advanced framework for whole body interaction. In: Proceedings of 3rd International Conference on Virtual and Mixed Reality, Springer Verlag, Berlin (2009)
7. Lee, J.C.: http://johnnylee.net/projects/wii/ (2008). Accessed Dec 2009
8. Paul, Dourish: Where The Action Is: The Foundations of Embodied Interaction. MIT, New York (2001)

Chapter 2
Springboard: Designing Image Schema Based Embodied Interaction for an Abstract Domain

Alissa N. Antle, Greg Corness, and Allen Bevans

Abstract In this paper, we describe the theoretical framing, design, and user study of a whole body interactive environment called Springboard. Springboard supports users to explore the concept of *balance* in the abstract domain of social justice through embodied interaction. We present the foundational theory of embodied conceptual metaphor, focusing on the *twin-pan balance schema,* which can be enacted spatially or physically. We describe how these enactments of the balance schema and the conceptual metaphor of balance in social justice can be used to design the interaction model for a whole body interactive environment. We present the results of our qualitative interview style user study with 45 participants. The study was conceived to explore how participants enact, perceive, and understand spatial, physical, and conceptual balance through whole body interaction with an abstract domain such as social justice. We conclude with a discussion of implications for whole body interaction design.

Introduction

As computing becomes embedded in the physical environment, we need to understand how to support users to enact appropriate input actions and understand related system outputs [7, 9]. Image schema and conceptual metaphor theory may provide insight into underlying motor-cognitive mechanisms that can be leveraged in interaction design for embedded systems [1, 6]. Most of the research to date on metaphor in human computer interaction has focused on the use of metaphor in the design of visual communication elements of graphical user interface or in understanding users' mental models of such interfaces. In this chapter, we focus on one way that metaphors may be used to design the interactional

A.N. Antle (✉), G. Corness, and A. Bevans
School of Interactive Arts and Technology, Simon Fraser University, Surrey,
British Columbia, Canada
e-mail: aantle@sfu.ca; gcorness@sfu.ca; alb19@sfu.ca

D. England (ed.), *Whole Body Interaction*, Human-Computer Interaction Series,
DOI 10.1007/978-0-85729-433-3_2, © Springer-Verlag London Limited 2011

mappings between input actions and output responses for whole body interaction in an abstract domain.

In previous works we explored the idea that conceptual metaphors, derived from image schemas and operating outside of conscious awareness, could be used to create systematic and predictable or "intuitive" relationships between specific human actions and specific system responses for a whole body, audio environment called Sound Maker [2]. We called these *embodied interactional models* and claimed that they constitute a design strategy that has several benefits [1]. Based on our investigation of Sound Maker, we found evidence that an embodied interactional model made it easier for both adult and child users to learn to use the system and resulted in an enjoyable experience [3]. We also found that users tended to interpret the input space, their actions in it and their effects on the system using a spatial perspective on meaning making rather than a body-centric (physical) interpretation.

In order to validate our previous findings and extend our work to include the visual modality and a very abstract domain, we have created another interactive environment, called Springboard. Springboard is a room-sized interactive environment where users can explore how solutions to issues in social justice can be *balanced* through *balancing* their bodies spatially (i.e. in a space) or physically (i.e. centre of gravity). This paper briefly describes the theoretical foundation, the design rationale, and the system implementation. Springboard is a research instrument that allows us to continue to empirically investigate the details and benefits of embodied interaction in embedded computational systems. We asked the following questions: What are users' general attitudes to this embodied interactive environment? Do they find it easy to use? Does incorporating an embodied metaphor for balance into the interaction model impact users' understanding of how to use the system? Is there any difference between users' interactions with and understandings of the system where its interaction model is structured using a spatial schema for balance compared to a body-centric schema for balance?

Theoretical Underpinning

Embodied Metaphor Theory

A conceptual metaphor is the interaction between a target domain and a source domain that involves an interaction of schemas and concepts. Image schemas in the source domain are used to structure understanding of concepts in the target domain through metaphorical elaboration. Johnson claims that metaphors arise unconsciously from experiential gestalts relating to the body's movements, orientation in space, and its interaction with objects [8]. He called these fundamental gestalts embodied schemas, also called *image schemas*. Johnson suggests that a cornerstone of human meaning-making is our ability to form conceptual metaphors by using the structural and inferential properties of image schemas to structure and organize abstract concepts.

There are only a few studies that apply embodied metaphor theory in human computer interaction. The general premise of this work is that interfaces or interaction models that are consistent with metaphorical elaborations of image schemas will be more effective, efficient and satisfying to use. For a general discussion of the role of image schemas and conceptual metaphors in user interfaces see [7], and in interaction models see [1].

The Meanings of Balance

Johnson presents an analysis of the meanings of balance that include experiences, perceptions and concepts of balance. He suggests that our experience of balance is so pervasive and basic that we are seldom aware of its existence. The structure of balance is a key element that pulls our physical experience together as a coherent whole. For example, a toddler learning to walk immediately experiences various states of bodily balance and imbalance (Fig. 2.1, left). We learn about balance with our bodies. The meanings of balance emerge through acts of balancing. Long before we have grasped the meaning of the word balance, we develop several image schemas for balance based on our physical experiences.

As children develop, image schemas related to balance begin to structure, and give coherent meaning to their perceptions. In the realm of visual perception, we soon learn to interpret visual imagery as balanced or imbalanced. An image with a black circle placed at the interior edge of a square is interpreted as less balanced than an image where the circle is in the middle of the square. The image schema for bodily balance (around a point) structures this interpretation. Balance or imbalance does not objectively exist in the images. Balance comes through our act of perception and our interpretation that utilizes a balance image schema.

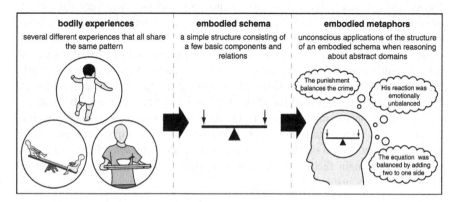

Fig. 2.1 Image schemas form from experience and are elaborated through embodied metaphor to structure abstract thought

Balance image schemas are also used to give meaning to balance in abstract domains such as psychological states, legal systems, mathematics, and social justice (Fig. 2.1, right). Through metaphorical elaboration, we interpret an abstract concept of balance based on its similarities with one or more image schemas for balance. For example, when we speak of social justice, we infer that justice involves a balance of factors such as rights, privileges, damages, and duties. Our understanding and judgments arise from the twin-pan balance schema (Fig. 2.1, centre). We treat factors metaphorically like forces or weights in the pans of a scale. The scale can be imbalanced by either side of the fulcrum having too much or too little metaphorical weight or force. For a detailed discussion of balance schemas and their metaphorical elaborations, see [8].

Design Rationale and System Implementation

Our multimedia interactive environment, Springboard, uses a camera vision system to sense and analyze data about a user's centre of gravity and foot position on an input platform. The system interprets sensed data to determine the degree of the user's body and/or spatial balance. This information is sent to the image and sound display engines that use it to determine which images and sounds to display. The design rationale and a brief system description follow.

An Abstract Domain: Social Justice

In our earlier work we explored the benefits of an embodied metaphorical interaction model in an acoustic environment. As pointed out by several reviewers, changes in sound parameters are more perceptual than conceptual and are more physical than abstract. The concept of balance in social justice is very abstract. It also lends itself well to visual representation. As such, it was chosen as a suitable domain to use in this phase of our investigations.

We chose to design a system based on three different issues in social justice so that we could create three content sets for our user study. We repeat the same task three times, each time with the same system but a different content set (and issue) in order to improve validity of the study. The issues we chose can each be conceptualized based on the metaphorical elaboration of the twin-pan balance schema. Each issue was represented through visual media and was complex enough to sustain user interest. Based on these criteria, we chose the following three issues that each have two main factors or metaphorical forces which must be balanced to achieve a socially just solution:

1. balancing ethical farming practices versus adequate quantity of food production (abbreviated food)

2. balancing resources used to build shelters versus quality of shelter production (shelter)
3. balancing the authority of state control versus community safety (safety).

We acknowledge that we have vastly simplified these complex social issues by conceptualizing them as the balance of two main factors. However, for the purposes of initially studying metaphor-based embodied interaction, we feel that the conceptualization is consistent with the twin-pan balance schema and adequate to reveal benefits or limitations to our approach.

Design Goals

Our main objective was to create a system that we could use as a research instrument to explore the benefits and limitations of using an embodied interaction model in a whole body environment that enabled users to explore the abstract idea of balance and imbalance in social justice. The interaction model is the mapping layer that relates input actions to changes in displayed images and sounds. A second objective was to explore the similarities and differences between using a spatial and a physical image schema as the basis for the embodied interaction model. From these objectives and our user study design requirements, we set four primary design goals.

The first goal was to create an interaction model that used the twin-pan balance schema to structure the input sensing space. The twin-pan schema can be enacted by a user either physically (e.g. moving or standing with their centre of gravity in or out of balance) or spatially (e.g. moving or standing in the centre of the input space or at the edges of the input space). The second goal was to create an interaction model that used the following three schema-concept pairings:

1. a spatial twin-pan balance image schema (i.e. based on body position being balanced or imbalanced in a space) that was linked to displayed images and sounds representing the concept of balance and imbalance for each issue (abbreviated "spatial" mode);
2. a body-centric twin-pan balance image schema (i.e. based on centre of gravity being balanced or imbalanced) that was linked to the same displayed images and sounds (abbreviated "body" mode); and
3. a combination of both spatial and body-centric twin-pan balance image schemas that was linked to the same displayed images and sounds (abbreviated "spatial + body" mode). The interaction model links image schematic input states to changes in output imagery and sounds, depicting various degrees of balance in each social justice issue. The system can be run using spatial, body or spatial + body modes of interaction.

A third design goal was that the whole body environment should support users to both move and think without privileging one modality more than others.

For example, input movements should not be too difficult or too trivial to enact. Similarly, changes in output images and sounds should be fairly easy to perceive and interpret (while moving). A fourth design goal was that the environment should support both imbalanced and balanced bodily states without causing physical harm to participants.

The Springboard Whole Body Interactive Environment

The Springboard whole body environment supports users to interactively explore images and sounds related to three social justice issues. The system is designed to be used by a single user. The active input space is a small raised platform (132×71×20 cm) made from a crib mattress spring, a board and black cloth (Fig. 2.2). Since standing in a balanced way is a normal state for most adults, we required an input space that upset this balance but not so much as to distract the user's attention away from the image display space. When a user steps onto the platform, their centre of gravity immediately becomes slightly out of balance and they will likely wobble on the platform. The rectangular design of the platform also supports lateral movement. By moving left or right, the user can also be out of balance spatially and the design of the platform ensures that it is even more wobbly at the edges than in the centre. States of bodily balance are determined as the user moves their body's centre of gravity and spatial position on the springboard input platform.

The spatial and body balance parameters for the input space are determined using a camera vision blob tracking and analysis system developed in the Max/Jitter programming environment. The user stands in front of a black background on the black

Fig. 2.2 Springboard input platform made from a crib spring, a board and black cloth

Springboard platform. This setup allows a simple background subtraction process to be used to isolate the user's image. The "balance" of the user can be calculated using a body balance index, which is based on the relation between the user's centre of gravity and feet, or a spatial balance index, which is based on their spatial position on the Springboard platform, or the combination of both. For the combination, the two indices are combined using a scaled addition process. The total balance index ranges from −10 to +10 where 0 reflects a completely balanced state. The total balance index is used to control the image and sound display engines.

A description of the image display engine follows. Each of the food, shelter and safety issues has two factors that can be balanced or imbalanced to various degrees, as described above. The factors are depicted with pairs of images displayed on a large vertical screen as shown in Fig. 2.3. For each issue, a set of images depicting different aspects of that issue were sourced and then tagged through a collaborative sorting process in order to categorize them in five numbered bins. For each issue, the bins range from (1) too much of the factor, to (5) too little of the factor with a central bin (3) for balanced factors. For example, for the shelter issue, an image of opulent interior of a private residence was tagged 5 (too much quality/resource consumption) and an image of a person sleeping in a cardboard box was tagged 1 (too little quality/resource consumption), as shown in Fig. 2.3. Each of the bins contains many images to support variation and multiple interpretations.

The display engine uses the current value of the total balance index (described above) in a random process controlled by a bell distribution curve to select pairs of images from the five bins. The center of the curve is determined by scaling the data from the total balance index (−10 to +10) to a floating point index from 1 to 5. The deviation of the bell curve is set so that when the control index is at x.0 the engine presents images only from that bin. For example, if the balance index is 3.5, the engine will display images from bin 3 and bin 4 with equal probability. To select pairs of images that represent the two factors or sides of twin-pan balance schema, the second image is selected using a mirror index derived by subtracting the balance index from the maximum for the index. For example, a balance index that would be

Fig. 2.3 Vertical display with pairs of images for issue: shelter (out of balance, bins 5 & 1)

mapped to bin 2 produces a mirrored index mapped to bin 4. For the food production issue, this might result in an image of mono-culture farms on one side, and chock full produce section at a large chain grocery store on the other side. Pairs of images synchronously fade in and out as the user's centre of gravity over their feet (body) and/or spatial position on the spring board platform (spatial) change. The end result is that the user's movements in and out of balance trigger metaphorically related changes in the images depicting the balance of two factors for each social justice issue.

The sound display engine for Springboard utilizes several approaches to representing the concept of balance through sonic aspects. Sound provides constant ambient information, responding to and guiding user actions. The obvious choice of a left-right channel panning was discarded. Panning is a representation of balance based on a cultural invention associated specifically with the technology of headphones. It is not based on a metaphorical elaboration of bodily or perceptually formed image schema. In addition, panning does not provide a clear resolution of change. We focus on more primary perceptually-based sound parameter changes such as pitch, timbre, and phase to achieve a sense of sonic balance and imbalance. For more details on sound design for Springboard, see [5].

User Study Methodology

An observational and interview style user study was conducted with 45 participants using Springboard as part of a larger study. The component of the study we report on here provides qualitative observations and verbal responses to post-task interview questions, which enable us to explore the impact on user experience of using image schematic input patterns to produce metaphorically related changes in image and sound content. We also compare the similarities and differences between using spatial and physical (body-centric) twin-pan balance schemas to structure the interaction modes.

Study Details

Twenty two (22) females and 23 males were recruited from the Simon Fraser University Surrey campus. All but three participants were aged 18–25 years old. All participants were daily computer users and 63% had been exposed to whole body interactive environments before. Participants were randomly assigned to one of the three interaction modes: spatial (n = 15); body (n = 14); and spatial + body (n = 16).

The study took place in a self-contained research lab that contained the Springboard system. Participants completed a training task and three identical tasks, each with a different content set (food, shelter, safety). Session duration ranged from 30 to 40 min. The tasks involved having the participant use Springboard to use their body to interact with each multimedia content set. Users were told to explore the images and sounds for as long as they liked, and to indicate when the images and sounds represented "balance" for each issue. They were not told what the issues were or how the system worked.

Qualitative Data Collection and Analysis

During each session we took detailed observational notes using a semi-structured data collection sheet. After each session, we conducted an interview with each participant. We asked open questions about their general likes and dislikes (attitudes), how easy or difficult they found Springboard to use, and how they thought the system worked.

Participant's verbal answers were recorded on audio and later transcribed. We used a bottom-up thematic analysis approach to identify themes that were related to the benefits or limitations of using an embodied interaction model. We also compared and contrasted responses between the three groups (spatial, body, spatial + body).

Results and Discussion

We present the results of our qualitative analysis, which address our research questions, through a discussion of the following themes.

General Attitude to Springboard

Overall, most of the participants were positive about their Springboard session. They found it "interesting", "novel", "cool", "thought provoking" and found the whole body interaction "a welcome change from sitting at a desktop computer" or being in a classroom. However, about half the participants also had criticisms of the session and Springboard. Many felt that they wanted more details of how to interact and instructions for the task. The open exploratory nature of the task was problematic for some participants. For example, when asked what they disliked, one participant said, "Well not really dislike but I guess if you weren't here I would have no idea what I'm supposed to be doing so it wasn't really clear, instructions or anything." Springboard is essentially a black room with the Springboard platform and a large display that offers participants few affordances or cues about how to interact with the system. Most participants quickly understood that they should position themselves on the Springboard facing the display. We designed the system intentionally to offer few clues to operation because we wanted investigate if participants would come to understand how their bodily and spatial states of balance impacted the depictions of balance and sonic balance based on metaphorical elaboration, either unconsciously or consciously. However, this raises the issue, also identified in [4], that physical objects (e.g. tangible user interfaces) can be designed or naturally provide affordances that encourage or constrain specific interactions such as image schema enactments. More unstructured whole body interactive environments (without controller artefacts) do not always have these affordances.

Enactment Versus Verbalization of Image Schemas

About a third of the participants were able to both enact and express verbally how the balance schema structured their interaction with Springboard. However, many other participants expressed that they "didn't really understand how the system worked". Despite this, we observed that most of these participants were able to use the system successfully to complete the tasks. Without being aware of it, participants enacted the spatial and body-centric balance image schemas as they interacted with Springboard. However, they were not able to verbalize a mental model of the system that included these balance schemas. This is consistent with image schema and conceptual metaphor theory since these mental structures are processed below the level of conscious awareness [8]. From this we suggest that if there is a specific user experience goal for whole body environment (e.g. explore balance in social justice) then the design must enable or afford users to enact image schemas and interpret metaphorically related system responses in ways that the designers intended. This can be done through the design of physical affordances and perceptual cues structured using one or more image schemas. For example, the spring board afforded moving in and out of balance, and the side-by-side visual layout mirrors the twin-pan balance structure. However, supporting users to enact or perceive image schematic structures does not necessarily require that users understand how the interaction model or system works. We suggest that it is important to consider these distinctions when designing whole body interaction based on embodied metaphor.

Image Schemas in Mental Models of Interaction

Participants provided verbal evidence that other image schemas and related metaphors occurred in their mental models of how they thought the system worked. For example, several participants initially thought that the system worked like an interactive video controller (metaphor: time is a linear path). "I was thinking that if I moved to the left the images would scroll backwards so if I shift left I could see previous images and if I moved my body to the right it would scroll forward but it wasn't doing that." Some participants thought that they should move towards images they wanted or liked. Similarly, one participant said that they should interact "by leaning towards the side that I think is social justice" (metaphor: force is emotional attraction). Some participants commented that they used force or pushed down to change the images (metaphor: force is change). Some participants thought that if they stepped to one side it would make images bigger. What is evident here is that participants used a variety of image schemas and metaphorical elaboration in their interpretation of the interaction model. However, they did not necessarily use the balance image schema! We suggest that cueing participants might be necessary to help them determine which schema they should use in cases where the physical characteristics of the system afford many input actions and interpretations.

Image Schemas in Interpretation

Many participants provided verbal evidence of using the schema of balance to structure their interpretation of Springboard content. For example, they used the word "balance" metaphorically in their verbal responses to our questions. They also used other words related to the twin-pan balance schema (e.g. "weight", "midpoint") in their responses. For example, one participant said "It was kind of like a teeter-totter, the more balanced you made it, I guess, the more the images represented a more balanced society." Another participant said, "It lets people know that society has to balance more, distribute more balance on the different classes of people .... to be equal to everyone." A third said, "Based on balance left and right you could weigh the options sort of in one direction or the other." This again raises the issue of whether participants need to be able to explicitly understand how the system works (with respect to the balance schema) to use it and make sense of content. We suggest, consistent with metaphor theory, that users do not need to explicitly understand metaphorical relations to use them to interpret their perceptions.

Spatial Versus Body-Centric Balance Image Schemas

There were no large differences in participant's responses between the three groups (spatial, body, spatial + body). There were two small differences that require further investigation. First, we found that more participants in the spatial group used words like "easy", "intuitive", and "simple" to describe what they liked about Springboard. Second, more participants in the spatial and spatial + body groups gave explanations of how Springboard worked that focused on the content rather than interaction. We interpret this cautiously as further evidence of the primacy of spatial schematic interpretations in whole body interaction, as seen in [2].

Conclusions

We present the theory, design, and results from an observational and interview style user study in which we investigate the benefits and limitations of using image schemas and embodied metaphors in an interactive environment that uses whole body interaction and depicts images and sounds from the abstract domain of social justice. Our findings suggest that using image schemas and related metaphors to structure interaction with multimedia content in an abstract domain like social justice is a promising approach. However, there are limitations. In particular, participants are often unaware of using schemas to structure interaction and interpretation, and use a variety of schemas and metaphors in their sense making. More work is needed to continue to explore the benefits and limitations of using embodied interaction models for whole body and tangible interaction in abstract application domains.

References

1. Antle, A.N., Corness, G., Bakker, S., Droumeva, M., van den Hoven, E., Bevans, A.: Designing to support reasoned imagination through embodied metaphor. In: Conference on Creativity and Cognition, pp. 275–284. ACM Press, Berkeley (2009a)
2. Antle, A.N., Corness, G., Droumeva, M.: Human-computer-intuition? Exploring the cognitive basis for intuition in embodied interaction. Int. J. Art Technol. 2(3), 235–254 (2009)
3. Antle, A.N., Corness, G., Droumeva, M.: What the body knows: exploring the benefits of embodied metaphors in hybrid physical digital environments. Interact. Comput. Spec. Issue Enactive Interfaces 21(1–2), 66–75 (2009)
4. Bakker, S., Antle, A.N., van den Hoven, E.: Embodied metaphors in interaction design. Pers. Ubiq. Comput. Special Issue on Children and Tangibles, (2011), in press
5. Droumeva, M., Antle, A.N., Corness, G., Bevans, A.: Springboard: exploring embodied metaphor in the design of sound feedback for physical responsive environments. In: Conference on Auditory Display, Copenhagen. http://icad.org/node/3059 (2009). Accessed 30 Sept 2010
6. Holland, S., Marshall, P., Jon Bird, J., Dalton, S., Morris, R., Pantidi, N., Rogers, Y., Clark, A.: Running up Blueberry Hill: prototyping whole body interaction in harmony space. In: Conference on Tangible and Embedded Interaction, pp. 93–98. ACM Press, Cambridge (2009)
7. Hurtienne, J., Weber, K., Blessing, L.: Prior experience and intuitive use: image schemas in user centred design. In: Langdon, P., Clarkson, J., Robinson, P. (eds.) Designing Inclusive Futures, pp. 107–116. Springer, London (2008)
8. Johnson, M.: The Body in the Mind: The Bodily Basis of Meaning, Imagination, and Reason. University of Chicago Press, Chicago (1987)
9. Svanaes, D.: Context-aware technology: a phenomenological perspective. Hum. Comput. Interact. 16, 379–400 (2001)

Chapter 3
Whole Body Interaction in Abstract Domains

Simon Holland, Katie Wilkie, Anders Bouwer, Mat Dalgleish, and Paul Mulholland

Introduction

There is little dispute that Whole Body Interaction is a good fit of interaction style for some categories of application domain, such as the motion capture of gestures for computer games and virtual physical sports. This reflects the observation that in such applications the mapping between user gesture and the desired effect is, broadly speaking, the identity function. For more abstract application areas such as mathematics, programming and musical harmony, finding appropriate mappings between gesture and effect is less straightforward. The creation of appropriate whole body interaction designs for such abstract application areas remains challenging. However, this is not to argue that whole body interaction is unsuited to abstract domains. Indeed, there is evidence, outlined below, that whole body interaction offers excellent affordances for some highly abstract applications areas.

In this chapter we consider an argument to this end, derived from conceptual metaphor theory and sensory motor contingency theory, concerning the suitability of whole body interaction to abstract application domains in general. In particular, we analyse a case study of a whole body interaction system for a highly abstract application area, advanced tonal harmony. This domain is generally considered challenging, irrespective of how it is approached, but whole body interaction appears to offer particularly interesting affordances for action and insight in this

S. Holland (✉), K. Wilkie, and P. Mulholland
The Music Computing Lab, Department of Computing, The Open University,
Milton Keynes, UK
e-mail: s.holland@open.ac.uk; k.l.wilkie@open.ac.uk; p.mulholland@open.ac.uk

A. Bouwer
Intelligent Systems Lab, Faculty of Science, Informatics Institute, University of Amsterdam,
Amsterdam, The Netherlands
e-mail: a.j.bouwer@uva.nl

M. Dalgleish
Department of Music (SPAL), University of Wolverhampton, Gorway Road, Walsall, UK
e-mail: m.dalgleish2@wlv.ac.uk

D. England (ed.), *Whole Body Interaction*, Human-Computer Interaction Series,
DOI 10.1007/978-0-85729-433-3_3, © Springer-Verlag London Limited 2011

domain, when appropriate conceptual metaphors and conceptual blends (see below) are harnessed in the design using whole body interaction. We analyse issues emerging from this case study and consider implications of these issues for whole body interaction design when dealing with highly abstract domains in general.

Conceptual Metaphor and Embodied Experience

Conceptual Metaphor theory is an important strand in current research on Embodied Cognition [19]. Conceptual Metaphor Theory [18, 21, 22, 25] posits that human capabilities for dealing with abstract concepts are always grounded in a small core of universal sensory-motor abilities, together with their associated low-level inferencing capabilities. More specifically, the theory hypothesizes that all cognitive capacities for dealing with abstraction are constructed by a process of association, mapping, composition and extension of maps, applied not just to entities, but also to roles, relationships and specialised inference capabilities, and grounded universally in low-level sensory motor resources for dealing with the body, objects, space and force [22] (Fig. 3.1).

Suggestive evidence for this theory comes from Linguistics and other areas of Cognitive Science including Psychology, Neuroscience and Human–Computer Interaction [22]. Conceptual Metaphor Theory has been applied variously in Mathematics (ibid.), Political Analysis [20], Human Computer Interaction [16] Music Theory [23, 26, 29], and Music Interaction Design [28] and Interactive Sound Generation [1, 2]. For an application to issues of balance in the abstract domain of social justice, see Chap. 2. Mathematics teachers have judged the theory

Fig. 3.1 A case study in Whole Body Interaction, described in this chapter. Different players play different roles

insightful and useful in teaching abstract mathematical concepts [10], and the theory has given rise to forms of analysis in HCI that have demonstrated that image schemas can help with design decisions for user interfaces [16, 17].

Broadly, there are three fundamental resources described in the theory: innate cognitive capacities, sensory motor schema, and conceptual metaphors. *Innate cognitive capacities*, such as subitizing,[1] grouping, pairing, and exhaustion detection, are shared with babies and some animals [22]. *Sensory motor schema*, also known as image schema, such as CONTAINMENT, CONTACT, CENTRE-PERIPHERY, and SOURCE-PATH-GOAL[2] are associated with various kinds of low-level, special-purpose inference (ibid). *Conceptual metaphors* enable the two already mentioned classes of fundamental cognitive resource to be applied to domains of arbitrary complexity by mapping innate cognitive capacities and image schemas onto more abstract domains. Examples of employment of conceptual metaphors include reasoning about abstract classes (based, in part, on concrete low-level reasoning about containers) and reasoning about arithmetic (based, in part, on innate reasoning about collections of objects).

Conceptual metaphors can be applied in two different ways: as *grounding metaphors*, and in *conceptual blends*. Grounding metaphors enable the simplest abstractions to be grounded directly in physical experience – for example arithmetic subtraction as grounded by taking objects away from a collection, or mathematical sets as grounded in experience of collections of objects. Conceptual blending works by allowing two or more conceptual metaphors to be used to create new expanded or composite metaphors by processes of composition, completion and elaboration [9]. These processes allow conceptual metaphors such as NUMBERS ARE COLLECTIONS OF OBJECTS and NUMBERS ARE LENGTHS to be blended in intricate ways, as analysed in detail in Lakoff and Núñez [22], to produce more highly developed abstract concepts such as real numbers, complex numbers and transfinite number systems.

While image schema and innate capabilities such as subitizing are considered universal, conceptual metaphors can, and do, develop differently between different individuals and cultures. The formation of conceptual metaphors can be affected by a combination of innate, developmental, individual and cultural factors.

At present, empirical evidence for the validity of conceptual metaphor theory is growing, if not conclusive. More empirical work is needed to establish the limits within which the various elements of the theory validly apply. However, there is good evidence from Mathematics Teaching, Psychology, Human–Computer Interaction and Linguistics that conceptual metaphor theory is at the very least

---

[1] Subitizing is the ability to make judgements, without counting, about numbers of items up to about three or four. It has been empirically demonstrated that this ability is present in babies and some animals. It appears that different brain areas are used for subitizing vs. counting. Subitizing is claimed to be one foundation, via conceptual metaphor and blending, for the concepts of number and arithmetic [22].

[2] A common convention is to capitalize the names of schema and conceptual metaphors.

pragmatically useful, for example to teachers and designers. In this chapter, we apply the theory to illuminate a case study in order to explore general implications for whole body interfaces for abstract domains.

A Complex Abstract Domain: Tonal Harmony

Tonal Harmony concerns the organisation of multiple simultaneous pitch sources, for example, two or more singers, or instrumentalists, playing independent but co-ordinated melodic lines. Tonal Harmony is generally considered the most technical part of music theory, requiring the mastery of demanding practical skills. Explicit understanding of tonal harmony involves understanding a wide range of abstract entities, relationships and terminology. These concepts span interlinked semi-hierarchical conceptual levels (for example, pitch, interval, scale, chord quality, voicing, mode, key and modulation). Each of these levels is associated with its own technical vocabulary. As well as being technically and conceptually demanding, tonal harmony is associated with practical obstacles to mastery. Generally, it is difficult for individuals without instrumental skills to get real-time experience of controlling multiple voices simultaneously in a flexible but precise manner – since without instruments or collaborators, we can only directly control a single voice. This is not the only route to mastery, but it is an important one.

To see how this relates to whole body interaction and conceptual metaphor, it will help to briefly consider two related theoretical perspectives, namely Sensory Motor Contingency Theory and Dalcroze Eurhythmics (Fig. 3.2).

Fig. 3.2 Dance mats and Wii controllers as used in the case study help to engage physical, spatial and navigational intuitions with the spatial conceptual metaphors reflected in the interaction design (described below)

Sensory Motor Contingency Theory

Sensory motor contingency theory [24] suggests that in order to learn to organize and respond appropriately to sensory input in some new domain or context, it is vital that one's motor actions have the power to perceptibly affect relationships in that domain. In diverse situations where this specific kind of feedback and experience is absent, competency has been observed to fail to develop. This principle has been demonstrated in numerous different contexts and time scales. Notable examples include the development of the visual perception systems of neonate kittens [11] systematic adaptation to sensory substitution in blind adults over months [3]; and opportunistic learned sensory substitution in sighted adults over minutes when carrying out simple tracking tasks [5].

Sensory motor contingency, assuming its applicability to the present case study, suggests that if we wish learners to develop their skills in engaging with, recognizing, identifying, memorizing, analyzing, reproducing, adapting and composing harmonic sequences, then their motor actions must have the capacity to actively manipulate those harmonic sequences to adequately fine levels of detail. However, in the domain under consideration, most novices cannot play musical instruments, and even if they can sing, singing only allows control of a single melodic line – not multiple voices. This argument can be taken too far. Trained singers, and players of single voiced instruments may be able to gain active experience of harmony by effectively multiplexing a single voice into multiple lines, or by mentally manipulating virtual lines. However, for those who cannot play a musical instrument and who are not active singers, conventional approaches to teaching harmony using books and passive listening may leave them at a distinct disadvantage, by a lack of experience of active control of the phenomenon of interest (Fig. 3.3).

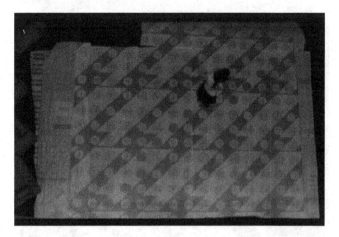

Fig. 3.3 An earlier whole body version of Harmony Space designed to use floor projection and camera tracking

Lessons from Dalcroze Eurhythmics

A related theoretical perspective, Dalcroze Eurhythmics, applies to musical rhythm rather than harmony, but shares key issues with tonal harmony. The music educator Emil Dalcroze (1865–1950) noticed that his students seemed unable to deal with technical and written aspects of rhythm if they lacked experience of enacting and feeling the relevant rhythms with their bodies. Simply hearing examples did not appear to be sufficient. Dalcroze proposed that students had to become competent in enacting representative rhythms bodily. Once this had been achieved, problems in dealing with technical and abstract aspects of rhythm were readily solved. In some cases, the requirement for bodily enacting a rhythm can be relatively undemanding, for example if the rhythm can be tapped with a single finger (a monophonic rhythm). However, some rhythms involve more than one independent stream of sounds, and are considerably harder to recognize, memorize, analyze and reproduce than monophonic rhythms [13].

In order to encourage competency in enacting rhythms, particularly ones involving multiple streams, Dalcroze invented a system of rhythmic 'gymnastics' or 'eurhythmics'. Amongst other things, this involved asking students to walk at a regular pace, while moving their arms in synchrony at, for example, twice or three times the rate.

We propose that these insights from Dalcroze Eurhythmics can be applied fairly straightforwardly in principle to tonal harmony. Students typically seem unable to deal securely with technical and written aspects of music connected with harmony if they lack experience of enacting, composing and modifying sequences of simultaneous pitches in real time. Simply hearing examples does not appear to be sufficient. We propose that to develop skills in harmony students need experience of enacting and manipulating representative harmonic sequences with their own bodies (Fig. 3.4).

Fig. 3.4 A player navigating a harmonic space

Harmony Space – A System for Exploring Tonal Harmony

Harmony Space [12, 15] is an interactive digital music representation system designed to give beginners and experts insight into a wide range of musical tasks ranging from performance and analysis to composition. When combined with whole-body interaction to create the Song Walker version [14], Harmony Space allows users to enact complex harmonic phenomena physically via mappings between (a) bodily movement and (b) conceptual metaphors and blends for musical abstractions. This approach affords rapid, concrete means of reasoning about and manipulating abstract musical entities and relationships by exploiting intuitions associated with bodily movement and navigation.

System Details

A previous design study [14] explored a version of whole body Harmony Space designed to work with camera tracking and floor projection (Fig. 3.3) However, we sought a simpler, more portable version that could nonetheless afford a similar degree of physical engagement. The Song Walker version employs four dance mats, four wireless controllers (wii remotes and nunchucks), various foot pedals, a large projection screen and a synthesizer. These are coordinated by a Harmony Space Server receiving data from controllers via HSp (Harmony Space protocol, a layer on top of OSC (Open Sound Control).

When operated by a solo player, one dance mat is used to navigate a proxy for the player (represented by crosshairs in the wall projection) around in the projected space. Squeezing the trigger on the wii remote visibly and audibly plays the chord associated with the current location and situation. When operated by multiple players, additional dance mats may be used simultaneously in a variety of collaborative ways, for example, to navigate key changes or to harmonically invert or otherwise alter the chords.

Conceptual Metaphors and Blends in Harmony Space

Harmony Space exploits a set of conceptual metaphors that link concepts in tonal harmony to spatial concepts. Many of these are elaborations of the postulated basic conceptual metaphor of pitch: *pitch intervals are displacements in three dimensions*. This conceptual metaphor stems from Balzano's theories [4] of harmonic perception, which retrospectively may be seen as positing a three-dimensional image schema for tonal harmony. As previously noted, conceptual metaphors typically emerge from a combination of innate, developmental, individual and cultural factors (though image schemas themselves are generally universal). Rich elaborations of the basic conceptual metaphor of pitch were afforded by early versions of

Harmony Space in a combined technical, and cultural process in three stages, as follows.

(a) Harmony Space introduces and embodies a set of metaphorical blends in which the basic conceptual metaphor of pitch interacts with itself in a series of layers. These represent interacting abstract layers of harmony; pitch alphabets, scales, keys, chord functions, tonal centres, roots, and bass lines, unified by the basic conceptual metaphor [15].

(b) The interactive digital nature of the tool facilitates the visual plotting of diverse music from the repertoire in spatial terms. This process affords reflection by interested users and music analysts on the emerging patterns and their musical meaning. Some patterns correspond to well known analytic concepts. Others have given rise to novel analytic and compositional insights.

(c) From the above technical and cultural process, new ways of discussing the technicalities of harmonic phenomena have emerged using a spatial, movement-based vocabulary as an alternative and complement to symbolic technical terms.

Some important candidate conceptual metaphors and blends employed in Harmony Space, both in the desktop and whole body versions, are outlined below (Fig. 3.5).

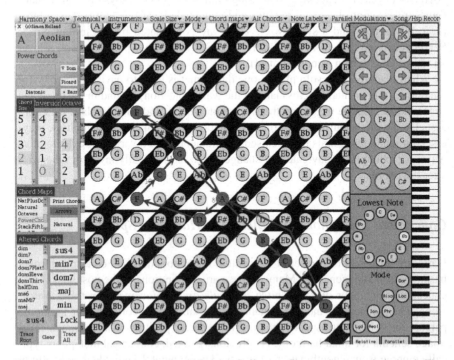

Fig. 3.5 A root trajectory showing David Bowie's Suffragette City, used in an analytical task. The *white shaded* 'preferred territory' is physically moved under the *dark nodes* and *gray arrows* that trace out the movement of the song, until the *white territory* fully contains the *dark nodes*

The following is an early attempt to identify and frame candidate conceptual metaphors for this domain. Some may prove to be overly specific, framed at the wrong level, or not truly universal. The current statements do not clearly distinguish candidate conceptual metaphors and surrounding explanation. For these reasons, candidates are not capitalized, as confirmed conceptual metaphors would be by convention. Still, this initial draft provides a basis for search, criticism, refutation and refinement. We believe this is a step towards illuminating the rich conceptual metaphorical structure of harmony.

Pitch

- Different musical intervals (octave, semitones, perfect fifths, major thirds, minor thirds) correspond to steps in different directions in space.
- In particular, semitones, fifths, and octaves are at right angles to each other in the plane, and octaves lie vertically (i.e., on the z-axis).
- The two main axes in the plane (semitones and perfect fifths) each have their own local vertical sense in the plane (this is an example of a conceptual blend).
- When moving in a straight line in any of the eight main directions in the plane, locations are repeated (depending on direction, this happens after 3, 4 or 12 steps).

Scales, keys and modes

- Common scales can be formed from the notes occurring in contiguous strips seven steps long in the fifths direction. Due to the repeating nature of the plane, these strips group into irregularly shaped two dimensional areas (as illustrated in Fig. 3.5).
- Key areas are scales spatially situated to represent preferred territory for journeys and chord elements (see the white area in Fig. 3.5).
- Diatonic materials are materials that restrict their elements and movement to preferred territory.
- Modulation is the co-ordinated movement of a preferred territory.
- A modal centre is a privileged location within preferred territory, typically where journeys start, end or rest.
- Mode changes occur when the privileged location moves within its enclosing territory.

Chords

- The most common chords (stacked thirds chords, as found in musical styles varying from classical and folk music to blues and jazz) are collections of two or more objects maximally compactly by local gravity to fit within a preferred territory.
- Triads are three element chords. Seventh chords are four element chords. Ninth chords are five element chords.
- Chord qualities are oriented geometrical shapes. Preservation of chord quality requires retention of shape and orientation. Altering the pitch of a fixed quality is change of location of the shape without rotation.

- The most common chord qualities, major and minor, correspond to the most frequent three-element chord shapes formed by compaction within the geometry of the most common scales.

Key centres

- The geometry of diatonic materials causes major and minor chord qualities to occur in groups within preferred territories. The spatial centres of these groups are the major and minor key centres (see Brower [6] for other perspectives).

Harmonic functions

- Different harmonic functions are associated with different locations within a territory.
- Due to the irregular shape of key areas, different chord qualities fit within the preferred territory at different locations. Thus different harmonic functions are associated with different chord qualities.

Inversion and voicing

- Inversion and voicing are movements of chord elements on the z-axis, displacing elements by an octave.

Harmonic movement

- Harmonic movement is spatial trajectory.
- Chord sequences, bass lines, and modulations are journeys.
- Composition is navigation, which may involve targets, directions, inertia, oscillatory movement and preferred territories.
- Due to the recurrence of locations in the plane, identical destinations may be reachable by alternative routes. Different routes correspond to different harmonic analyses.
- Journeys may segment in one way when viewed geometrically, but in another way when compared with an external clock ("Harmony vs. Hypermeter").
- Tonal movement corresponds to trajectories along the diagonal from top right to bottom left or vice versa.
- Modal movement corresponds to trajectories along the diagonal from top left to bottom right or vice versa.
- Tonal and modal movement are at right angles to each other.
- Tonal and modal tensions can be adjusted by swerves in direction.
- Tonal and modal ambiguity arise where direction of movement and location of territory is ambiguous.

The above candidate conceptual metaphors are arcane when expressed in words. They are more easily absorbed physically, visually and aurally. Their physical, spatial nature and their emphasis on navigation makes them well suited for enacting through whole body interaction. Furthermore, the occurrence of related interacting spatial metaphors at different levels (pitch, key, inversion, modality) offers opportunities for collaborative navigation.

Whole Body Interaction vs. Desktop

Harmony Space has existed previously principally as diverse desktop prototypes [14]. Beneath the different user interaction layer, the semantics of the Song Walker and desktop versions are essentially identical. However, the types of reasoning elicited from users by the two versions appear to contrast interestingly in some respects.

When a user controls a harmonic sequence in real-time on the desktop system using a mouse and alphanumeric keyboard, some operations must be carried out on the keyboard more or less simultaneously. This requires a certain amount of learning and expertise about the details of the keyboard control system, which can get in the way of direct engagement with the domain. Furthermore, spatial movements of various kinds in the various dimensions of the harmonic domain are much more simply mirrored using dance mats and wii controllers than by alphanumeric key sequences and mice.

When two or more players control a harmonic sequence in real time using the dance mat version, appropriate simple spatial movements can be collaboratively taught with minimal preamble, with directly perceived musical results. Thus, the affordances offered by the design that relate to conceptual metaphors and conceptual blends in the conceptual structure of the domain can be enacted and experienced more directly using the dance mat version than a desktop version.

Asymmetrical Collaboration

As well as the potential advantages of whole body interaction for engaging with spatial phenomena, there are also potential advantages for supporting collaborative roles.

Typically, when musicians collaborate to produce harmony, each musician contributes one part (which in some cases may contribute more than one voice – and in other cases single voices may be split between musicians). From many points of view, especially for experts, this more or less symmetrical distribution of roles is highly appropriate. However, where players are novices, or where there is a desire to gain insights into the abstract structures of tonal harmony, one drawback of the conventional approach is that that this process leaves these abstractions intangible and invisible.

By contrast, when Harmony Space is used collaboratively, the roles do not have to be split voice-wise, but may be split asymmetrically into heterogeneous spatial navigation and selection tasks, corresponding to abstractions of interest (Fig. 3.6).

Contrasting simultaneous asymmetrical roles available include the navigation of: the root path; changes of key; inversions and voicing; chord size; chord maps; altered chords; and bass lines. For particular pieces of music, typically only two or three of these roles are required at a time. The combinatorial interplay of these factors yields the detail of harmonic sequences.

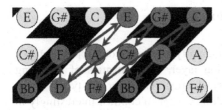 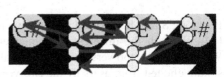

Fig. 3.6 In the study, some players collaborated to play the chord sequence of John Coltrane's Giant Steps. The *left hand figure* shows the path navigated by one player to control the root path. The *right hand figure* shows the path navigated simultaneously by another player controlling the key changes. The trace of the performance corresponds to a detailed abstract harmonic analysis of the piece

One key motivation for an asymmetrical approach is that experiencing these different roles allows players to enact aspects of the distinct conceptual metaphors whose blending together, we hypothesize, plays a key role in the understanding and mastery of tonal harmony. For example, movement in space can correspond under different metaphors variously to root movement and key movement. Deeper understanding comes from experiencing how these different kinds of movement can interact.

With multiple dance mats, players can readily see what other players are doing, and the rhythms to which they are working.

By rotating roles while performing, analyzing and composing, beginners can learn something about how different conceptual metaphors have been tacitly blended together in a variety of ingenious ways by composers over some 400 years.

Empirical Observations

Recent trials with eight pairs of users, some complete beginners, some musical experts, are being analyzed formally elsewhere. Here we limit ourselves to general observations. As regards the performance of pieces, all participants could perform one or more moderately complex songs after a few minutes training. Songs performed included:

- Ticket to Ride (The Beatles),
- Isn't She Lovely (Stevie Wonder),
- Pachelbel's Canon,
- Giant Steps (John Coltrane),
- Billie Jean (Michael Jackson).

Participants asked to harmonically analyse a piece, such as Suffragette City by David Bowie, were able to do so. This task required identifying the mode of the piece by physically shifting territory by means of a dance mat until the trace of the harmonic journey fell entirely within the preferred territory (see Fig. 3.5).

All participants could compose and modify simple chord sequences in musically intelligent ways. In a simple-open ended collaborative navigational composition task, one pair of beginners spontaneously focused particularly on inversions and explored these carefully, with much discussion and multiple attempts. Another pair of users deployed altered chords in a similarly careful way to musically positive effect. The care with which most beginners collaboratively composed musically sensible chord paths was surprising. Several users commented on the degree of physical engagement they brought to the tasks.

To illustrate this, one initially skeptical user was able to learn to play the complete harmony of Pachelbel's canon after about 10 min, At this point he said variously "I haven't got this musically in my head at all", "I don't have a sense of what's going on cognitively – how the visual representation is helping me remember it", and "visually overwhelming". However about 30 min later, having played several more songs, he commented "Love the kinaesthetic quality" and "Once you're used to it, you could dance songs" (in the sense that Song Walker allows one to generate the harmony for a song by dancing to it).

Comments on the degree of physical engagement might be unremarkable in the case of, for example, arcade games, but are unusual in the context of tasks that are generally taught in knowledge intensive ways using rule-based, symbolic, and quasi-mathematical approaches. Also, conventional approaches to learning these tasks generally take one or two orders of magnitude longer (Fig. 3.7).

The user trial was not designed to look for evidence of long-term adoption by participants of the conceptual metaphors enacted. However, there was anecdotal evidence that this happened. For example, days after the trial, one non-musically trained participant returned to discuss the harmonic structure of a song that he

Fig. 3.7 Two players improvise collaboratively using the whole body interface. The bass player plays his instrument normally and controls frequent key shifts with his feet with the dance mat. The second player navigates a chord sequence. Both players sometimes lead and sometimes follow. The game was played too fast for reflective thought and was considered highly engaging

knew, but which had not featured in the trial. Without since having had any access to the interface, he correctly identified the path this song would trace, and went on to ask insightful questions about the musical implications of this path.

Conclusions

Taking into account the theoretical issues and the case study, what lessons can be drawn for whole body interaction in general? Let us marshal the key theoretical points to help us synthesize a concrete proposal. As already noted, conceptual metaphor theory posits that all human capabilities for dealing with abstract concepts are grounded in low-level sensory motor resources for dealing with the body, objects, space and force. More specifically, conceptual metaphors are developed by various developmental and cultural processes to allow abstract concerns to be manipulated using resources borrowed from universal image schemas. This allows abstractions to be grounded directly in physical experience. To go beyond this, and in order to be able to deal with abstraction of arbitrary complexity, we need conceptual blending to allow two or more conceptual metaphors to be melded by processes of composition, completion and elaboration. In all cases, an audit trail, from the abstractions back to physically grounded experience may be identified. This does not create a panacea for instantly simplifying any domain, but it does in principle relate any abstract topic to the physically-related, low-level skills to which humans are well suited.

It remains a non-trivial task to analyse conceptual metaphorical structures in any specific domain, though as noted, progress has been made in areas such as Mathematics, Human Computer Interaction, Music Theory and Harmony. How then, can this be applied to whole body interaction design in the general case? In effect, we are arguing for an elaboration of the approach to interaction design advocated by Dourish [7]. Like Dourish, we argue that collaborative, physically engaged interaction allows a wider range of human mental resources to be brought to bear on problems than sitting at a desk in isolation thinking abstract thoughts. In a difference of emphasis to Dourish, we see the direct exploitation of conceptual metaphors in interaction design as a particularly powerful way to bring these resources to bear on abstract problems domains. In particular we advocate the following key steps when designing for whole body interaction.

(a) The crafting of user interaction metaphors specifically to reflect and exploit the physical grounding of conceptual metaphors and blends in the given domain.
(b) The exploitation of cues to prompt the user to foreground physically grounded mental resources in manipulating the conceptual metaphors and blends exploited by the interface.

The good news is that the previously rehearsed theoretical arguments suggest that by this process, it should be possible to usefully apply whole body interaction to *any arbitrary abstract domain*. Of course, limitations will apply. Zbikowski [30] points out how conceptual metaphors can vary greatly in the *density of image-schematic correspondences* between source and target domains. The fewer the correspondences, the less useful a conceptual metaphor is likely to be. Strong conceptual metaphors can form the basis of more effective whole body interaction designs than weak ones. Zbikowski [29] and Eitan and Timmers [8] identify some rather weak conceptual metaphors in music, for example those concerning crocodiles and waterfalls, while Lakoff and Núñez [22] identify some extraordinarily strong conceptual metaphors in mathematics, for example in their conceptual analysis of Euler's equation. The candidate conceptual metaphors in Harmony Space are highly dense (assuming they are validated) as many spatial metaphors are. However, we hypothesise that conceptual metaphors need not necessarily be explicitly spatial in nature to effectively support whole body interaction. What matters is that the density of image-schematic correspondences between source and target domains should be high, and the length of chains in conceptual blends not too long. Of course, the success of this approach will always remain dependent on the identification of conceptual metaphors in the domains of interest, as does the closely related approach that employs conceptual metaphors to analyse interaction designs, pioneered by Wilkie et al. [27].

We offer the present case study as an existence proof of the value and reach of the explicit use of conceptual metaphors in whole body interaction design. We have demonstrated in at least one abstract domain that this approach affords the performance of complex technical tasks that otherwise require extensive abstract symbolic knowledge.

References

1. Antle, A.N., Corness, G., Droumeva, M.: Human-computer-intuition? Exploring the cognitive basis for intuition in embodied interaction. Int. J. Arts Technol. **2**(3), 235–254 (2009)
2. Antle, A.N., Droumeva, M., Corness, G.: Playing with the sound maker: do embodied metaphors help children learn? In: Proceedings of the 7th International Conference on Interaction Design and Children, Chicago, pp. 178–185. Association for Computing Machinery, New York (2008)
3. Bach-y-Rita, P.: Brain Mechanisms in Sensory Substitution. Academic, New York (1972). Studies **64**(1), 1–15 (2005)
4. Balzano, G.J.: The group-theoretic description of 12-fold and microtonal pitch systems. Comput. Music J. **4**(4 Winter), 66–84 (1980)
5. Bird, J., Holland, S., Marshall, P., Rogers, Y., Clark, A.: Feel the force: using tactile technologies to investigate the extended mind. In: Proceedings of Devices That Alter Perception Workshop (DAP 08), Seoul (2008)
6. Brower, C.: A cognitive theory of musical meaning. J. Music Theory **44**(2), 323–379 (2000)
7. Dourish, P.: Where the Action Is: The Foundations of Embodied Interaction. MIT Press, Cambridge (2001). ISBN 978-0-262-54178-7
8. Eitan, Z., Timmers, R.: Beethoven's last piano sonata and those who follow crocodiles: cross-domain mappings of auditory pitch in a musical context. Cognition **114**(3), 405–422 (2010)
9. Fauconnier, G., Turner, M.: The Way We Think: Conceptual Blending and the Mind's Hidden Complexities. Basic Books, New York (2002)
10. Gold, B.: Mathematical Association of America Online Book Review. http://www.maa.org/reviews/wheremath.html (2001). Accessed Oct 2010

11. Held, R., Hein, A.V.: Adaptation of disarranged hand-eye coordination contingent upon re-afferent stimulation. Percept. Mot. Skills **8**(1958), 87–90 (1958)

12. Holland, S.: Learning about harmony with harmony space: an overview. In: Smith, M., Wiggins, G. (eds.) Music Education: An Artificial Intelligence Approach. Springer, London (1994)

13. Holland, S., Bouwer, A., Dalgleish, M., Hurtig, T.: Feeling the beat where it counts: fostering multi-limb rhythm skills with the haptic drum kit. In: Proceedings of TEI 2010, Boston, Cambridge (2010)

14. Holland, S., Marshall, P., Bird, J., Dalton, S., Morris, R., Pantidi, N., Rogers, Y., Clark, A.: Running up Blueberry Hill: prototyping whole body interaction in harmony space. In: Proceedings of the Third Conference on Tangible and Embodied Interaction, pp. 92–98. ACM, New York (2009)

15. Holland, S.: Artificial intelligence, education and music. Ph.D. thesis, Institute of Educational Technology, The Open University (1989)

16. Hurtienne, J., Blessing, L.: Design for intuitive use – testing image schema theory for user interface design. In: Proceedings of the 16th International Conference on Engineering Design, pp. 1–12. Paris (2007)

17. Hurtienne, J., Israel, J.H., Weber, K.: Cooking up real world business applications combining physicality, digitality, and image schemas. In: Proceedings of the 2nd International Conference on Tangible and Embedded Interaction, Bonn, pp. 239–246. ACM, New York (2008)

18. Johnson, M.: The philosophical significance of image schemas. In: Hampe, B., Grady, J. (eds.) From Perception to Meaning: Image Schemas in Cognitive Linguistics, pp. 15–33. Walter de Gruyter, Berlin (2005)

19. Klemmer, S.R., Hartmann, B., Takayama, L.: How bodies matter: five themes for interaction design. In: Proceedings of the 6th Conference on Designing Interactive Systems (DIS'06), pp. 140–149. University Park, 26–28 June 2006.. ACM, New York (2006)

20. Lakoff, G.: Moral Politics: How Liberals and Conservatives Think. University of Chicago Press, Chicago (2002)

21. Lakoff, G., Johnson, M.: Metaphors We Live by. The University of Chicago, London (2003)

22. Lakoff, G., Núñez, R.: Where Mathematics Comes from: How the Embodied Mind Brings Mathematics into Being. Basic Books, New York (2000)

23. Larson, S.: Musical forces and melodic patterns. Theory Pract. **22–23**, 55–71 (1997–1998)

24. O'Regan, K., Noe, A.: A sensorimotor account of vision and visual consciousness. Behav. Brain Sci. **24**(5), 883–917 (2001)

25. Rohrer, T.: The body in space: dimensions of embodiment. In: Ziemke, T., Zlatev, J., Frank, R., Dirven, R. (eds.) Body, Language, and Mind: Embodiment, pp. 339–378. Walter de Gruyter, Berlin (2007)

26. Saslaw, J.: Forces, containers, and paths: the role of body-derived image schemas in the conceptualization of music. J. Music Theory **40**(2 Autumn), 217–243 (1996)

27. Wilkie, K., Holland, S., Mulholland, P.: What can the language of musicians tell us about music interaction design? Comput. Music J. **34**(4), 34–48 (2010)

28. Wilkie, K., Holland, S., Mulholland, P.: Evaluating musical software using conceptual metaphors. In: Proceedings of the 23rd British Computer Society Conference on Human Computer Interaction, Cambridge, pp. 232–237. British Computer Society, Cambridge (2009)

29. Zbikowski, L.M.: Metaphor and music theory: reflections from cognitive science. Music Theory Online **4**, 1–8 (1998)

30. Zbikowski, L.M.: Conceptual models and cross-domain mapping: new perspective on theories of music and hierarchy. J. Music Theory **41**(2 Autumn), 193–225 (1997)

Chapter 4
Mirrored Motion: Augmenting Reality and Implementing Whole Body Gestural Control Using Pervasive Body Motion Capture Based on Wireless Sensors

Philip Smit, Peter Barrie, Andreas Komninos, and Oleksii Mandrychenko

Abstract There has been a lot of discussion in recent years around the disappearing computer concept and most of the results of that discussion have been realized in the form of mobile devices and applications. What has got lost a little in this discussion is the moves that have seen the miniaturization of sensors that can be wirelessly attached to places and to humans in order to provide a new type of free flowing interaction. In order to investigate what these new sensors could achieve and at what cost, we implemented a configurable, wearable motion-capture system based on wireless sensor nodes, requiring no special environment to operate in. We discuss the system architecture and discuss the implications and opportunities afforded by it for innovative HCI design. As a practical application of the technology, we describe a prototype implementation of a pervasive, wearable augmented reality (AR) system based on the motion-capture system. The AR application uses body motion to visualize and interact with virtual objects populating AR settings. Body motion is used to implement a whole body gesture-driven interface to manipulate the virtual objects. Gestures are mapped to corresponding behaviours for virtual objects, such as controlling the playback and volume of virtual audio players or displaying a virtual object's metadata.

Introduction to Motion Capture

Humans have always had difficulties interacting effortlessly with computers. The difference in language is perhaps too great to ensure natural and graceful communication; therefore it could be supposed that interaction may be improved in some ways by taking away some of the physical barriers between the machine and the user.

P. Smit (✉), P. Barrie, A. Komninos, and O. Mandrychenko
School of Engineering and Computing, Glasgow Caledonian University,
70 Cowcaddens Road, Glasgow, UK
e-mail: philip.smit@gcal.ac.uk; peter.barrie@gcal.ac.uk; andreas.komninos@gcal.ac.uk;
oleksii.mandrychenko@gcal.ac.uk

D. England (ed.), *Whole Body Interaction*, Human-Computer Interaction Series, 35
DOI 10.1007/978-0-85729-433-3_4, © Springer-Verlag London Limited 2011

Today many artificial intelligent technologies like speech and image recognition systems are commercially available to make people feel that the device is reacting to them in a more intuitive way. We took this concept a step further and investigated how a wireless sensor-based system could be implemented to allow the capture of human body movement and gestures in real time.

Motion-capture is not limited to man-machine interfacing only, but also has applications in a diverse set of disciplines, for example in movie and computer game production, sports science, bioengineering and other sciences to which the analysis of human body movement is a major focal point. Motion capture systems have tended to be complex, expensive, purpose-built setups in dedicated and strictly controlled environments that maximize their efficiency. However, in the context of pervasive computing, the design of a system to capture motion at any time and any place is constrained by several parameters that are not considered in traditional systems. Such constraints are the durability, wearability (and discreetness of the system when worn), independence from specially configured environments, power consumption and management and connectivity with other pervasive systems. We aimed to address these problems in our study, and as such began to think about how to develop a low-cost, real-time motion-capture system.

The approach we took was to use sourceless sensors to establish the orientation of the human anatomical segments, from which posture is then determined. Sourceless sensors do not require artificial sources (e.g. IR illumination or artificial magnetic fields) to be excited. Instead, they rely on "natural phenomena", e.g. the earth's magnetic field and gravity, to act as stimulus [4]. Such sensors need to report their readings so these can be processed and translated into body movement. To achieve this, we thought it would be appropriate that wireless technology was used to connect the sensors, thus forming a Wireless Body Area Network (WBAN). Wireless sensors make the system unobtrusive, increase its wearability and compared to a wired solution, allow for a much wider range of applications. In the following sections we present our investigation into the development of a low-cost, low-power WBAN of sensors, as an enabler for HCI applications. We also present an outline of applications where this has been successfully used and discuss future opportunities for this system.

Background to Motion Capture

Wearable sensor systems have been used in the past with success in several contexts of which particular focus seems to have been placed within the domains of Pervasive Healthcare [6, 10, 15] and Interaction with Mixed or Virtual Reality systems [12, 19], and Mobile Systems [9]. Wearable sensors have also been used to investigate Interaction in such domains as Computer Gaming [2] and the acquisition of varying levels of Context Awareness [8, 18]. In such respects, while much progress has been made, this progress only partially fulfills the objective of capturing of full body motion in pervasive computing landscapes. There are only a few systems we are aware of which meets this objective; one is in [21], although this system relies on a set of wired sensors and a heavy backpack to power it, limiting its wearability and configurability, as sensors have to be used as a complete set. Two commercial systems work on a similar principle with [21], using sets of sensors wired to a hub, which transmits aggregated data wirelessly using Bluetooth or 802.15.4 (XSens,[1] EoBodyHF[2]). Wired sensors limit the wearability of these systems.

Our work's fundamental aim is to investigate the use of a low-cost distributed computing infrastructure with sensors to provide a means of capturing environmental and human activity as part of our research group's current interest areas (pervasive healthcare, mobile spatial interaction and mobile audio-video interaction). For HCI researchers there are exciting opportunities due to the standardization, miniaturization, modularization and economies of scale presented by the new technologies available for the creation of wireless sensor networks. Of special interest is wireless body area network (WBAN) technology. Using modern silicon Micro-Electro-Mechanical Systems (MEMS) manufacturing techniques, sensors (such as gyros, magnetometers and accelerometers) have become inexpensive, small and can now be worn on the body or integrated into clothing [20]. Such sensors, coupled with low power processors that may integrated the necessary wireless componentry, (such as the 32-bit Freescale MC1322x platform), provide the basic fabric for increasingly powerful wireless sensor networks.

System Design

From reviewing the existing literature, we identified a set of heuristics against which a pervasive motion capture system must perform well. Our criteria were as follows:

- **Connectivity**: Pervasive systems do not work in isolation. Any sensor-based system must allow its components to communicate with each other and coordinate its behavior. It must, however, also be able to communicate its components' status to external systems in the environment.
- **Power**: A pervasive system must not rely on external sources of power, as these are not omnipresent. It should have its own power source and appropriate power management features that allows it to operate for lengthy periods of time.
- **Performance**: The performance and responsiveness of a pervasive motion capture system must be such that it affords the real-time capture of bodily motion and its transmission to external systems with minimal latency.
- **Wearability**: Systems must be light, easily wearable and discreet. Discretion can be achieved by embedding sensors in everyday objects or garments, or by designing them so that they can be easily concealed.

In designing the Mirrored Motion demonstrator, we considered these heuristics as appropriate to informing our system characteristics.

---

[1] XSens http://www.xsens.com

[2] EOWave Systems http://www.eowave.com

Connectivity and Power

Our system is comprised of sensor "nodes" that can be attached to key locations on a user's body, monitoring the movement of major body parts (limbs, torso, head). One of the off-body nodes acts as a "coordinator", gathering data from all nodes and relaying to external systems for further processing. To coordinate the communication between the peripheral and the coordinator nodes, the Bluetooth and IEEE 802.15.4 standards were considered suitable candidates. We also considered 802.11x (Wi-Fi) but this was quickly rejected, as its power consumption is too high for continuous use. A shortcoming of Bluetooth is that it is limited to eight nodes per network, which would be insufficient for covering even just the basic major parts of a human body. In contrast, IEEE 802.15.4 can have 65,536 nodes in a network (star or mesh topologies) and can work over similar node-to-node distances as Bluetooth. It can operate with a smaller network stack size, reducing the embedded memory footprint. For the flexible and extensible HCI applications to be considered, the larger node count is useful to create networks that integrate on and off-body nodes and have potentially multiple interacting users. IEEE 802.15.4 data rates are in the range of 20–250 kbps, although in actual use the higher rate cannot be attained due to protocol overheads. Although lower than Bluetooth, this data rate has been shown in our experiments to be sufficient for body-motion frame rates. Because of its characteristics in allowing multiple node connectivity and very low power consumption, we selected 802.15.4 as the preferred communication protocol. The wireless module used in the system is a Panasonic PAN4555.

Wearability and Performance

Sensors used in each node for the first prototype were a 3-axis accelerometer and a magnetometer per node. A magnetometer–accelerometer sensor can produce accurate orientation information when the only force experienced by the sensor is gravity. However, any additional forces will result in the reference vector produced by the accelerometer to be inaccurate. In a revision to our original design, miniature MEMS gyros were added to the sensor pack. Gyros measure angular velocity and this helps to reduce the effects of non-gravity forces (Fig. 4.1).

These sensors were originally packaged in a rather large form, roughly the size of an average mobile phone, as pre-configured development kits were used to prove the concept. Once satisfied with the performance of the system, we re-designed the hardware and created custom sensor packs that were optimized for size. Each pack is relatively small (less than 4 × 3 in.). They are attached to the user's body with Velcro straps, making them easy to wear and remove. Their small size makes them easy concealable under normal clothing. Because this is an experimental platform we created a modular construction allowing the removal and addition of the sensor and wireless components. The necessary connectors and modules take up extra space. A custom version could be created with a smaller footprint, with all parts

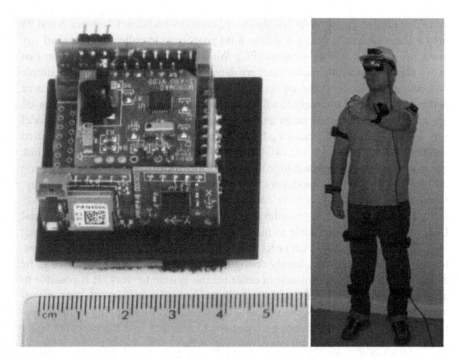

Fig. 4.1 Our custom-designed sensor pack containing three-axis accelerometer, gyro, magnetometer and 802.15.4 comms (*left*). On the *right*, a user demonstrating the small size and wearability of the packs, Velcro-strapped on his body. The cable attaches his VR headset to the host PC

integrated onto a single PCB. Sensor nodes are placed on each of the tracked human limbs (upper and lower arm, head, torso, upper and lower leg) to track the orientation of each. The raw data acquired by the sensor WBAN is transmitted wirelessly to an external system (in our experiments, a typical PC). We set a data acquisition target for our system to achieve real-time performance at a sampling rate of 30 Hz, as this would, in theory, allow us the re-creation of a user's skeletal model on an external system with a refresh rate that would yield about 25–30 FPS, which is adequate for real-time video. The posture of the skeleton is calculated in real-time through forward kinematics. Kinematics simplifies computations by decomposing any geo-metric calculations into rotation and translation transforms. Orientation is obtained by combining (or fusing) these information sources into a rotation matrix – an algebraic format that can be directly applied to find the posture of the user. The result is a simple skeleton model defined as a coarse representation of the user.

The Sensor Network

The sensor nodes were successfully tested at a 30 Hz sample rate but this appeared to be the upper limit. Our empirical results show that the coordinator could handle up to 360 packets per seconds (i.e. up to ~12 nodes) with latency between 5 and 25 ms for the coordinator (using a simple 8-bit processor) to collect and forward any given frame to the external systems (PC). We would like to point out however that in our current system the packet rates are dependent on the constraints of the simple processing hardware and the application running on it. A lightweight application or better processor will probably handle much higher packet rates. In order to provide a synthesis of human movement and position within the system, a skeletal model was developed on the PC receiving the motion data. Similar models have been used successfully in the past [5, 13, 14]. Our model uses the lower torso as the root link and tracks the position of each limb as a set of links connected to each other starting at the root. The skeleton model we produced is easily extensible and can be augmented to incorporate many more nodes, such as to track palm, finger or foot movement. Because the receiver (coordinator) node on the PC is connected using a serial USB connection, it is possible to have multiple WBANs on the user's body, each with up to 12 sensor packs (in order to maintain very low latency levels). Our system is, in this respect, very highly configurable, as not all of the nodes need to be attached to the body or activated in order for the system to work. It is possible to arrange the system in such manner as to detect only arm movement, torso movement, leg movement or any combination of these, simply by strapping on the appropriate sensor packs and indicating to the capture interface which sensors are being work by checking the relevant boxes (see Fig. 4.2).

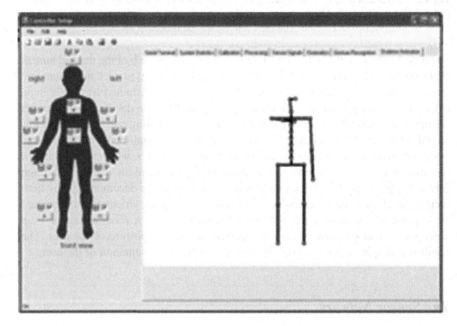

Fig. 4.2 The motion capture interface (PC). A user can indicate which sensor packs are being worn by checking the relevant boxes on the human outline shape. The skeleton model on the right is constructed in real-time

A calibration procedure has to be enacted at the start of a motion capture session by the user. Posture calibration is performed with the user assuming a predefined reference posture (standing up straight, arms down), as in [5]. The calibration takes approximately 2–3 s to complete, which can be considered to be a low overhead for the human actor. The captured data is sent from the coordinator to the PC and is then processed through a configurable low-pass filter before going through the skeletal transformation. At this stage, the PC can then display a stick-figure animation as shown in Fig. 4.2. The calibration interface and sensor placement guide on the human is also shown in Fig. 4.2.

Whole Body HCI

Achieving motion capture solves only one part of the problem in creating novel human-computer interfaces. We developed a demonstration application based on our sensor system, in which the movement is captured from the user and then the skeleton is covered with a digital skin, using DirectX and integrated into a synthetic 3D environment as shown in Fig. 4.3. In this demonstrator, the user is equipped with a VR headset as well as the motion capture system. The 3D world is the start of the experimentation with interaction. This experiment provides

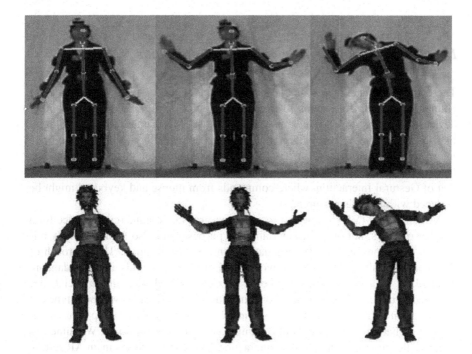

Fig. 4.3 Real-time mapping of user body movement to a 3D virtual avatar in an immersive world

smooth motion tracking from first (with 2/3D head mounted display) and third person perspectives that immerse the users in a synthetic experience using real movements and synthetic visual feedback, so, for example, when the user holds up their hands in front of them in the real world they see their hands in a 3D virtual world (videos of this can be viewed on our website at http://www.mucom.mobi). In another application, we augmented our nodes with an optical proximity sensor, to allow a sensor node to be mounted within a shoe to undertake a field investigation of foot motion. Further to this, we began investigating how our equipment can be used to accurately detect gait and foot clearance for elderly persons, helping solve and investigate issues in fall prevention. This is particularly important as until now, people could only be monitored in specialized labs (with expensive video equipment); now it is feasible to monitor an elderly person in their own environment and for extended periods of time, at relatively low-cost. A recent laboratory-based trial compared an existing video-tracking system with our foot-mounted sensor system. The results show a high degree of correspondence between the two data sets.

Continuing in the domain of pervasive healthcare, we also produced a prototype of a Marble Maze game that was used with a wobble board. The user stands on the board and makes small movements in order to guide the marble through the virtual maze, helping improve body balance and posture for rehabilitation patients. We used one sensing node to detect the movement of the wobble board with a high level of success.

Introduction to an Augmented Reality Application

There is significant interest in the development of more "natural" methods for Human Computer Interaction. Keyboards, joysticks, mice, displays and other devices are hardware interfaces in widespread use. Many intelligent technologies like speech and image recognition systems are commercially available to facilitate interaction through the use of naturalistic human-computer interface modalities. One interaction modality that has been the focus of considerable research lately is that of Gestural Interaction, where commands from mouse and keyboard might be replaced with a user's gestures [3].

Virtual reality (VR) has been a focus of research and commercial practice for a number of years, not only for entertainment purposes but also for industrially relevant applications such as 3D product design and visualization. The approach of Augmented Reality, where virtual worlds and objects, or worlds and metadata are mapped on to views of the real world, mixing the real with the artificial, has emerged in the computer science world in addition to VR. However, both types of visualization suffer from problems of control – how can a user manipulate virtual objects as naturally as they would manipulate real physical ones? We aimed to examine the concept of naturalistic interaction with virtual objects in an AR setting by investigating how our wireless-sensor-based system could be used to recognize gestures made by the user's body and help create a wearable AR system that could be deployed and used without the need for fixed infrastructure.

The approach we took was to develop a system based on the Mirrored Motion system, a VR display headset and a web camera attached to the user's head. The sensors provide raw data subsequently used for the recognition of the user's gestures, whilst the camera gives a live video feed on which virtual objects are superimposed. The web camera works with the sensor on the user's head to obtain the camera's orientation and as such, synchronize the panning and rotation of the virtual world to match the web camera movements.

Background to Augmented Reality

AR technology enhances a user's perception of and interaction with the real world. The key feature of the augmented reality technology is to present auxiliary information (visual, audio, haptic etc.) in the sensory space of an individual, though in our work we concentrate on augmenting the environment with visible virtual objects. The virtual objects display information that the user cannot directly detect with his or her own senses. The information conveyed by the virtual objects helps the user to perform real-world tasks. This new form of human-computer interaction can be applied to various industry areas [11]. AR is an emerging technology area and as such, applications that could benefit from AR technology are still not fully explored. Typical examples are seen in engineering, military and educational domains. AR technology for digital composition of animation with real scenes is being explored to deliver adverting content or bring new digital entertainment experience to users.

Our system represents an exciting opportunity to engage in interaction design research. For the purposes of AR, orientation sensors coupled with a web camera provides evident opportunity for orientation in a virtual world accordingly to the direction that camera faces. The skeletal model built from our sensors' data supplies the receiver with rotation matrices and linear angles that can be used to recognize human gestures [16]. We aimed to extend the surrounding spatial environment with supplementary information through AR. We wanted to use the system not only to help visualize virtual objects for AR, but also interact with the objects through gestures.

System Design

AR technology is not a new concept. Apart from studies in AR visualization, many applications already exist in advertising, industry, robotics, medicine, sport, military and many other spheres. Additionally, several researchers have proposed to use gesture recognition in conjunction with AR [7, 20]. However, we are not yet aware of any AR systems based on full body motion capture and that utilize gesture interaction, which do not require extensive infrastructure support and which can be used in pervasive computing settings. From reviewing the existing literature, we identified defined two goals [2, 18] to be implemented:

- **Gesture recognition**. The proposed system must recognize user's gesture in 3D space independently on the user's location. Gestures can be trained before recognition.
- **Extending reality**. The system must provide means for presenting auxiliary information in the field of view of a user's VR headset. Providing the particular gesture is recognized the system is to change the state of correspondent virtual object.

In designing the AR demonstration, we considered these goals as appropriate to inform our system characteristics.

Gesture Recognition

As described earlier, our system is comprised of sensor "nodes" that can be attached to key locations on a user's body, monitoring the movement of major body parts (limbs, torso, and head). One of the off-body nodes acts as a "coordinator", gathering data from all nodes and relaying to external systems (e.g. a PDA, a server or a desktop computer) for further processing. The approximate frequency of streaming data is 20 Hz. While our system is capable of full body motion capture, in this application we used an upper body set of sensors, as we were more interested in torso and hands gesture recognition. An internal processing system provides us with an updatable skeleton model of the user which is a method also used by other researchers, e.g. [9]. In general terms, gesture recognition consists of several stages, like feature extraction, preprocessing, analyzing and making a decision. Our experimental method consists of using linear angles between any two links in the skeletal model as a dataset that is fed into the gesture recognition algorithms described below (see Fig. 4.4).

At the preprocessing stage we perform work to filter the noise caused by rapid movements and inaccuracy of the measurements (around 3–5°). A magnetometer-accelerometer-gyro sensor can produce accurate orientation information when the forces experienced by the sensor are gravity or low accelerated movements. Any additional forces will result in the reference vector produced by the accelerometer to be inaccurate.

Analyzing sequences of linear angles and performing the gesture recognition itself was implemented with the help of AMELIA general pattern recognition library [1], which we used as a basis to implement our own customized Hidden Markov Model. Hidden Markov models (HMMs) are the basis of most gesture recognition algorithms used today. However, traditional HMM-based gesture recognition systems require a large number of parameters to be trained in order to give satisfying recognition results. In particular, an n-state HMM requires n^2 parameters to be trained for the transition probability matrix, which limits its usability in

Fig. 4.4 Gesture recognition architecture

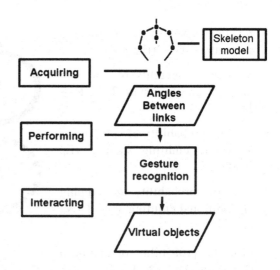

Skeleton model

Acquiring

Angles Between links

Performing

Gesture recognition

Interacting

Virtual objects

environments where training data is limited [13, 17]. The reduced model that was used in our system uses a constant number of parameters for each state to determine transition probabilities between all states. As there are many different notation conventions in use for Hidden Markov Models, here we utilize a convention we believe makes our model easy to understand. We thereby define our augmented hidden Markov model $(S = \{E,N\}, S_b, S_e, T,O)$ by a set of states S, a designated beginning state S_b, a designated ending state S_e, a state transition probability function T, and an observation probability function O. The augmented HMM behaves essentially the same as a regular HMM, with only a few points of departure. The set of states S is divided into disjoint sets of emitting states E and non-emitting states N. The difference between the two is that when entered, emitting states emit an observation belonging to the observation set θ according to the observation probability function $O: E \times \theta \rightarrow [0,1)$. The model always begins in the beginning state $S_b \in S$, and until it ends up in the ending state $S_e \in S$ it makes transitions according to the transition probability function $T: (S - S_e) \times S \rightarrow [0,1)$. T must also satisfy that the sum of transition probabilities out of any state is 1. In the reduced parameter model, we use the following parameters, depicted also in Fig. 4.5.

Our system allows users to record their own gestures for predefined actions that control the behaviour of virtual objects (e.g. selecting/deselecting an object, turning on and off a virtual appliance such as a virtual radio, controlling the behaviour of a virtual object such as start/stop playback of music), some of which are depicted in Fig. 4.6. As such, different actors may use diverse gestures for the same action. Typically, to record one gesture an actor repeats it for three to four times, as in [5, 17]. Once a few "recordings" of a gesture have been made, the system is then trained on the captured motion data set in order to be able to recognize the gestures. A general gesture tends to be 2–3 s in time. After training, the user can perform gestures in different sequences as well as performing actions that are not gestures. Our system recognizes gestures with the probability of

- τ_i is the probability of remaining in an emitting state, $T(E_i, E_i)$

- η_i is the probability of going to the next emitting state $T(E_i, E_i + 1)$

- ς_i is the probability of skipping at least one emitting state $T(E_i, N_i+1)$

- k_i is the probability of skipping an additional emitting state $T(N_i, N_i+1)$

- p_i is the probability of ending a skip sequence $T(N, E_i+1)$

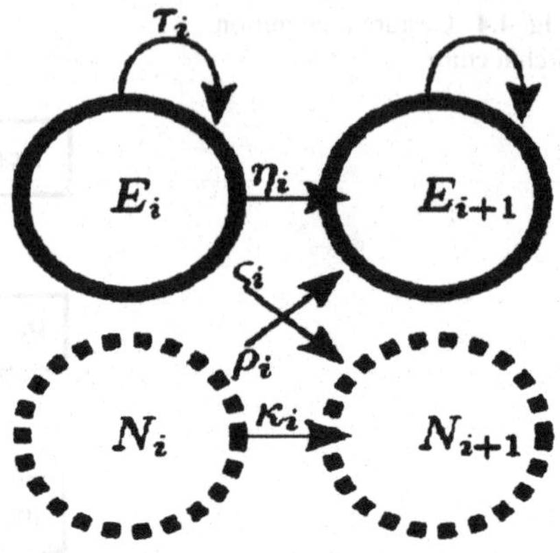

Fig. 4.5 Transition probability parameters for the HMM

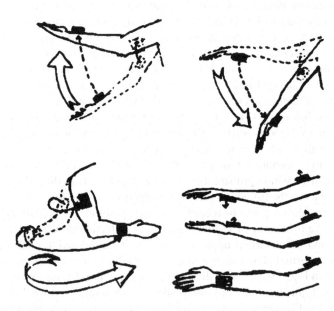

Fig. 4.6 Examples of naturalistic gestures designed to control a virtual radio in the AR system. The top gestures show raising the (*left*) and lowering (*right*) the volume. The *bottom left* shows skipping a station. By modifying the position of just one node (carpal), we can achieve a large number of distinct gestures (*bottom right*)

80–90% (determined experimentally). Examples of our gesture recognition systems are available to view online in video form from our website (http://www.mucom.mobi).

At this point in time, our system has two limitations: Firstly, saving of the recorded gestures training data is not yet implemented (due to development-time constraints) but we consider it as a simple goal. Secondly, our current recognition model does not allow a gesture to stop in the actor's relaxed position. For example, if a user stands still and tries to record a gesture, finishing it at the relaxed posture, the recognition system will not determine when the gesture ends. However, this limitation will be removed in the near future.

Extending Reality Using Whole Body Interaction

There are differing approaches to augmenting reality and presenting synthetic visual information overlaid on real world views. Magic Lens applications rely on the use of a camera-enabled device that acts as a viewer, through which additional information pertaining to real objects or completely virtual 3D objects can be viewed. Another mode is the use of special glasses, on which simple graphics or text is rendered. For our approach, we used a set of VR goggles connected to a webcam. Live video that comes from a web camera is constantly placed in front of a viewer in a 3D world. In order to ensure that the 3D world's game camera corresponds with some fidelity to the live video feed from the webcam, the system must be calibrated by starting at a pre-determined real-world location whose coordinates are mapped to a pre-determined point in the virtual world. The user sees a combined image from real video and virtual objects. Virtual objects are placed in front of the dynamic web camera feed. The coordinates of the video are not updated, therefore live view always stays on the same place – in front of the viewer, whereas coordinates of the virtual objects are updated. We combined a web camera with the head sensor, which helps map the camera orientation (and hence the user's view of the real world) in 3D space. As a user moves his or her head, the virtual world moves accordingly. The virtual objects that are in front of the human actor will come in and out of the user's field of view, when the viewer looks to the left or to the right (up or down). In order to provide a synthesis of live video feed and virtual objects to the user, so that an augmentation of reality can be implemented, Microsoft's XNA gaming development tools were used. In our AR application, a user sees a mixture of real and virtual objects. In order to interact with virtual objects or metadata pertaining to real objects, these must somehow be selected. To select a virtual object, we used data that comes from the sensor on the right hand. We transform pitch and rotation to the Y and X movements of a cursor in the virtual world. To select a virtual object, the user thus uses their right arm to "point" a crosshair cursor to the virtual object they want to select. Every virtual object has its own bounding form. For simplicity, we used bounding spheres only.

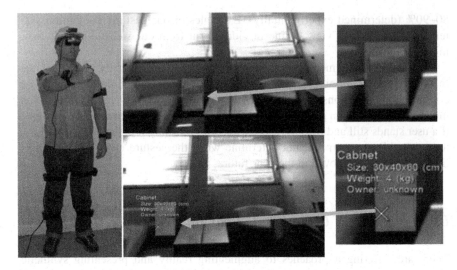

Fig. 4.7 The user points an arm-controlled cursor (visualized to the user as an X) at the virtual object (marked by the *arrow*), which is then highlighted. Metadata for that object is subsequently displayed

We took advantages of the XNA ray technique to understand whether a ray (game camera – cursor – infinity) intersects with the bounding spheres of virtual objects. When the cursor line of sight intersects and hovers over an object, it becomes selected (Fig. 4.7). We found this method of selection in preliminary tests easy to understand and one that is well received as it affords more precise and flexible control than using head direction for selecting (one can look and point in different directions).

Conclusions and Further Work

We have described how we defined a set of criteria for a pervasive body motion capture system and created a system informed by these, which was then used to investigate whole and partial body interaction in a series of demonstrators. Throughout our development we aimed to make use of easily available, low-cost components, keeping the cost per node to approximately £150. Given the many different environments (e.g. healthcare, gaming, VR, AR etc.) in which we wished people to interact with and benefit from our work, we needed to ensure that the system was additionally highly configurable, to allow a wide range of interaction opportunities to be investigated. Overall we were successful in delivering a high-performance, truly pervasive, extensible and highly wearable system that fulfils the criteria for such systems.

We have described how we implemented gesture recognition with the pervasive body motion capture system and created augmented reality, which might be used in different fields such as entertainment, sports, military etc. Throughout our development we aimed to make use of our existing low-cost nodes. Overall we were successful in delivering a high-performance, truly pervasive, extensible and highly wearable system that fulfils the criteria for augmented reality systems. In Fig. 4.4, the user's only restriction to mobility is the headset connection, in this picture connected to a desktop PC, but equally able to be connected to a portable laptop/tablet. However, our system at the moment does not support the motion of the user's body between locations in the real/virtual world. We assume that the user remains fixed and as such we have only used the upper body sensor set as a means to trap gestures. In the near future, we plan to take advantage of our ability to capture motion from the entire body, in order to allow the user to move through the AR world. We would be particularly interested in examining how our MEMS-based system performs in inferring user location (e.g. while walking) and how the accuracy of our system might be enhanced through the fusion of GPS data, where available. Additionally, a hybrid positioning system as described would be of great interest to examine in scenarios where indoor-outdoor transitions occur for the user.

We believe that our system will prove an extremely useful tool for a range of interaction opportunities; aside from our previous projects we are working on applying our system in several areas. We are particularly interested in its potential in mixed reality situations for gaming. We also wish to investigate issues in human-human interaction through embodied agents, controlled through the motion capture system. We are looking into the control of VR agents, as well as robotic agents for which the metaphor of "transferring one's soul" will be used to investigate response and interaction with other humans. Finally, we are interested in pursuing applications in tangible interfaces and semi-virtual artifacts, as well as gesture-based whole-body interaction with large situated displays. We hope to be able to create new types of human-computer interfaces for manipulating program windows, arranging or opening files using ad-hoc large projected or semi-transparent situated displays.

References

1. AMELIA: A generic library for pattern recognition and generation. http://ame4.hc.asu.edu/amelia/ (2010) (link valid 08/2010)
2. Antifakos, S., Schiele, B.: Bridging the gap between virtual and physical games using wearable sensors. In: Proceedings of the Sixth International Symposium on Wearable Computers (ISWC 2002), pp. 139–140, Seattle (2002)
3. Azuma, R.: A survey of augmented reality. Presence Teleoper. Virtual Environ. 6(4), 355–385 (August 1997)
4. Bachmann, E.: Inertial and magnetic angle tracking of limb segments for inserting humans into synthetic environments. Ph.D. thesis, Naval Postgraduate School (2000)
5. Bodenheimer, B., Rose, C., Pella, J., Rosenthal, S.: The process of motion capture: dealing with the data. In: Computer Animation and Simulation, pp. 3–18, Milano. Eurographics, Springer, London (1997)
6. Bonato, P.: Wearable sensors/systems and their impact on biomedical engineering. Eng. Med. Biol. Mag. IEEE 22(3), 18–20 (2003)

7. Buchmann, V., Violich, S., Billinghurst, M., Cockburn, A.: FingARtips: gesture based direct manipulation in Augmented Reality. In: GRAPHITE 2004: Proceedings of the 2nd International Conference on Computer Graphics and Interactive Techniques in Australasia and South East Asia, Singapore (2004)
8. Clarkson, B.P.: Life patterns: structure from wearable sensors. Ph.D. thesis, Massachusetts Institute of Technology (2002)
9. Crossan, A., Williamson, J., Brewster, S., Murray-Smith, R.: Wrist rotation for interaction in mobile contexts. In: Proceedings of the 10th International Conference on Human Computer Interaction with Mobile Devices and Services, pp. 435–438. ACM, Amsterdam (2008)
10. Jovanov, E.: Wireless technology and system integration in body area networks for m-Health applications. In: Proceedings of the 27th Annual International Conference of the IEEE Engineering in Medicine and Biology Society, Shanghai (2005)
11. Lyu, M.R., King, I., Wong, T.T., Yau, E., Chan, P.W.: ARCADE: augmented reality computing arena for digital entertainment. In: 5th IEEE Aerospace Conference, Big Sky (2005)
12. Martins, T., Sommerer, C., Mignonneau, L., Correia, N.: Gauntlet: a wearable interface for ubiquitous gaming. In: Proceedings of the 10th International Conference on Human Computer Interaction with Mobile Devices and Services, pp. 367–370, Amsterdam. ACM, New York (2008)
13. Molet, T., Boulic, R., Thalmann, D.: Human motion capture driven by orientation measurements. Presence Teleoper. Virtual Environ. **8**(2), 187–203 (1999)
14. O'Brien, J.F., Bodenheimer, R.E., Brostow, G.J., Hodgins, J.K.: Automatic joint parameter estimation from magnetic motion capture data. In: Proceedings of Graphics Interface 2000, pp. 53–60, Montréal (2000)
15. Ouchi, K., Suzuki, T., Doi, M.: LifeMinder: a wearable healthcare support system using user's context. In: Proceedings of the 22nd International Conference on Distributed Computing Systems, pp. 791–792, Vienna (2002)
16. Rajko, S., Oian, G.: HMM parameter reduction for practical gesture recognition. In: IEEE International Conference on Face and Gesture Recognition, Amsterdam (2008)
17. Rajko, S., Oian, G., Ingalls, T., James, J.: Real-time gesture recognition with minimal training requirements and on-line learning. IEEE Conference on Computer Vision and Pattern Recognition, Minneapolis (2007)
18. Seon-Woo, L., Mase, K.: Activity and location recognition using wearable sensors. Pervasive Comput. IEEE **1**(3), 24–32 (2002)
19. Svensson, A., Björk, S., Åkesson, K.P.: Tangible handimation: real-time animation with a sequencer-based tangible interface. In: Proceedings of the 5th Nordic Conference on Human Computer Interaction, Lund (2008)
20. Tognetti, A., Lorussi, F., Tesconi, M., Bartalesi, R., Zupone, G., De Rossi, D.: Wearable kinesthetic systems for capturing and classifying body posture and gesture. Conf. Proc. IEEE Eng. Med. Biol. Soc. **1**, 1012–1015 (2005)
21. Vlasic, D., Adelsberger, R., Vanucci, G., Barnwell, J., Gross, M., Matusik, W., Popovic, J.: Practical motion capture in everyday surroundings. ACM Trans. Graph. **26**(3), 35 (2007)

Chapter 5
Sharing and Stretching Space with Full Body Tracking

David M. Krum, Evan A. Suma, and Mark Bolas

Abstract New opportunities emerge when mixed reality environments are augmented with immersive displays and full body, real-time tracking. Such systems enable the creation of experiences where users "share space" with other virtual humans in the virtual environment. These systems can portray responsive 3D virtual humans that react to position, motion, and gesture. The tracking data can also be used in analyzing physical and social responses to virtual characters. Additionally, such systems can use tracking data to identify opportunities for altering a user's perception of the environment. This is helpful in situations where redirection or reorientation of the user might be done to "stretch space," i.e. imperceptibly rotating or changing the environment around the user, so that a straight-line walk becomes a curve, preventing the user from ever encountering the walls in the physical space. We believe that allowing users to co-inhabit virtual spaces with virtual humans and decoupling physical size constraints from these virtual spaces are two important building blocks for effective mixed reality training experiences.

Introduction

The Institute for Creative Technologies (ICT) at the University of Southern California is a University Affiliated Research Center focused on the development of engaging, memorable, and effective interactive media to revolutionize learning in training, education, and other fields. In support of these applications, the Mixed Reality Lab researches and develops immersive technologies and techniques to build mixed reality environments.

D.M. Krum (✉), E.A. Suma, and M. Bolas
University of Southern California, Institute for Creative Technologies, 12015 Waterfront Drive, Playa Vista, CA 90094–2536, USA
e-mail: krum@ict.usc.edu; suma@ict.usc.edu; bolas@ict.usc.edu

D. England (ed.), *Whole Body Interaction*, Human-Computer Interaction Series, DOI 10.1007/978-0-85729-433-3_5, © Springer-Verlag London Limited 2011

Mixed reality is a term that describes environments and experiences that combine elements that are real with elements that are virtual. For example, mixed reality experiences might be provided by physical rooms where windows are simulated by display screens, or by head mounted displays (HMDs) that use cameras and graphics engines to overlay virtual objects over a view of the real world.

To create effective mixed reality training scenarios, it is important to immerse users in simulated experiences that convincingly replicate the mental, physical, and emotional aspects of a real world situation. The Mixed Reality Lab's early work in this area was known as the FlatWorld project, which created a system of "digital flats" as building blocks for mixed reality environments [6]. Our current research direction has been influenced by two high impact aspects of FlatWorld: the ability to create highly navigable environments and the ability to present virtual human characters. Our most recent research has thus recently centered on the use of full body tracking systems and immersive displays in order to support realistic physical locomotion and strong engagement with virtual human characters.

To provide full body tracking, we have been building and refining the Intelligent Reality Sizable Tracked Augmented Graphics Environment, or IR STAGE, which is a full motion capture stage. We constructed the IR STAGE with the following two goals in mind: (1) provide accurate full body motion capture to support sharing space with virtual human characters; and (2) accomplish head tracking over an area large enough to conduct experiments with stretching virtual space. To achieve these goals, we segmented the space into two separate units. IR STAGE 1 is a 36 × 40 ft space that is optimized for full body tracking in a manner similar to the motion capture setups used by the film industry. A total of 46 PhaseSpace Impulse motion capture cameras are arranged at multiple heights in a circular pattern with a typical radius of 15–20 ft and aimed in at the center region. This provides accurate and robust tracking of LED markers that can be placed anywhere on the body, making it suitable for our projects in sharing space with virtual humans, though the most precise tracking is limited primarily to the central region of the space. In contrast, IR STAGE 2 is optimized for head tracking over an entire 36 × 36 ft space all the way out to the borders. To achieve this goal, a total of 52 PhaseSpace cameras were hung from a ceiling mounted grid. To spread out the tracking over such a wide area, 44 cameras were placed at a height of 13 ft, pitched downwards at a 45° angle, and aimed in various directions to cover the space. In our tests, ceiling-mounted cameras were the least accurate in tracking marker height, so we also placed an additional eight cameras around the borders at a height of 6 ft. We found that arranging LED markers in a circular perimeter about the head-mounted display provides reliable rigid body head tracking throughout the entire space, which supports our work in stretching space. Though the two IR STAGE units are currently optimized for their respective goals and can currently operate independently, our long term vision is to unify the system into a single 80 × 36 ft space that can robustly provide both head tracking and full body motion capture throughout the entire workspace.

Previous Work

Our current research direction has evolved from several bodies of prior work, including efforts related to large tracked spaces, redirected walking, and our group's own work with mixed reality environments and virtual human characters.

In film and theater, a key element of stagecraft has been the flat, a modular, movable panel used to present background scenery. The FlatWorld project updated the flat concept to create "digital flats" for mixed reality, with new features like 3D imagery, 3D audio, and 4D sensory actuators like fans for wind and rumble floors for vibration. Digital flats can be easily positioned and projected upon to simulate walls or viewports, such as windows and doors. They can also be combined with physical props, like chairs and tables, and standard flats, representing solid walls, to create rooms, alleyways, and other structures. Many users can freely navigate these environments at the same time. Furthermore, flats and props can be quickly re-staged in a number of different arrangements, satisfying training requirements for reconfigurable environments. Other particularly notable FlatWorld innovations include the use of semi-transparent screens for portraying virtual humans, and adaptive projection, allowing transient effects, like bullet holes, to appear on a wall or floor.

Virtual humans can play important roles in learning and training systems as opponents, collaborators, spectators, instructors, and guides. The goal is to create virtual human characters that are treated just like real humans, or create reactions similar to those that real humans create. A key metric for such virtual humans is "co-presence", which is the perception that character has a physical, social, and emotional existence. The ICT has produced a variety of virtual human characters. One notable example, co-developed by our lab, is SGT Star, an information guide employed by the US Army Accessions Command to speak about Army careers at public events. In our lab, SGT Star is presented on a semi-transparent screen, providing a simulated 3D appearance. This presentation seemingly pulls the character off of a flat projected screen, enabling motion parallax cues between the character and background scene. However, since users cannot walk past the character (into the screen) and the character and cannot emerge from the screen, the character still inhabits a different space which is unreachable and virtual.

Physical locomotion (walking, running, etc.) has been recognized as essential for simulations in which the soldier interacts directly with the surrounding environment. Virtual locomotion techniques that simulate walking (e.g. joystick or button presses) have been shown to be inferior to real walking in many experiments, including studies of spatial orientation [2], attention [13], search task performance [10], and sense of presence [15]. Additionally, since virtual locomotion does not realistically portray the energy and effort of real world movement, it might provide negative training in scenarios where tactical movement and coordination are important, such as urban combat. Despite the advantages of real walking, however, physical workspace constraints and motion tracking hardware limitations have historically made it impractical for deployment in large-scale virtual environments.

The Department of Defense (DoD) has long been interested in methods for allowing soldiers to physically walk around in unlimitedly large virtual training worlds. A number of hardware-based solutions have been developed, such as omnidirectional treadmills [3, 11] and large hamster-ball contraptions [16]. Walking-in-place techniques have also been explored as a middle ground between real walking and virtual locomotion [5, 14]. However, advances in wide-area tracking technology have made it possible to construct tracking spaces that are large enough to support real walking for many applications [17, 18]. Unfortunately, these large tracking spaces still have finite boundaries which ultimately limit the size of the virtual environment to fit within the available physical space.

To relax the physical size restrictions imposed by the tracking space, Razzaque proposed a technique known as redirected walking, which subtly rotates the virtual environment to steer the user's walking path away from the boundaries of the tracking area [8]. This technique can be augmented using a visual distractor to provoke head turns, making it easier to apply the rotation imperceptibly [7]. Alternatively, it is also possible to apply a scale factor to walking movements in the forward travel direction, allowing the user to cover greater distances in the virtual world [4]. Since all of these techniques introduce a visual–vestibular conflict by manipulating the mapping between real and virtual motions, it is important that rotational and scale gains be applied slowly and gradually, so that the user does not notice and, perhaps more importantly, does not experience motion sickness.

Sharing Space with Virtual Humans

Characters in virtual reality environments often appear to be two dimensional or distant (either perceived or real). These shortfalls may weaken engagement, and thus the efficacy of training. By incorporating a wide field of view HMD and full body tracking, we aim to convince users they are sharing the same volumetric space with virtual humans. This will help enhance the illusion that the virtual human is a sentient entity with whom the user can socially relate.

Humans have a strong drive to relate socially with objects that display even only a glimmer of personality. In fact, while many humans may not consciously perceive that they are interacting with unintelligent objects in a social fashion, they often still fall into the human tendency to ascribe personalities and emotions to things, like animals, computers, and cars [9]. Removing barriers to this tendency can elicit more realistic responses to virtual human characters.

By employing full body tracking, and wide field of view displays, like Fakespace Labs Wide5 HMD (providing up to 150° of horizontal field of view), we are attempting to create uniquely compelling experiences with virtual humans. In the following sections, we will describe a number of anecdotes and experiments we have performed using a wide field of view HMD and full body tracking for shared space experiences with virtual humans.

Avatars and Self-Representation

In many virtual environments, user avatars are either invisible, incomplete, or do not correctly follow the movements of the user. Full body tracking allows a correct self-representation of the user's own body in the virtual environment, increasing the level of self-immersion and placing the user on the same level as the virtual human.

The importance of self-representation became apparent to us in one virtual scene which utilized an environment from a Unity game engine demo. This scene presents a wooden bridge over water. The roughhewn construction of the bridge, with some broken wooden planks and large gaps in between, invites careful placement of the user's feet. Without a good representation of the user's feet, the scene feels artificial. There is no way for the user's feet to visually interact with the treacherous bridge. By adding trackers to the user's feet, the user is able to place each foot on the appropriate plank, avoid holes, and thus respond to the precariousness of the bridge.

Puppeteering

Full body tracking can also enable virtual puppeteering, allowing a virtual character to be voiced and animated in real time. While an autonomous virtual character is certainly a goal, virtual puppeteering could have a role in custom character control, multitasking (or supervisory) control of multiple characters, and studying user reactions to virtual characters.

In an early experiment with puppeteered characters, we placed a number of tracking markers on an operator's arms. These markers controlled the arm movements of a virtual character. The user, wearing a Wide5 HMD, would approach and reach out towards the virtual character. The virtual character (following the operator's movements) would begin to wave his hands more and more wildly, and then progress to knocking the user's hands away and pushing the user away. These actions were startling to us as users since we, as experienced VR users, do not expect virtual characters to strike out or push us away. Such events can cause users to become a little more wary of the virtual characters and afford them a little more personal space.

Another example of virtual human puppeteering is at FITE/CHAOS, a military training installation at Camp Pendleton, California (see Fig. 5.1). An actor, fluent in Pashto, a language of Afghanistan, is wearing a motion capture suit, studded with LED markers, and wearing additional markers around his mouth. This enables him to control the character in real-time and speak with proper lip syncing. The actor's cultural and linguistic knowledge, as reflected in his speech and movements, is carried through the motion capture system and embodied by the virtual character.

Fig. 5.1 Virtual character being puppeteered at Camp Pendleton, California

Virtual Human Presentation

While projection screens are often used to present virtual characters, they fall flat in several respects. Without stereoscopic displays, the characters are only presented in 2D. Without head tracking of the user, the characters and scenes cannot be portrayed with the proper perspective. Furthermore, a projector and a screen can only display a correct perspective for a single user, since only one image can be displayed at a time. An additional issue for projection screens is that they seemingly create a barrier between the space of the user and the space of the character. The user cannot walk past the screen into the character's space, and the character cannot emerge from the screen to enter the user's space.

We are using wide area tracking and a wide field of view display to create scenes where the user and the virtual human can freely move around and past each other. This allows the user to have a stronger sense of personal space, which can overlap with the virtual character's personal space, and allow non-verbal social interactions.

We presented a user with a virtual character, an American Old West outlaw, on both a projected screen (Fig. 5.2) and then later in an HMD on the IR STAGE (Fig. 5.3a, b). While the character was engaging on the projected screen, there was a more interesting response on the IR STAGE. When the character approached, the user took a step back, as noted by the initial position (marked by the green line) and the final position (marked by the red line) as seen in Fig. 5.3a, b. We theorize that this may have been in response to several factors: (1) avoiding the character due to the 3D stereo imagery of the HMD, (2) maintaining a visual framing around the character so as to keep the character in full view, or (3) maintaining an appropriate social distance (proxemics) from the character.

Fig. 5.2 A virtual character on a projected screen

With a typical projector and screen configuration, only one image is displayed, so every observer views that same imagery. This leads to problems with the eye gaze and gestures. If the virtual human tries to gaze or point at a particular person in a crowd, it may look like the virtual human is looking and pointing at everyone. By equipping each user with a head mounted projector, using retroreflective screens, and employing a tracking system, we can provide each user with personalized perspective correct imagery. This system, called REFLCT (Retroreflective Environments For Learner-Centered Training) is designed to unobtrusively deliver mixed reality training experiences (see Fig. 5.4a, b) [1]. The REFLCT system:

- Places no glass or optics in front of a user's face.
- Needs only a single projector per user.
- Provides each user with a unique and perspective correct image.
- Situates imagery within a physical themed and prop based environment.
- Can be low power, lightweight, and wireless.
- Works in normal room brightness.

Each user only sees the imagery from their own projector, since the retroreflective screens bounce light straight back towards the light source. This system allows each user to experience a perspective correct viewpoint, enabling each user to unambiguously perceive whether a virtual character is establishing eye contact, gesturing, or pointing a weapon at them. Furthermore, since no bulky optics cover the users' eyes, trainees can also establish eye contact with each other.

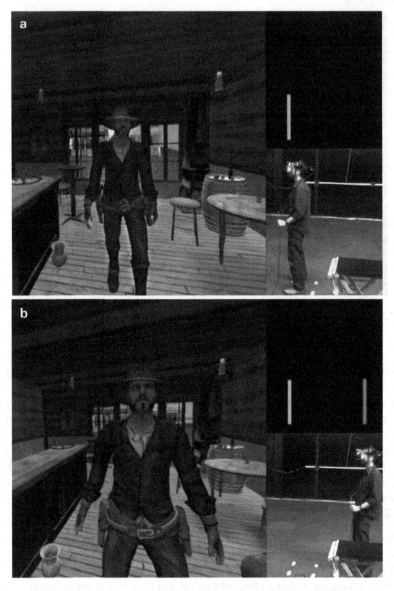

Fig. 5.3 (**a, b**) Stepping back in reaction to a virtual character on the IR STAGE

Stretching Space in Virtual Environments

We are particularly interested in combining redirection techniques with mixed reality stimuli to provide a more compelling illusion of walking through a virtually unlimited space. We believe the use of passive haptic feedback, physical props, and different walking surfaces can be used to augment this sense of immersion.

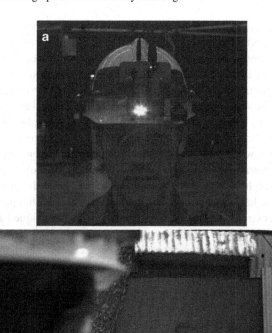

Fig. 5.4 (**a, b**) The REFLCT head mounted projector and associated projected imagery

Our first experiments with mixed reality redirection involved combining a scaled translational gain technique with a force-sensitive push cart. We constructed a heavy wheeled cart that was tracked in the IR STAGE, allowing us to render a virtual representation for the user to interact with when wearing the HMD. The amount of force the user applied to push the cart was used to calculate a scale gain on their virtual motion, effectively stretching the physical space to allow travel over greater virtual distances. To test this apparatus, we designed a hospital scenario in which the user was instructed to push a gurney through a building. Our preliminary tests have suggested that the spatial manipulations are less noticeable to the user when pushing the cart. We believe there are two possible explanations for this phenomenon. First, pushing on the cart provides distraction which may prevent the user from noticing the scaling. Secondly, since pushing the cart requires physical exertion, it may be that the increased physical effort psychologically prepares the user to move over a greater distance.

We have also begun experimenting with a redirection technique that leverages change blindness to stretch the physical space without manipulating the mapping between physical and virtual motions [12]. This technique alters the structure of the environment in subtle ways behind the user's back. Since the human visual system relies upon transient optical motion to detect changes to a scene, these structural alterations are very difficult to detect when they are applied outside the user's field of view. It is important to note that the user's motions are never scaled or rotated; instead, we simply structure the environment in such a way that the user naturally follows the path we lay out in the virtual world. For example, by moving a door in the corner of a virtual room, we can get the user to exit the room and proceed in a different direction without noticing. To demonstrate this approach, we have constructed a military training scenario where the user walks through a 3,000 ft² virtual village with multiple buildings while staying within a 900 ft² physical area (see Fig. 5.5a, b). We have also tested the change blindness technique in an interior office building environment. Our formal studies of this technique have shown it to stunningly effective. Out of 77 participants, each experiencing the redirection technique 12 times, only one person noticed the scene changes. Perhaps more importantly, we found that despite the changing environment, participants were able draw coherent sketch maps of the environment. A pointing task also revealed that they were able to maintain their spatial orientation within the virtual world.

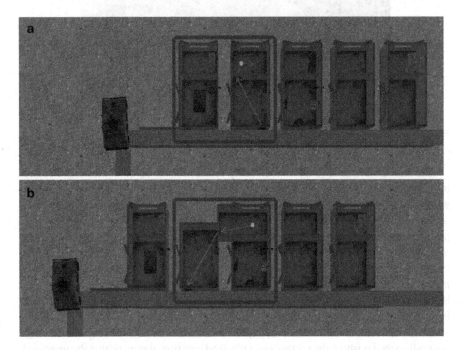

Fig. 5.5 (**a**, **b**) Users search multiple houses for a stash of hidden weapons. When the user enters the back room of each building (**a**), the doorway and the surrounding environment is altered, without affecting the user's view of the room (**b**). The user can explore the entire village without walking outside of the physical space

In addition to being nearly imperceptible, change blindness redirection is also well-suited for combining with mixed reality stimuli. For example, in our military training scenario, we repeatedly redirect the user over a 30 ft long gravel walkway. When exiting a virtual building, the tactile sensation of walking on a different surface contributes to the sense of being outside and walking on an expansive, continuous roadway between buildings. We are continuing to look for novel ways to leverage the advanced motion sensing capabilities of the IR STAGE to augment the illusion of stretching space, particularly those that engage the user's whole body.

Conclusion

The construction of the IR STAGE will continue to enable a variety of experiments that examine how humans perceive virtual environments and virtual human characters. We can explore how humans respond to virtual humans when several barriers between their worlds are dissolved. This will lead to opportunities for more believable characters, better rapport, improved assessment of intent, and better non-verbal communication. Furthermore, real-time tracking data allows systems to multiply the physical space available for locomotion. Redirection and other techniques can be applied to full effect when users are distracted and unable to see manipulations of the environment that steer them away from walls. As we expand the lexicon of redirection, it will become feasible to create training scenarios that are longer and more elaborate, with users roaming freely while completely immersed in their virtual world.

We feel that the IR STAGE and related infrastructure will be a valuable scientific apparatus that can provide the means to answer a variety of questions in immersion, interaction, and human perception.

References

1. Bolas, M., Krum, D.M.: Augmented reality applications and user interfaces using head-coupled near-axis personal projectors with novel retroreflective props and surfaces. In: Pervasive 2010 Ubiprojection Workshop, Helsinki (2010)
2. Chance, S.S., Gaunet, F., Beall, A.C., Loomis, J.M.: Locomotion mode affects the updating of objects encountered during travel: the contribution of vestibular and proprioceptive inputs to path integration. Presence 7(2), 168–178 (1998)
3. Darken, R., Cockayne, W., Carmein, D.: The omni-directional treadmill: a locomotion device for virtual worlds. In: User Interface Software and Technology (UIST), Banff, Alberta (1997)
4. Interrante, V., Ries, B., Anderson, L.: Seven league boots: a new metaphor for augmented locomotion through moderately large scale immersive virtual environments. In: IEEE Symposium on 3D User Interfaces, pp. 167–170, Charlotte (2007)
5. Kaufman, R.E.: A family of new ergonomic harness mechanisms for full-body constrained motions in virtual environments. In: IEEE Symposium on 3D User Interfaces, Charlotte (2007)

6. Pair, J., Neumann, U., Piepol, D., Swartout, B.: FlatWorld: combining Hollywood set design techniques with VR. IEEE Comput. Graph. Appl. **23**(1), 12–15 (2003)

7. Peck, T.C., Fuchs, H., Whitton, M.C.: Evaluation of reorientation techniques and distractors for walking in large virtual environments. IEEE Trans. Vis. Comput. Graph. **15**(3), 383–394 (2009)

8. Razzaque, S.: Redirected walking. Dissertation, University of North Carolina at Chapel Hill (2005)

9. Reeves, B., Nass, C.: The media equation: how people treat computers, television, and new media like real people and places. Cambridge University Press, Cambridge (1996)

10. Ruddle, R.A., Lessels, S.: The benefits of using a walking interface to navigate virtual environments. ACM Trans. Comput. Hum. Interact. **16**(1), 1–18 (2009)

11. Schwaiger, M., Thümmel, T., Ulbrich, H.: Cyberwalk: implementation of a ball bearing platform for humans. International Conference on Human-Computer Interaction, pp. 926–935, Beijing (2007)

12. Suma, E., Clark, S., Finkelstein, S., Wartell, Z.: Exploiting change blindness to expand walkable space in a virtual environment. In: IEEE Virtual Reality, Exploiting change blindness to expand walkable space in a virtual environment. In: IEEE Virtual Reality, pp. 305–306, Waltham (2010)

13. Suma, E., Finkelstein, S., Reid, M., Babu, S., Ulinski, A., Hodges, L.F.: Evaluation of the cognitive effects of travel technique in complex real and virtual environments. IEEE Trans. Vis. Comput. Graph. **16**(4), 690–702 (2010)

14. Templeman, J.N.: Virtual locomotion: walking in place through virtual environments. Presence **8**(6), 598–617 (1999)

15. Usoh, M., Arthur, K., Whitton, M.C., Bastos, R., Steed, A., Slater, M., Brooks, F.P.: Walking > walking-in-place > flying, in virtual environments. In: ACM SIGGRAPH, pp. 359–364, San Antonio (1999)

16. Virtusphere. http://www.virtusphere.com (2010). Accessed 23 Oct 2010

17. Waller, D., Bachmann, E., Hodgson, E., Beall, A.C.: The HIVE: a huge immersive virtual environment for research in spatial cognition. Behav. Res. Methods **39**, 835–843 (2007)

18. Welch, G., Foxlin, E.: Motion tracking: no silver bullet, but a respectable arsenal. IEEE Comput. Graph. Appl. **22**(6), 24–38 (2002)

Chapter 6
Waggling[1] the Form Baton[2]: Analyzing Body-Movement-Based Design Patterns in Nintendo Wii Games, Toward Innovation of New Possibilities for Social and Emotional Experience

Katherine Isbister and Christopher DiMauro

Abstract This chapter describes research conducted to analyze and better understand what is compelling about particular body-movement-based design patterns in Nintendo Wii games, towards innovating new possibilities for social and emotional experience with movement-based games and other interactive experiences. The authors analyzed games from diverse genres, to generate a bottom-up set of dimensions and characteristics of the mechanics, that can help build a foundation for heightening social and emotional engagement and enjoyment through design of novel mechanics, and/or through combining and extending successful existing mechanics. Key findings include the prevalence of kinesthetic mimicry, the value of whole body versus piecemeal movement, tensions between precision and loose movement in design, and the value of using Laban's dimensions of Effort as a lens through which to understand which sorts of movement patterns are more engaging.

Introduction

The Wii gaming platform, released in December 2006, has been lauded in the gaming community and in the popular press for introducing physical play to a broader gaming audience [7–9]. Attention has been devoted to the health benefits of the additional movement, and the value of the platform to nontraditional audiences such as senior citizens, but there has not been systematic and detailed analysis of the kinds of design choices that are being made in crafting game gestures themselves.

---

[1] Waggling is a derogatory term for swinging the Wiimote back and forth as a game mechanic.

[2] Wario Ware Smooth Moves christened the Wiimote the 'form baton' in their humorous instructions to players about how to hold it in various positions (see http://www.youtube.com/watch?v=ab4dse9AMPM).

K. Isbister (✉) and C. DiMauro
NYU-Poly, Six Metrotech Center, Brooklyn, NY 11201, USA
e-mail: isbister@poly.edu; chrisdimauro@gmail.com

D. England (ed.), *Whole Body Interaction*, Human-Computer Interaction Series,
DOI 10.1007/978-0-85729-433-3_6, © Springer-Verlag London Limited 2011

Recently, researchers in the CHI community have begun to conduct studies demonstrating that physical games increase engagement [1, 12] and social interaction [10]. These studies point to general effects based on presence or absence of body movement in gaming, but do not dissect at a finer-grained level of detail what sorts of motions create what sorts of effects and why.

Our research approach is to use an understanding of social psychological and communication findings about sociality and emotion as a lens for better understanding how specific design choices can impact players [6]. In the present project, we are working to create a taxonomy of the sorts of body movements and gestures employed in popular and well-regarded Wii games, toward building a more detailed understanding of what seems to be effective and why. In particular, we are interested in which sorts of movement mechanics create social and emotional engagement and enjoyment for players.

Game designers have known for many years that engaging the whole body in thoughtfully crafting game mechanics can lead to powerful social connections and positive emotional experiences [3, 13]. In recent years, game studies scholars [2] have begun to articulate a framework for understanding how game mechanics can promote certain beliefs and worldviews. It is our belief that game designers can consciously craft whole-body interactions that encourage social and emotional engagement and connection, and we are interested in uncovering any existing patterns along these lines toward advancing them in our laboratory with our own game mechanic explorations.

Research Strategy

We examined games that were best sellers and/or well reviewed by the gaming press. We also asked Wii developers to recommend games with interesting movement mechanics that we should examine. The games we analyzed were: Wario Ware Smooth Moves, Mario Party 8, Boogie Superstar, Wii Cheer, Boom Blox, Star Wars: The Force Unleashed, Wii Sports, Super Mario Galaxy, and Super Monkey Ball: Banana Blitz. The games represent a mix of genres – rhythm games (Wii Cheer, Boogie Superstar), party games (Wario Ware Smooth Moves, Mario Party 8, Wii Sports, Super Monkey Ball), and action/adventure games (Star Wars: The Force Unleashed, Super Mario Galaxy).

For each game, we used a combination of user manuals, web-based walk-throughs and press explanations (e.g. Fig. 6.1b), and play of our own, to create a list of the movement-based mechanics in the game. Then we made notes during play-through, about each movement mechanic. We described the mechanic itself, how the particular mechanic fit into the overall game feel, goals, back story, and any underlying rhetoric that could be discerned (using Bogost's notions of procedural rhetoric [2]). For example, here is a brief initial description of a specific movement-based mechanic. In Star Wars: The Force Unleashed, you can fling an object or a person to the ground, using a hurling motion with the nunchuk part of the Wii controller (typically held in

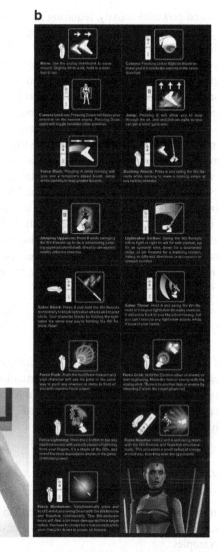

Fig. 6.1 The Wii controller (**a**) consists of the 'nunchuk' (*left*) and the 'wiimote' (*right*). (**b**) GamePro online included this player control taxonomy in an article about Star Wars: The Force Unleashed (see http://www.gamepro.com/article/previews/173628/star-wars-the-force-unleashed-page-3-of-5/)

the left hand, see Fig. 6.1a). This motion feels forceful and aggressive, and represents one of the fantasy powers that Jedi Knights have in the Star Wars universe – to use 'the force' to act on the physical world. Using the nunchuk for this mechanic allows the player to focus the Wiimote main controller (held in the other hand at the same time) movements on the operation of his/her light saber, a primary combat weapon in the Star Wars universe. Interestingly, in the films themselves, hurling people to the ground is a mind-powered activity, requiring no physical movement at all. But in the game, using a forceful movement of the nunchuk seems to amplify and make more satisfying the exercise of this particular power.

The goal was to generate a bottom-up set of dimensions and characteristics of the mechanics, that can help us build a foundation for exploring heightening social and emotional engagement and enjoyment through designing our own mechanics, or combining and extending those we've observed.

We also decided, after making our first pass at notations about the individual movement mechanics, that it would be valuable to perform a more systematic analysis of the movement qualities in each mechanic. We knew about previous work in movement analysis to better understand digital interactions, which made use of Laban's Movement Analysis system [11, 15], and we were particularly interested in the three dimensions of Effort, as they seemed to have potential for characterizing a wide range of movement-based mechanics. In the Laban system, a movement can be characterized in its Effort qualities as direct or indirect, strong or light, and bound or free. We went back and played through the games and made note of where each movement mechanic seemed to fall along these three dimensions.

Analysis

The goal of this research was to uncover systematic qualities of movement mechanics that may contribute to fun game play, in particular social and emotional engagement during play. What follows are patterns we found, through bottom-up analysis of the observations that we made and collected (via published reviews) about the game mechanics in the games we examined.

Kinesthetic Mimicry

All of the movement mechanics were patterned (to some degree) after real-world physical movements and activities that players already knew how to perform. Here are some examples:

- Holding the Wiimote sideways and pretending to use it as a steering wheel (Wario Ware)
- Pretending to box by punching while holding the Wiimote in the hand (Wii Sports)
- Pulling a block out of a pile by slowly moving the Wiimote backward (Boom Blox)
- Copying dance movements while holding the Wiimote in the hand (Wii Cheer, Boogie Superstar, Wario Ware)

Some movements were more fanciful than others – for example, in Wario Ware Smooth Moves one mini-game required the player to hold the Wiimote in front of her nose as if it were an elephant's trunk, while pretending to be an elephant.

In contrast, the movements in Wii Sports and in Boom Blox were based more literally upon existing real-world movements (playing sports, playing a Jenga-like puzzle game).

Some game mechanics mimic real-world activities in which a tool is held in the hand (e.g. bowling, tennis, fighting with a sword/light saber) and some mimic movements that would normally not require an object held in the hand (e.g. dancing, boxing). The form factor of the Wiimote is condusive to imagining some sorts of real-world objects (tennis racket, light saber, long block from Jenga, vacuum cleaner) and not others (e.g. a ball that is to be thrown or rolled, a hula hoop around one's waist). In our play-throughs, the lack of direct physical correspondence did not seem to heavily affect how fun the mechanic was. That is to say, it was still fun to pretend to keep a hula hoop going by holding the Wiimote at one's waist, even though it felt nothing like a real hula hoop.

It makes sense that designers would craft movement mechanics that leverage familiarity with real-world movements, making it easier to quickly train players, and helping them understand the consequences of their actions in the game world. However, we observed a tension between this approach and the typical console-style control structure for games that was in place pre-motion controller, which seemed to have direct effects upon how engaging the experience was.

Console game controllers, which have not changed much since the home consoles of the 1980s (see Fig. 6.2), combine a set of buttons and joysticks/d-pads

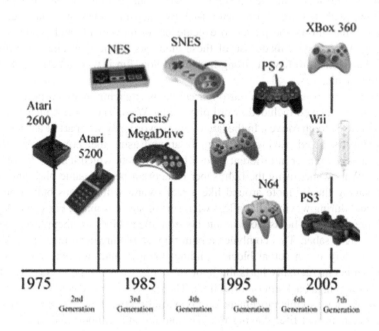

Fig. 6.2 Today's game controllers have the same basic structure that emerged around 1995 (Image taken from http://blog.echovar.com/?m=201001)

in a single object that is held between both hands during game play. The player can rapidly access all of the buttons on the controller while gripping it. This produces a play stance in which the player is relatively still, eyes focused on the screen, hands together in front of her gripping the controller, fingers rapidly manipulating buttons and joysticks. The player who is accomplished can rely on touch and need not look at the controller. Rapidly pressing buttons is not much like performing real-world physical movements, and so game mechanics evolved which transposed physical challenges into button pressing challenges. Perhaps the best example would be fighting games (e.g. Mortal Kombat and Street Fighter), which developed a system of special attacks that could be accessed by memorizing and quickly pressing certain combinations of buttons, requiring a highly precise set of movements that corresponded to tight control of an on-screen avatar's actions. Of course, mastering these movements is hardly like memorizing actual combat sequences for real-world physical combat, and yet, the quick reflexes and mental calm required to execute these movements has some kind of parallel to real-world physical expertise. A player can become very accomplished in console-based combat, and acquiring these skills takes time.

Tensions Between Precision and Loose Movement Style in Design

The Wii's controller combines the typical joystick and button structure of a console controller, with a novel form-factor (the two separate elements, nunchuk and Wiimote) that allows the player to execute broad movements and gestures. The games that we played made use of these elements of the controller in different ways, that seemed to have a strong impact on how fun it was to perform a given game mechanic.

The clearest example from our observations is engaging in sword play. Two of the games we played included sword play – Star Wars: The Force Unleashed, and Wario Ware Smooth Moves. In the latter game, sword play was part of a mini-game that simply involved waving the Wiimote around using the 'boxer form' (Wario Ware trains the player in different holds of the Wiimote which it calls 'forms'). In the Star Wars game, using the light saber is a core aspect of game play, and combines waving the Wiimote around like a real sword, with various button presses before and during waving, that affect what sort of strike is made. For example, the player presses A and holds the Wiimote horizontally to block another player's strike with her light saber. This combines a button press requirement and a pure kinesthetic mimicry of an actual block. Holding down A and swinging the Wiimote toward an enemy actually hurls the light saber itself toward the enemy. The light saber boomerangs back after a brief time. The player of course is not really throwing the Wiimote, so this movement is only partially kinesthetically similar to what would occur in real life. Waving the Wiimote around without holding down any buttons executes moves that one would expect, and this feels the closest to full kinesthetic mimicry.

When playing Star Wars: The Force Unleashed, it is easiest to engage in the movements that do not require button presses, and that are most directly related to real-world analogs. (These are the same movements that are enabled in the Wario Ware mini-game). It is far more complex and less immediately engaging to combine button presses with broad movements, and doing so took away from engagement and immersion for us in our play sessions. It is clear from reviews (e.g. http://uk.wii.ign. com/articles/910/910269p1.html) that the designers were constrained by needing to provide button-based game-play mechanics while also trying to exploit the Wii's motion capabilities, and it is also clear that these movements were more accessible and engaging to those already entrained in the button-pressing prior releases of the game (as opposed to our team, which had not played prior versions).

Not all combinations of movement and button presses were of necessity awkward feeling at first. For example, when removing pieces in Boom Blox, the player needed to hold down A and then move her hand slowly backward to pull a block out. This felt kinesthetically similar to grasping a real block, and was quite intuitive.

Some Wii games avoid the conflict between tight, button-based control and broader movement by strictly containing the role of movement in game play. In Mario Galaxy, for example, there was very little use of broad movement. Rather the Wiimote was used in a two-handed fashion, in which the nunchuk's joystick (held in the left hand) maneuvered the game avatar, and the Wiimote (held in the right hand) was mostly used as a way to point at and interfere with enemies. Reviewers enjoyed this novel two-handed mode of gameplay (e.g. http://uk.wii.ign.com/ articles/732/732898p1.html), regardless of the lack of broad movement. In some sense, one could say that the designers of this game used movement to make relatively small tweaks to the basic controller paradigm, which managed to add value to game play while preserving its main contours.

In any case, this continuum (from pure broad movement to mostly button and joystick control schemes), and the artful blending of these modes of game play, seems an important design dimension to consider in crafting movement mechanics.

Piecemeal Versus Full Body Motion

Another pattern we observed, was that it was rare to find movement mechanics that resulted in whole-body movement. Of the games we examined, only Wii Sports and Wii Cheer elicited smooth, full body motion from players (see for example this videoclip posted on Youtube: http://www.youtube.com/watch?v=TvHrF0cpx7o& mode=related&search=).

What was far more common, was a semi-active player – games like Boogie Superstar and Star Wars: The Force Unleashed encouraged broad arm movements and a standing play position, but left the player's torso, hips, and legs relatively motionless, with little weight shifting going on. Some games had so little movement that they could be played in the usual seated gaming position, such as Mario Galaxy and some of the Wario Ware and Super Monkey Ball minigames (e.g. driving, throwing things). Other games required brief bursts of relatively full-body movement (such as the Wario Ware dancing and hula hoop minigames).

We noticed in our play sessions, that the full body movement games seemed to elicit more engagement, and to more quickly result in fun for players and those who observed them. As one of our observers put it, it is more fun to watch someone engage in whole-body movement, and also more fun to perform the whole body movement.

These observations can be grounded in some known phenomena from social science: the physical feedback effect [14] and emotional contagion [4]. Research has demonstrated that if a person moves as if she is happy, she will tend to label herself as more happy afterward – vigorous and joyful full body game mechanics may be making use of this physical feedback effect. Watching others who are feeling a strong emotion causes us to also feel a bit of this strong emotion (emotional contagion [4]), – and since full body movements provide more legible displays of emotion, they may contribute to stronger positive emotions in spectators during play sessions as well. We are currently developing game prototypes that allow us to conduct controlled comparison of game versions, to test out whether these effects hold true, under more rigorous experimental conditions.

Laban Effort Dimensions and Engagement

In our first pass-through of game play, we noticed that some kinesthetic mimicries of activities were a lot more fun than others. Our second play pass-through, in which we noted Effort qualities of the movement mechanics, gave us an intriguing piece of the puzzle as to why this might be. Let us consider the example of dancing. Three of the games required players to engage in dance or dance-like activities: Boogie Superstar, Wii Cheer, and the Wario Ware dancing mini-game. In our play-testing, we enjoyed the Wario Ware and Wii Cheer dance mechanics far more than those in Boogie Superstar. Looking at the Laban Effort qualities, we found that movement mechanics for both Wii Cheer and Wario Ware dancing were free, whereas Boogie Superstar had very bound movement qualities. The movements in Boogie Superstar were typically sustained (performed over and over again in a regular fashion), whereas the movements in the other two dance games were mostly sudden (lots of changes in what was required of the player). All three games had mostly light (versus strong) movements.

In our experience, performing the Boogie Superstar movements (such as swinging both arms in front of the body, back and forth, to a tight rhythmic metronome), felt mechanical and constrained, whereas the dancing in the other two games felt more silly and joyful. We believe the Laban Effort dimensions help illuminate why this was so. Dancing while playing Boogie Superstar does require performance of movements that could be part of real-life dance, but the tight tempo constraints and repetition do not feel like real improvisational, casual dancing, and don't seem to generate the same buoyant state in the player. Thus it may be important for designers who are aiming for kinesthetic realism to have particular *physical and emotional end states* in mind to aim for, which are derived from certain *qualities* of the movements they are trying to imitate with the movement mechanics.

It's also worth noting that both Wii Cheer and the Wario Ware dance mini-game seemed to have looser criteria for recognizing a movement as correct, which allowed people to put more of their own movement 'spin' on performance. That is to say, one could play both Wii Cheer and the Wario Ware dance mini-game with far more improvisation in footwork, hip wiggles, weight shifts, and the like. This may have also contributed to the increased engagement we felt when playing these games.

Social Interaction

Although all of the games we tried out were designed to allow group play, it was far more common for a game to have a turn-taking mechanism that resulted in serial solo play, rather than multi-player simultaneous play. This is not to say that the 'audience' wasn't highly engaged during the other player's turn – far from it. Many of the games were highly performative – watching others play was very interesting and created strong engagement and lots of positive interpersonal dynamics (see [16] for a fascinating study of interpersonal dynamics in group console play).

In terms of multi-player mechanics, most of what we observed was competitive in nature. For example, sports matches against one another (Wii Sports) and parallel dance performances that were scored and compared (Boogie Superstar, Wii Cheer).

One interesting opportunity for cooperative play was the use of both controller pieces in Mario Galaxy. One player could operate the nunchuk, and the other the Wiimote, making for a somewhat easier and very engaging form of cooperative play. We also found that it was great fun to play Wii Cheer in multi-player mode without any real regard for scoring, but instead, as a non-competitive group activity.

Our research team felt, on the whole, that cooperative game mechanics seemed underdeveloped, and we see this as an opportunity area for creating engaging movement mechanics. We are currently developing social game prototypes that explore and extend some of the informal activities we found ourselves engaging in during our play sessions [5].

Movement and Its Relation to Story and Game World

Earlier in this chapter, we presented the example of picking someone up using 'the Force' and hurling them away, in Star Wars: The Force Unleashed. This movement mechanic is executed with a button press and then a quick flick of the nunchuk to fling the person. The ease with which one can accomplish this movement and its powerful effects give the player a visceral vicarious experience of what it might be like to be a Jedi knight who can control people effortlessly. So one can say that the story and game world resonate well with how this mechanic is enacted.

In the games that we examined, we found for the most part only very thin story worlds, with very little opportunity for this kind of projection and exaggeration. Most of the games instead worked with well-known activities (sports, dancing, cheer leading, parlor games like Jenga) and did not really provide the player with a strong avatar or story world to project into.

Perhaps it is simply the case that quick, casual games like these are not well suited to deep story worlds that might require more complex and extended play sessions [8]. However, we suspect there is opportunity in further examination and development of story and character-based movement mechanics that exploit the unique visceral experience of having movement qualities radically different from one's own everyday body. We are working on prototypes in our lab that push further on this aspect of engagement with movement mechanics.

Conclusions

In our detailed examination of movement mechanics in Wii games from several genres, we have generated some insights into what makes certain movement mechanics more fun than others, and that may lead to better elaborated design guidelines in future, for creating engaging movement mechanics.

We were able to unpack kinesthetic mimicry a bit, delving into what makes some games a more faithfully engaging mimicry of a certain activity than others. We observed that whole-body movement seems to lead more easily to a positive experience for players and spectators, and we observed emergent coop play patterns that we believe can be fruitfully extended and developed.

Our lab group is using this analysis to aid in the evolution of a design pattern language for movement-based game mechanics, and to help us push the envelope with our own movement mechanic prototypes. We imagine that these explorations may also be of value in broader HCI contexts, such as the development of interaction schemes in virtual worlds or with accelerometer-enabled mobile devices.

References

1. Bianchi-Berthouze, N., Kim, W.W., Patel, D.: Does body movement engage you more in digital game play? And why? In: Proceedings of the International Conference of Affective Computing and Intelligent Interaction, LNCS 4738, pp. 102–113, Lisboa (Sept 2007)
2. Bogost, I.: Persuasive Games: The Expressive Power of Videogames. MIT Press, Cambridge (2007)
3. Fluegelman, A. (ed.): The New Games Book: Play Hard Play Fair Nobody Hurt. Doubleday, New York (1976)

4. Hatfield, E., Cacioppo, J.T., Rapson, R.L.: Emotional Contagion. Cambridge University Press, Cambridge (1994)
5. http://socialgamelab.bxmc.poly.edu/projects/socialgaming/
6. Isbister, K.: Better Game Characters by Design: A Psychological Approach. Morgan Kaufmann, San Francisco (2006)
7. Isbister, K., Straus, R., Ash, J.: Wriggle! Creating a platform for dynamic and expressive social-emotional play. Presented at CHI Workshop on Supple Interaction, San Jose (2007)
8. Juul, J.: A Casual Revolution: Reinventing Video Games and Their Players. MIT Press, Cambridge (2009)
9. Kalning, K.: Meet the man behind the Wii: Nintendo's Shigeru Miyamoto talks about the console's success. MSNBC, July 17, 2008, downloaded 23 Oct 2008. http://www.msnbc.msn.com/id/25710005/ (2008)
10. Lindley, S., Le Couteur, J., Bianchi-Berthouze, N.: Stirring up experience through movement in game play: effects on engagement and social behaviour. In: CHI 2008 Proceedings, pp. 511–514, Florence (2008)
11. Loke, L., Larssen, A.T., Robertson, T., Edwards, J.: Understanding movement for interaction design: frameworks and approaches. Pers. Ubiquit. Comput. 11(8), 691–701 (2007)
12. Peirce, C., Fullerton, T., Fron, J., Morie, J.F.: Sustainable play: toward new games movement for the digital age. Game Cult. 2, 261–278 (2007)
13. Santiago, K.: I am more than my thumb: a body-based interface experiment seeking to engage the entire body, using the game 'cloud'. Masters in Fine Arts, thesis submitted to the Interactive Media Division, School of Cinema-Television (May 2006)
14. Strack, F., Martin, L.L., Stepper, S.: Inhibiting and facilitating conditions of the human smile: a nonobtrusive test of the facial feedback hypothesis. J. Pers. Soc. Psychol. 54, 768–776 (1988)
15. Sundström, P., Ståhl, A., Höök, K.: In situ informants exploring an emotional mobile messaging system in their everyday practice. In a special issue of IJHCS Eval. Affective Interfaces 65(4), 388–403 (2007)
16. Voida, A., Carpendale, S., Greenberg, S.: The individual and the group in console gaming. Proc. CSCW 2010, 371–380 (2010)

Chapter 7
Exploring Bodily Engaging Artifacts Among Golfers, Skaters and Dancers

Carolina Johansson and Jakob Tholander

Abstract To reveal qualities for design of interaction that allow for full body experiences three full body movement activities with artifacts (golf, skateboard and an interactive movement companion) were studied. The study revealed interaction qualities for engagement of a rich array of senses and bodily capabilities for being-in and moving-in the world. We show how successful design of movement-based and bodily interactive artifacts rely on qualities that allow users to connect their actions to the surrounding physical and social world. We introduce four key qualities for whole-body movement-based interaction.

Introduction

HCI continues to move towards experience-oriented technologies that aim at bringing in a larger range of bodily, sensory and social aspects of human experience, and to design for rich human experiences where body, mind and world come together in new exciting ways. Such work include design frameworks for somaesthetic experiences [8], conceptualizations of feeling and body in interaction [5], examples of technologies for bodily engagement [3, 7], as well as approaches and principles for engaging in design of movement based interaction [6].

Here, we hope to unravel some of the magic of people's deep engagement and their skilled reflection in activities in which body-artifact experiences are central. We are especially concerned with the experience of body and movement in relation to artifacts and to pin-point central experiential and interactional qualities in that relationship, and to transfer some of these qualities in the design of whole-body interaction with movement based artifacts.

We have investigated two very popular and much loved practices with non-digital artifacts (skateboard and golf) in order to dig out some experiential aspects not yet

C. Johansson (✉) and J. Tholander
MobileLife at Stockholm University, Forum 100, 16440 Kista, Sweden
e-mail: lina@sics.se; jakobth@dsv.su.se

D. England (ed.), *Whole Body Interaction*, Human-Computer Interaction Series,
DOI 10.1007/978-0-85729-433-3_7, © Springer-Verlag London Limited 2011

covered by interactive artifacts, and to compare these practices to a new interactive device designed for movement and bodily engagement (a prototype of a tangible movement partner called the BodyBug). Although they differ in many ways; golf and skateboarding are for example long-time established activities while the BodyBug is a brand new technical device, there are interesting aspects to compare and gain design insights from.

This work revealed several design insights relating to the qualities of whole-body interaction and experience with artifacts. We focus on three core qualities: the importance of creating interactive artifacts that do not shield the user from the material, physical, and social environment, artifacts that give open-ended responses for individual subjective experiences, and artifacts that allow perceptual modalities to be used in a complimentary fashion to allow for continuous attention from body and environment. We argue that the qualities we have identified are of critical importance for the crafting of artifacts that aim for graceful and sustained bodily interaction.

First, we present examples of people engaging in full body movement with non-digital artifacts; their deep and prolonged engagement with these, and how graceful movement and reflections on movement are key elements in their experience. Next, we present examples from users of the BodyBug and how we can find traces of similarly engaged and graceful movements in the interaction. However, as the interaction with the BodyBug sometimes breaks down in undesirable ways, we trace the source of such breakdowns in the way that the feedback and response leads the user's perception to become overly focused on the artifact without allowing the user to stay connected the physical surrounding. We would like to emphasize that the BodyBug is successful in many ways, but in a study focusing on how it allows users to interact with the world, challenges and difficulties are revealed.

Studies of Golfers, Skateboarders and Body Buggers

Golf and skateboarding were chosen as both being activities with non-digital artifacts and also for their seemingly difference in character (for example in skateboarding you cover a large space at a fast pace where in golf you are more centered and focused on one specific movement, i.e. the golf swing. The BodyBug (see Fig. 7.1) is an example of a technical artifact developed for movement-engaging interaction [1]. It is a portable and mobile device created in order to encourage and support free and natural full-body movement interaction. The BodyBug system consists of a wearable interactive robot. It can be compared to a Tamagotchi-like gadget that climbs on a string and feeds on and responds to bodily movements. A built-in accelerometer is used to sense the user's movement and a small display on the back shows textual feedback, instruction, and illustrations with buttons for navigating between games. In our study we used five games that were played by moving around in different ways.

The studies were performed with an open-ended approach aiming at capturing the central aspects of body-artifact-movement relationships. Our data was collected "in the wild", i.e. in settings where the activities ordinarily takes place (skateboarding

Fig. 7.1 The BodyBug

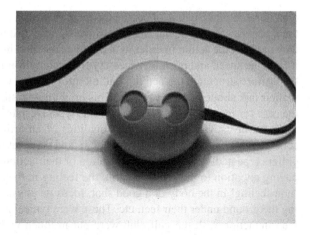

hall, golf driving range and dance studio). We observed and filmed the activity and held semi structured interviews around the participants' experience of body, movement and artifact. Here, we primarily focus on the participants' experiences and ways of talking about body and movement, and how they related to the artifacts used for their activity.

Golfers and Skateboarders on Body, Artifact and Movement

Simply by observing golfers and skateboarders one could see an aesthetic as well as a functional engagement in their actions and movements. The golfers for instance always tried to finish their swing in a balanced posture which both is a sign of appropriate technique and a way of mirroring the swing of highly skilled golfers. Similarly skateboarders position themselves on the board both to maximize balance and efficiency in movement, as well as to make the tricks with grace and attitude to impress their peers.

In general descriptions of their experiences, golfers and skateboarders emphasized the importance of the social dimensions and possibility of learning and being amongst friends. Within that context, the actual performance of the physical actions is of course central to their descriptions, but not brought up as the sole and primary reason for engaging in the activity.

The Role of the Artifact in Golf

Throughout our observations of the golfers' verbalization and the instructor's illustrations of movements and bodily action, the golf club and its specific qualities was rarely focused upon or explicitly talked about. The path and position of the golf club in relation the ball is of course the main reason as to why they are performing their actions in a particular manner. However, they rarely reflect on the fact that they perform the action in order to manipulate the club in a certain manner, making it have the speed and position necessary for accomplishing a particular shot. While the artifact structures the activity and the movements, it seldom comes into focus in their talk about their movements. This might not be surprising and is supposedly the case for most physical activities of this type. Despite this, it provides an opportunity to investigate how particular qualities of an artifact shape the moves and actions users perform with it. In interviews and observations, we could see how the golfers repeatedly emphasized the relation of their actions to the physical world by paying attention to the sound of a hit, the feeling in the hands of a bad shot or the 'non-feeling' in the body of a good shot, focus on physical distance of a shot, feeling the ground under their feet, etc. These were typical for how the golfers through the interaction with the golf club were put in touch with the physical world, and how that in turn gave them opportunities to reflect on their movements and interpret the results of their swings.

Golfer Talk on Experience and Body

Both in the instructional situations and the interviews, the golfers put substantial effort into making their experience of playing golf and the golf swing 'talkable', often through the use of a technical language. Already at a fairly basic level, players talked about technical aspects of their movements that have been proven of importance for carrying out a successful golf swing. This included aspects such as "*I try to lower my shoulder during the backswing*", "*At the end of my backswing I try not to make sure that my weight never goes beyond the inside of my left foot*", "*I try to cock my wrists earlier in the backswing*". For example, at the beginning of a lesson:

Lars: *I feel that I do it in three steps: first here coming up, then I try turning my body, and then*
Instructor: *And how does it feel?*
Lars: *It feels mechanical, but it's starting to get better.*

By describing a sequence of steps, Lars here verbally together with illustrative moves (see Fig. 7.2) deconstructs his experience of the golf swing for the purposes

Fig. 7.2 Body positions

of talking about it with the instructor, thereby allowing him to describe and communicate aspects of how he experiences his swing. This is a form of intellectualization that does not only have a communicative role, but it is also a part of the overall experience in the golfers pleasurable strive to improve his swing and his game. The experience of swinging the golf club is closely intertwined with intellectual aspects of the movement.

The dynamic whole is broken down into smaller constituents in order to make aspects of the experience shared with someone else. The talk about the bodily experience is thus bound to a particular activity and a specific form of social interaction. This reflects one of the challenges of what in phenomenology has been called 'languaging' or verbalising human experience [9], which in HCI translates to the methodological problem of representing people's experiences such as bodily actions and movement for purposes of understanding human technology relationships.

Skateboarders on Body and Movement

Contrary to the golfers, both in interviews and in-action observations the skateboarders described bodily experiences and movement in a more holistic manner. They emphasized the sense of speed, feeling free with the board, the smoothness of actions, and how the experience not only comes from the specific actions on the board, but from the whole context provided by friends, the culture of skateboarding and the environment. The skateboard was rarely a primary element of what they talked about; instead focus was on the embodied experience (Fig. 7.3).

Fig. 7.3 Skateboarder on the ramp

Generally, they were not particularly detailed in describing the bodily moves and actions involved in keeping the balance. Instead they focused on the totality of the feeling by emphasizing things like "*you feel it when you go in the turns, you then kind of feel, I don't know how to explain it*", as a means for successfully doing the tricks. When getting more into details on aspects of movement in our interviews, the skateboarders did not break down the activity into sub actions in the same manner as the golfers. For example, Viveka, a 22 year-old working at a skateboard hall, emphasized the role of balance and ways of moving with the board, but she did not describe specific details such as body positions or shifts in stance. She said things like "*you kind of feel it*" and "*you have to relax and feel it*" and how "*movement is actually everything*".

Describing the Movements of Friends

The skaters spent more time watching their friends and taking in the actions surrounding them in the hall than actual time on the board. We asked two skateboarders standing on the side to make in situ commentaries on the actions of their friends. With quite some detail regarding they described the relation between movements and the skateboard and how that affected the techniques for doing tricks. For instance, Sabina who had only been skateboarding three times as a part of school project described what she was looking for when observing her much more experienced friends: "*I am trying to see how they twist the board and how they place their feet. It's like, they change feet from having been standing like this. Then, when they make half the trick only one foot end up on the board*". Clearly, the surrounding environment with its jumps, other skaters and interweaving actions plays a big part in the overall experience of skateboarding.

When commenting on his friend, a 17 year-old talked about bodily control and described different movements in some detail: "*The tiniest things is about body movement, turning the shoulders with the board, how you stand, the placement of the feet, everything*". Compared to the golfers however, he did not describe it in a technicalized language in terms of body positions or angles but focused on timing and feeling: "*You go for the feel. After a while this feeling has settled like a little hole so you know exact, you feel now go*" (Fig. 7.4).

Experiencing Movement with the BodyBug

In the BodyBug sessions, the participants joined in pairs and sometimes played together or sometimes took turns watching each other play. In the five different games that were played, the participants' movements ranged from free improvisation

Fig. 7.4 Skateboarders talking about tricks

to guided movement from the BodyBug such as jumping, stepping and spinning in a specific fashion.

Users of the BodyBug had different ways of characterizing and systemizing their movements: "*It feels as if one moved very circular all the time*" and "*To move it up then down, to interchange between high and low position, I liked that – it became like a sphere*". Another participant classified her movement experiences as "*Base-movements*". Free movement involving the whole body was preferred by the participants and was considered both natural and fun. When moving this way the artifact faded from immediate focus of attention and shifted towards the actual movement in relation both to the artifact and the physical environment; "*My favorite game was Stop, where it felt as if I could move around as I wanted*". This shows the importance of how the artifact responds to the users' actions, and the possibilities for interpretation it opens up for.

As the BodyBug was moving on the string, communication with the eyes and making sounds many participants thought of the BodyBug as a living thing that they interacted with. They talked about how they tried to figure out what it would like about their movement, wondering what it was thinking and in general referring to it in terms such as "*this little guy*". This artifact-being-alive aspect might have been one reason as to why they talked about their movement as its purpose being to 'please' the BodyBug. "*I felt like I tried to make it happy*". Many felt they had moved too much: "*I exaggerated the movements, I did too much*", which pinpoints this experience of them not moving for their own enjoyment or for a particular aim, but in order to 'satisfy' the bug (Fig. 7.5).

Fig. 7.5 Moving with the BodyBug

The Role of the Artifact

"Because I'm very guided by this [pointing at the BodyBug] it follows that one doesn't really have an eye on the room in general". As the participants' focus was often exclusively on the BodyBug giving instructions on the small screen or by its eyes, the participants had difficulties connecting with their physical

surrounding. Often, they were close to bumping into each other and thus not being aware of one another or the room: "*it feels a bit ... inside. That one is in one's own sphere*".

The BodyBug has two modes of communicating: audio by different noises and playing tunes, and visual by text on the small display or movement cues by the eyes. It was evident that the visual form was dominating: "*It was a little bit difficult to understand when I did right or wrong because I couldn't look at the display when spinning around*". The often repeated feeling that the display was too small also proves this visual domination: "*it was too hard to see exactly what it wanted, especially when one is moving around*". Other participants did pay more attention to the audio cues given. However, also in this case the visual stole the attention at occasions as she also admits to "*sneaking a peak*" at the display. Some users expressed frustration over not getting the right feedback even though they felt they had performed a correct move.

This 'artifact-focused' interaction is in part due to how the BodyBug responds to the users actions. It gives a discrete kind of feedback that evaluates whether you have moved right or wrong, without leaving room for the users' own interpretation. In comparison, a non-technical device as a golf club or skateboard provides an open-ended response that allows the users' to have a richer range of possible interpretations of their experience with the artifact.

Discussion

Our findings reveal the following key qualities for design of interactive artifacts that connect body and world in an intriguing way:

- make it valuable to engage with the physical environment
- avoid perceptive modalities (in our case vision) that remove attention from body and environment
- the response should not be discrete but open up for individual experience and interpretation
- the artefact should allow users to continuously be socially aware.

Both skateboarders and golfers emphasized the connection to the physical environment for the accomplishment of challenging interaction with the artifact. Skateboarders talked about "surfaces" such as slopes or rails and how they were used to carry out tricks. Similarly, golfers spent time on practicing the moves required to hit the ball from different slopes or bouncing the club on the ground. Also among BodyBug users, we observed interaction and movement of the engaged, sustained and often graceful character where user, artifact, and physical surround worked as complimentary aspects in the interaction. However, in many cases the movement got detached from the world around the user who only focused on the feedback of the artifact, without relating to how the feedback corresponded to the physical world. The visual, textual and sound feedback of the BodyBug seemed to detach the users from their bodily engagement with artifact and world as complementary aspects.

The interdependency between user, artifact and physical environment is one of the primary qualities for the kind of rich, sustained and graceful interaction that we saw in golf and skateboarding. In this relationship, the response, or feedback, of the artifact comes out of how it is applied to the physical world and how the user interprets and experiences the response of that application. Hence, it is not primarily the feedback from the artifact itself that determines the outcome of the action carried out by the user. Rather, it is the user's interpretation of the response in relation to artifact and world that makes up the experience.

This challenges designers of experience-oriented artifacts for body and movement to view the artifact as a medium for engaging in movement based activities, while not letting it become the sole and primary focus of the movement. This would allow the "outcome" of the activity not to be determined by the output of the system, but to be determined by the experience of the user. Rather than making users mind-focused we should aim for designing artifacts that allow them to become movement- and body-focused, so that they can continuously be bodily engaged with and connected to social, material and physical aspects of their surrounding world. Thereby, users can engage with movement-based interactive artifacts in a way that can be increasingly developed and mastered over time, and provide possibilities for a deep connectedness between our bodies and the physical world.

Reflections

Our findings relate to the perspective of embodied interaction which emphasizes the importance of understanding human action as intrinsically intertwined and inseparable from the social and material aspects in which it occurs [2]. More specifically, aspects of the qualities discussed above have also been identified in other kinds of activities and settings. For instance the notion of awareness, primarily social and contextual, has been a long-standing issue in CSCW e.g. [4]. Similarly, in pervasive computing the importance of designing with reference to the contextual aspects of interaction are commonly emphasized, emphasizes designing for a "heads up" experience to avoid that people get occupied watching their screens and loses attention to the physical surrounding. However, in our work we have identified the importance of supporting users in staying connected to their physical surrounding in their moment-to-moment bodily engagement and interaction with a device. This requires designing for the possibilities for users to adapt their actions to the responses of the device, and to the physical surrounding, in each particular moment of interaction.

Current and Future Work

We are currently designing a whole-body movement interaction based on the qualities presented in this paper. Our focus is on how to design responses to user's actions in a fashion that inspires interesting movements conducted with reference to the surrounding physical and material circumstances. This work is conducted together with children and teachers of a local elementary school and based in a gym-hall setting and the project explores learning about energy through moving with wiimotes attached to the body.

We are also extending the initial design qualities presented in this paper, to a set of eight interactional qualities that contribute to a perspective on interaction that can inspire researchers and designers to explore technology that enable a deep connectedness between the whole human being and the physical world in which we live and act. These qualities are explored in creating design work and design exercises for new scenarios for movement based interaction, and inspire designers into novel ways of thinking of and designing for moving bodies in the world. These qualities will be presented in a paper at NordiCHI 2010 [10].

References

1. BodyBug by Movinto Fun. http://www.bodybug.se/. Accessed Oct 2010
2. Dourish, P.: Where the Action Is. MIT Press, Cambridge (2001)
3. Fagerberg, P., Ståhl, A., Höök, K.: eMoto: emotionally engaging interaction. Pers. Ubiquit. Comput. **8**(5), 377–381 (Sept 2004)
4. Kjeld, S.: The problem with "awareness": introductory remarks on "awareness in CSCW'", *Computer Supported Cooperative Work (CSCW)*. J. Collab. Comput. **11**(3–4), 285–298 (2002)
5. Larssen, A.T., Robertson, T., Edwards, J.: The feel dimension of technology interaction: exploring tangibles through movement and touch. In: Proceedings of TEI'07, Baton Rouge, pp. 271–278. ACM Press, New York (2007)
6. Loke, L., Larssen, A.T., Robertson, T., Edwards, J.: Understanding movement for interaction design: frameworks and approaches. Pers. Ubiquit. Comput. **11**(8), 691–701 (2007)
7. Moen, J.: From hand-held to body-worn: embodied experiences of the design and use of a wearable movement-based interaction concept. In: Proceedings of TEI '07, Baton Rouge, pp. 251–258. ACM Press, New York (2007)
8. Schiphorst, T.: Soft(n): toward a somaesthetics of touch. In: Proceedings of CHI 2009, Boston, 4–9 Apr 2009, pp. 2427–2438. ACM Press, New York (2009)
9. Sheets-Johnstone, M.: The Corporeal Turn. An Interdisciplinary Reader. Imprint Academic, Exeter (2009)
10. Tholander, J., Johansson, C.: Design qualities for whole body interaction – learning from golf, skateboarding and bodybugging. In: Proceedings of NordiCHI 2010, Reykjavik (2010)

Chapter 8
Whole Body Large Display Interfaces for Users and Designers

Garth Shoemaker and Kellogg S. Booth

Abstract A body-centered model of human-computer interaction holds promise to change the way both users and designers of computing systems go about their daily work. From the users' perspective, a body-centered interaction model allows them to fully capitalize on the wealth of skills that have evolved over millennia of evolution. Users can exploit their natural abilities of grasping and pointing, they can employ the power of proprioception and specialized processing in different spaces, and employ the rules of social interaction that govern everyday life. All of these things could be integrated into computing systems in such a way that interaction becomes based on our everyday knowledge. From a designer's standpoint, a body-centered model of interaction makes users the focal point of the design and implementation process. Instead of wrestling with device communication and protocols, the designer treats users as the initiators of all action. This is both a philosophical and a practical shift in process with deep ramifications.

Why Whole Body Interaction

Ever since the introduction of the mouse and the WIMP (windows, icons, menus, pointers) model of human computer interaction, users have been required to use computers in the same consistent manner, regardless of the task at hand. The scenario is familiar: a single user sits at a desk mounted with an often modest-sized monitor, and performs input using both a mouse and keyboard. The devices stay the same regardless of the task, as does the configuration of the workspace. This is in sharp contrast with the real world, where people are not so constrained by input and output devices. A person can work on a table (small or large), can stand to work at a whiteboard, or can move about a room interacting with multiple collaborators.

G. Shoemaker (✉) and K.S. Booth (✉)
Department of Computer Science, University of British Columbia, 201-2366 Main Mall,
Vancouver, British Columbia V6T 1Z4, Canada
e-mail: garths@cs.ubc.ca; ksbooth@cs.ubc.ca

D. England (ed.), *Whole Body Interaction*, Human-Computer Interaction Series,
DOI 10.1007/978-0-85729-433-3_8, © Springer-Verlag London Limited 2011

Physical real estate (space) available to a person is almost always much more than the real estate available on standard desktop monitors. Furthermore, the physical world offers a much richer set of input devices. A person can use pens and pencils, scissors, straight edges, paint brushes, miter saws, pool cues, and violin bows. Regardless of the task at hand, there is a work space configuration and a set of tools, sometimes highly specialized, that are appropriate. Work and interaction in the physical world is much more flexible, fluid, and dynamic than work that is constrained by the limitations of a traditional desktop computing system.

Despite the dominance of the traditional desktop computer configuration, we are currently entering a new phase of computing interaction, foreseen by Nielsen [17] and others, where users are adopting different computer form factors that are optimized for varying tasks. Very small devices such as personal phones are growing in power and capabilities. They offer more than just the benefits of portability. For example, the Apple iPhone contains a gyroscope and compass that makes possible powerful augmented reality applications. These applications simply would not make sense on a desktop machine. Tablet devices such as the Amazon Kindle and Barnes & Noble Nook e-readers are also changing the way we interact with computers. The ability to access any of several million book titles is a capability that desktop computers could easily offer, but is a proposition that only becomes attractive with the form factors of e-readers.

Large display devices also offer benefits for interaction (Fig. 8.1). The form factors of such displays mimic the properties of large physical work surfaces, such as

Fig. 8.1 A mockup of users collaborating around a large display. Direct communication with other users, and use of other physical and interactive surfaces, plays as important a role as the display itself

whiteboards and tables. As with whiteboards and tables, large displays can foster collaboration and support tasks such as brainstorming and casual data reference.

As computing form factor design draws more and more inspiration from the physical world, the way in which we interact with the virtual world becomes more physical, more literal and more direct. Users cohabit a space with surfaces and tools, rather than being separated from the virtual world by the hard unyielding surface of the display, only able to interact indirectly by way of mouse and keyboard. This is an important shift in computing that should be recognized and understood.

This chapter presents a whole body model for interaction that can potentially benefit users and system designers/developers/researchers alike. Body-centered interaction is both a philosophical approach for designing interactions, and a practical means of supporting system design. It is well suited to emerging computing form factors. From a user's viewpoint body-centered interaction results in techniques that leverage the natural capabilities of users. From a designer's viewpoint, body-centered interaction eases development, and helps the designer keep the user central to the design process. We examine both of these viewpoints, with a particular emphasis on interaction techniques for large displays.

Related Work

Two areas of research are particularly relevant to our exploration. We first consider the use of both large physical surfaces and large interactive displays. We then look at work related to body-centered interaction.

Large Surfaces and Large Displays

Large physical surfaces play an important role in supporting everyday tasks. As such, they ought to be a critical component of the whole workspace "toolbox" [19]. One reason is that people make use of physical desks for organizing artefacts, and they develop complex approaches for doing so [15]. Whiteboards and tack-boards are widespread in homes and offices, and play quite different roles from desks, due to their vertical orientation [21]. Looking at the history of large work surfaces, Buxton notes that the invention of the blackboard in the nineteenth century, replacing smaller slates, is considered a major milestone in the advancement of educational technology [4], and thus it is ironic that today there is a movement to replace large shared blackboards with individual laptop computers [12], potentially undoing gains that we have benefitted from for the bulk of the last 200 years.

Large display surfaces offer the same benefits as large physical surfaces, with the added ability of showing interactive dynamic virtual content. This is made possible by the computer. Examples of tasks that benefit from large displays are storing personal information [27], supporting brainstorming activities [5], and allowing casual engagement in public spaces [26]. Domains where large surfaces are used include hospitals [28] and control rooms [22].

Body-Centered Interaction

There is a rich history of work investigating the relationships between human bodies and virtual interaction techniques, both within and outside of the research community. Artists have often been at the forefront of this exploration. A very early example of this is the VIDEOPLACE project by Krueger et al. [13], which made use of a shadow embodiment of the user to mediate interaction. Utterback has explored this theme in depth, with a number of examples looking at body-virtual interaction from different perspectives [29]. More recently, Lozano-Hemmer has explored shadows in other ways, including his "Under Scan" interactive video art installation [14].

Two examples of work in HCI related to whole body interaction are Jacob et al.'s notion of Reality-Based Interaction (RBIs) [10] and Klemmer et al.'s investigation of "how bodies matter" [11]. The paradigm of Reality-Based Interfaces for interaction design stresses a number of themes related to modeling the real world in the virtual world. These themes include *naive physics*, *body awareness and skills*, *environment awareness and skills*, and *social awareness and skills*. The themes serve to unify individual ideas that have recurred in the HCI literature. Klemmer et al.'s work on "how bodies matter" investigates a sub-set of RBI, but identify five themes of their own: *thinking through doing*, *performance*, *visibility*, *risk*, and *thick practice*, which serve to provide insight into the creation of interaction techniques that combine both physical and computational worlds. The lessons from these two approaches are consistent. They suggest that we should build on real world experience and capabilities when designing virtual interactions, while simultaneously taking full advantage of the "more-than real" power that is possible when we are not constrained by physicality. As Jacob et al. point out, computing systems should not settle for perfectly mimicking the real world. They should offer something beyond what the physical world offers, otherwise no benefit is derived.

How Can Body-Centered Interaction Help Users?

The ultimate purpose of interaction design is to aid users in the accomplishment of their goals. Here we consider body-centered interaction in the context of large display use, and consider how a body-centered approach to interaction design can better support users.

There is a wealth of knowledge regarding the human body and how it relates both to itself and to the environment. Medical doctors, psychologists, and sociologists have spent centuries developing a deep understanding of how humans function at various levels of abstraction, from low-level signal processing to higher level cognition. We can draw on this knowledge to aid in the development of a body-centered approach to design.

Interaction Spaces

Until recently all computer interaction occurred in the same sensorimotor space. A keyboard and mouse was within easy reach, and a monitor was also roughly at arm's length. With the introduction of a more heterogeneous work environment, where there may be a number of large and small display surfaces scattered about the room, it is important to consider how the human brain functions when working in different spaces.

We are not aware of it at a conscious level, but the human brain uses different approaches and internal representations to coordinate sensorimotor operations in different spaces [6]. Three interaction spaces are of interest to us: *personal space*, *peripersonal space*, and *extrapersonal space* [9]. Personal space is that occupied by the body, peripersonal space is the region within easy reach of the hands, and extrapersonal space is whatever lies beyond peripersonal space. Interaction in each of these different spaces can result in distinct performance characteristics. It is believed that interaction in personal and peripersonal space is more optimized than interaction in extrapersonal space, because most of our real world interaction experience is inside the bounds of peripersonal space.

Properties of the different spaces can have a significant impact on the efficacy of interaction techniques, and even the basic theoretical underpinnings of HCI. For example, Fitts's law was originally developed to describe physical human pointing performance in peripersonal space [8]. It may not generalize to virtual interaction outside of a users' reach, which is a common scenario on large displays when devices such as laser pointers are employed. A hint of this is provided by Pratt et al. [20], who demonstrated that the visual context of a target can modulate pointing performance. Their conclusion that allocentric information interacts with Fitts's law implies that pointing performance could be sensitive to different internal spatial representations that might be used for the three spaces. As Pratt et al. comment, "… existing models of motor control will need to be examined, reinterpreted, or possibly replaced", a conclusion that is particularly relevant when applied to large display situations and multiple-space interaction.

The unification of interaction spaces is another topic of relevance. Although the brain uses different representations and approaches to interacting in different spaces, there are ways to "bridge the gap" between spaces, allowing the brain to work in one space using the same approach that it uses in another. It has been found that the brain can naturally bind personal and peripersonal space [30], but binding extrapersonal space is more difficult. Researchers have nevertheless found two ways of binding extrapersonal and personal space that ease interaction at a distance. First, it has been shown that a person's image in a mirror binds the two spaces [16]. Second, body shadows can bind the two spaces [18]. These are approaches that can also be employed in a body-centered computing environment. One example is the authors' previous use of shadows to support interaction on large screen displays [23].

Social Conventions

Humans have developed complex rules for social interaction. Some rules are specific to particular cultures, but others are universal. They govern how we talk to one another, how we move in shared spaces, and how we coordinate work. With large displays, and any computing environment that is meant to support collaboration, it is useful to recognize and incorporate a knowledge of these social guidelines. This is yet another aspect of the body-centric approach to interaction design.

One important aspect of social interaction is the notion of private space, as described by Felipe and Sommer[1] [7]. Private space is the region around a person's body outside of which they attempt to keep other people during normal interaction. As described by Sundstrom and Altman [25], private space is more complex than simple private/non-private, and changes fluidly depending on the situation. A computing system that possesses knowledge of private space, and is able to accurately model how private space varies based on different factors could use this knowledge to coordinate interactions with multiple users. For example, a system could use proximity information to determine when different users transition between close collaboration and independent work. This is something that has already been investigated in the HCI community at a high level [2], but the intricacies of proximity have not been fully explored.

There is more to social interaction than physical proximity and private space. Complex cues such as eye gaze, body lean (posture), and smiling also convey important information [3]. A computing system that is able to capture these cues could make direct use of them, but many of these cues are subtle enough that they are difficult to capture. It is nevertheless possible to make use of these cues indirectly by incorporating direct user-user interaction into the system design. For example, user-user interactions can be used for manipulation of data, rather than requiring users to interact with a device or display as the focus of interaction. In this way the system is taken "out of the loop" and users are able to employ their natural communicative abilities in a context in which they are directly applicable.

Example Interaction Techniques

We have designed and implemented a number of interaction techniques derived from our approach, described in detail elsewhere [24]. We provide a brief overview here.

Based on our knowledge of interaction spaces, and the scale of interaction for large displays, we have developed techniques in which users interact with the display through a virtual shadow proxy. The shadow serves the role of unifying

---

[1] "Private space" in this context is sometimes referred to in the literature as "personal space." We call it "private space" to disambiguate from the definition of "personal space" used in the previous section that discussed interaction spaces.

Fig. 8.2 Two body-centered interaction techniques. *Left*: body-based tools that are accessed directly on the user's own body. *Right*: Digital data sharing protocols that are governed by natural social conventions

personal and extrapersonal space. It also allows users to reach over longer distances, which is useful for large displays. Two other techniques (Fig. 8.2) emphasize other aspects of how human behavior is strongly connected to our bodies. The first is *body-based tools*, which allows users to select interaction modes by reaching to predefined body locations. This approach relies on the power of proprioception, making mode selection a personal operation, and thus avoiding the need for public tool bars and menus that clutter the workspace. The second technique is a set of sharing protocols in which real-world physical actions result in the copying of virtual data between users' personal data stores. The protocols involve users directly handing virtual content to one another. Proximity of users' hands is used by the system to govern access. This incorporates common social conventions directly into the process of sharing digital data.

How Can Body-Centered Interaction Help Designers?

A body-centered approach to interaction can aid in the design and development process. A shift of focus from devices and displays to users and context serves to both emphasize the role of the user, and to abstract away irrelevant implementation details. Here we describe both the shift of focus and a concrete example of a body-centered development approach.

From Device-Centered to Body-Centered

In typical software development, the developer measures the state of various input devices and then causes the system to respond to those state changes. For example, the

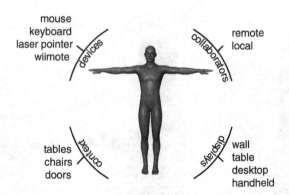

Fig. 8.3 In the body-centered approach to application development, the user is at the core of the design and development process. Other contextually relevant objects are considered in relation to the user. The user is the source of all action

software might measure the movement of a mouse or the motion of a magnetic marker being tracked by a sensor. This is a *device-centric* model of application development. What is actually of interest, however, is what the user is doing. As developers, we are not really interested in how the mouse moves, but instead we want to know how the user's hand moves. We are similarly not interested in the magnetic marker, but how the user's head is positioned and oriented so a proper perspective view can be rendered in a virtual or augmented reality setting. Devices are typically just a means of measurement, not ends in themselves. As Baecker and Buxton observe [1], "an input device is a transducer from the physical properties of the world into logical parameters of an application." A shift to a *body-centric* model of application development occurs when a developer provides a system that ignores the specifics of measurement and instead responds directly to what the user is actually doing. From a developer's standpoint, the body-centric interaction approach shifts the design and development process from a *device-centric* activity to a *body-centric* focus (Fig. 8.3).

Body-Centered APIs

Application programming interfaces (APIs) allow developers to create software applications without requiring knowledge of the low-level details. It follows then that body-centric development should be supported through the use of a body-centric API, or *BAPI*. A properly designed BAPI allows developers to query the state of users, including the locations and limb poses of individual users, and relationship between users and devices, displays, and each other using a single model of the entire scene.

As an example of how a BAPI can be used, the following pseudo-code traverses a scene model to determine interesting properties of the users in a collaborative application.

```
Set allUsers = BAPI::getAllUsers
FOR each user in allUsers
  Set userLocation to user->location
  Set upperArmAngle to user->upperArmAngle
  Set closestCollaborator = user->closestCollaborator
  Set display to user->gazeTarget
  IF user->isTouchingDisplay(display) = true THEN
    Set location = user->touchLocation(display)
    CALL handleDisplayTouch with location
  END IF
END FOR
```

One of the major strengths of using a BAPI is that the details of sensing are abstracted away from the developer. In large display environments there are many things to be measured (e.g. user locations in a room, limb poses, identity of users, locations of numerous displays). It is rare that one sensing approach will be able to measure everything. With a BAPI, there is a sensor-fusion layer beneath the BAPI that combines signals from a number of sensing platforms into a single coherent model of the environment (scene) in which users are working. It is this scene that is queried by the BAPI. The developer does not need a working knowledge of individual sensing platforms.

A Body-Centric Application Case Study

Body-centric interaction approaches are best evaluated in the context of a real-world computing environment. It is particularly useful to be able to integrate new interaction approaches into existing systems, with the goal of discovering how use of these existing systems might change with the adoption of new interaction metaphors. We describe here such an integration that was used to explore the viability of the approaches described in the previous sections.

Traditional operating systems, such as Microsoft Windows or Apple OS X, were developed with many assumptions being made regarding how they would be used. For example, the systems assume input by a single user, at a single point (defined by a cursor), on a relatively small display. When integrating new interaction approaches, such as our body-centric approaches, it is necessary to abstract away the constraints of traditional operating systems to support the concepts inherent in body-centric approaches. Our current implementation of body-centric interaction techniques integrates into the Microsoft Windows 7 operating system (Fig. 8.4). Implementations for other platforms would be similar.

In integrating our body-centric interaction approach into Microsoft Windows 7, we had several design requirements we wished to fulfill. These include the following:

1. The system should allow interaction using body-centric interaction techniques for any native software application.

Fig. 8.4 Body-centric interaction techniques, specifically shadow embodied bimanual reaching at a distance, integrated in the Microsoft Windows 7 operating system. The user is shown dragging objects in Microsoft Visio

2. Appropriate visual feedback, such as body shadows and tools, should be shown over top of all other on-screen content, such as windows and toolbars.
3. Bimanual interaction should be supported for a single user.
4. Simultaneous interaction by multiple users should be supported.

The approach used for supporting these design requirements is described in the following sections.

Application Universality

We wish our body-centric interaction approach to appear native to the operating system. Users should be able to switch seamlessly between any native applications, while using our techniques. There are features available to developers of Windows 7 applications that make this possible.

One problem that has to be addressed is displaying visual feedback over top of all applications. Our application must be able to render on the very top, while another application (e.g. Microsoft Word) holds focus. This is accomplished using several properties of Windows Forms in the .NET architecture. The TopMost property of a Form object forces an application to render on top of all other applications, regardless of whether or not it has focus.

We wish the other applications to be visible, however, and therefore we must be able to render our application using transparency. This is a somewhat complicated process, involving setting the TransparencyKey of the Form, then using dwmapi.dll in some atypical ways. The details of this are beyond the scope of this chapter, but resources are available on the web that describe the process. The advantage of this approach is that the bulk of the body-centric application is entirely transparent, revealing the native applications in use, and the body shadow is rendered partially transparent, so that the user is able to interact using it as feedback.

Event Management

Users must be able to trigger events. In our implementation, using Nintendo Wii Remotes for input, each of possibly several users can trigger a single stream of click events with each hand. These event streams must be compressed into a single event stream to be consumed by the operating system, due to the assumption on the part of the OS of a single cursor.

Input events from the Wii Remotes are coalesced into a single event stream using the approach shown in Fig. 8.5. When a button on a Wii Remote is pressed the following series of events occurs:

1. Test if the cursor is locked. If it is, then exit.
2. Lock the cursor.
3. Move the cursor to the location on the screen determined by a projection onto the screen of the location of the hand holding the Wii Remote.
4. Send a mouse down event to the operating system.
5. Continuously update the location of the cursor, until the Wii Remote button is released.
6. Send a mouse up event to the operating system.
7. Unlock the cursor.

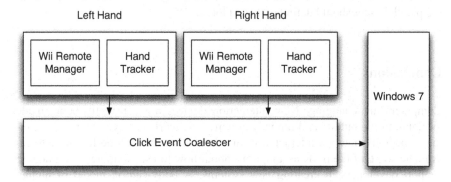

Fig. 8.5 Input events from multiple users and multiple hands are coalesced into a single event stream understandable by the operating system. In this manner body-centric input can be supported by a single cursor at the level of the OS

This approach allows for control of the system cursor by a single hand of a single user at any one time. While a hand is controlling the cursor no other hand is able to take control. Any attempt will result in no action being performed. Denial of access to the cursor is ideally communicated to the user through visual feedback, for example by displaying a red "x" at the location of the hand that attempted, but failed, to take control of the system cursor.

The described approach for coalescing events into a single event stream imposes constraints on interaction, but this is unavoidable, based on the limitations of current operating systems. It is expected that these limitations can be relaxed in the future, when operating systems incorporate richer support for multi-touch and multi-user interaction.

User Observations

Observations that were part of the case study of users interacting under Windows 7 with our body-centric approach reveal several interesting findings. First, it is clear that traditional WIMP design elements are not appropriate for very large displays. Small text at the peripheries of a display, including text shown in menus and on toolbars, is frequently illegible due to a combination of distance and perspective distortion. This stresses the importance of new methods of accessing modes or commands, such as our body-based tools, that are collocated with the user and thus are always within reach and in sight. One means of integrating support for body-based tools into the OS would be for the body-based tools to operate as macros. Different body tools could activate different key combinations or menu selections, depending on bindings specific to the currently active application.

The event coalescing approach functioned well in our trials. Although it was clear that locking out access to the cursor based on priority limited user interactions to some degree, this was manageable with sufficient feedback to users of cursor state. Nevertheless, when operating systems make it possible, a means of performing parallel input should definitely be explored.

Conclusions

Computers are changing. New interaction devices are constantly being made available to the public, and the way in which we work and live is rapidly evolving, especially how we interact with digital media. This is a perfect time to re-evaluate some of the basic assumptions about how to use computers, and how to support developers in creating new systems. A body-centric model of human computer interaction recognizes how we work in the real world, and respects the natural abilities of human beings. It is an approach that fits well with emerging new computing form factors. We believe that a body-centric approach will help guide the evolution of these new devices so they become more than just individual islands of computation, but instead become part of an ecosystem of expanded functionality.

References

1. Baecker, R.M., Buxton, W.: Readings in Human Computer Interaction: A Multidisciplinary Approach. Kauffman, San Francisco (1987)
2. Ballendat, T., Marquardt, N., Greenberg, S.: Proxemic interaction: designing for a proximity and orientation-aware environment. In: Proceedings of ITS'10, Saarbrücken (2010)
3. Burgoon, J.K., Buller, D.B., Hale, J.L., deTurck, M.A.: Relational messages associated with nonverbal behaviors. Hum. Commun. Res. **10**(3), 351–378 (1984)
4. Buxton, B.: Surface and tangible computing, and the "small" matter of people and design. In: IEEE International Solid-State Circuits Conference Digest of Technical Papers, pp. 24–29, San Francisco (2008)
5. Cherubini, M., Venolia, G., DeLine, R., Ko, A.J.: Let's go to the whiteboard: how and why software developers use drawings. In: Proceedings of CHI'07, pp. 557–566, San Jose (2007)
6. Colby, C.L.: Action-oriented spatial reference frames in cortex. Neuron **20**, 15–24 (1998)
7. Felipe, N.J., Sommer, R.: Invasions of personal space. Soc. Probl. **14**(2), 206–214 (1966)
8. Fitts, P.M.: The information capacity of the human motor system in controlling the amplitude of movement. J. Exp. Psychol. **47**(6), 381–391 (1954)
9. Holmes, N.P., Spence, C.: The body schema and multisensory representation(s) of peripersonal space. Cogn. Process. **5**(2), 94–105 (2004)
10. Jacob, R.J., Girouard, A., Hirshfield, L.M., Horn, M.S., Shaer, O., Solovey, E.T., Zigelbaum, J.: Reality-based interaction. In: Proceedings of CHI'08, pp. 201–210, Florence (2008)
11. Klemmer, S., Hartmann, B., Takayama, L.: How bodies matter: five themes for interaction design. In: Proceedings of DIS'06, pp. 140–149, University Park (2006)
12. Kraemer, K.L., Dedrick, J., Sharma, P.: One laptop per child: vision vs. reality. Commun. ACM **52**(6), 66–73 (2009)
13. Krueger, M.W., Gionfriddo, T., Hinrichsen, K.: VIDEOPLACE – an artificial reality. In: Proceedings of CHI '85, pp. 35–40, San Francisco (1985)
14. Lozano-Hemmer, R.: Under Scan. Emda & Antimodular, Turin (2007)
15. Malone, T.W.: How do people organize their desks?: Implications for the design of office information systems. ACM Trans. Inf. Syst. **1**(1), 99–112 (1983)
16. Maravita, A., Spence, C., Sergent, C., Driver, J.: Seeing your own touched hands in a mirror modulates cross-modal interactions. Psychol. Sci. **13**(4), 350–355 (2002)
17. Nielsen, J.: Noncommand user interfaces. Commun. ACM **36**(4), 83–89 (1993)
18. Pavani, F., Castiello, U.: Binding personal and extrapersonal space through body shadows. Nat. Neurosci. **7**, 13–14 (2004)
19. Plaue, C., Stasko, J., Baloga, M.: The conference room as a toolbox: technological and social routines in corporate meeting spaces. In: Proceedings of Communities and Technology, pp. 95–104, State College (2009)
20. Pratt, J., Adam, J.J., Fischer, M.H.: Visual layout modulates Fitts law: the importance of first and last positions. Psychon. Bull. Rev. **14**(2), 350–355 (2007)
21. Rogers, Y., Lindley, S.: Collaborating around vertical and horizontal large interactive displays: which is best? Interact. Comput. **16**, 1133–1152 (2004)
22. Salo, L., Laarni, J., Savioja, P.: Operator experiences on working in screen-based control rooms. In: 5th ANS International Topical Meeting on Nuclear Plant Instrumentation, Controls, and Human Machine Interface Technology, LaGrange Park (2006)
23. Shoemaker, G., Tang, A., Booth, K.S.: Shadow reaching: a new perspective on interaction for large displays. In: Proceedings of UIST '07, pp. 53–56, Newport (2007)

24. Shoemaker, G., Tsukitani, T., Kitamura, Y., Booth, K.S.: Body-centric interaction techniques for very large wall displays. In: Proceedings of NordiCHI '10, Atlanta (2010)
25. Sundstrom, E., Altman, I.: Interpersonal relationships and personal space: research review and theoretical model. Hum. Ecol. **4**(1), 47–67 (1976)
26. Tang, A., Finke, M., Blackstock, M., Leung, R., Deutscher, M., Lea, R.: Designing for bystanders: Reflections on building a public digital forum. In: Proceedings of CHI '08, pp. 879–882, Florence (2008)
27. Tang, A., Lanir, J., Greenberg, S., Fels, S.: Supporting transitions in work: Informing large display application design by understanding whiteboard use. In: Proceedings of GROUP '09, pp. 149–158, Sanibel Island (2009)
28. Tang, C., Carpendale, S.: An observational study on information flow during nurses' shift change. In: Proceedings of CHI '07, pp. 219–228, San Jose (2007)
29. Utterback, C., Achituv, R.: Text rain. In: SIGGRAPH Electronic Art and Animation Catalog, p. 78, Los Angeles (2002)
30. Vaishnavi, S., Calhoun, J., Chatterjee, A.: Binding personal and peripersonal space: evidence from tactile extinction. J. Cogn. Neurosci. **13**(2), 181–189 (2001)

Chapter 9
Observations on Experience and Flow in Movement-Based Interaction

**Anton Nijholt, Marco Pasch, Betsy van Dijk,
Dennis Reidsma, and Dirk Heylen**

Abstract Movement-based interfaces assume that their users move. Users have to perform exercises, they have to dance, they have to golf or football, or they want to train particular bodily skills. Many examples of those interfaces exist, sometimes asking for subtle interaction between user and interface and sometimes asking for 'brute force' interaction between user and interface. Often these interfaces mediate between players of a game. Obviously, one of the players may be a virtual human. We embed this interface research in ambient intelligence and entertainment computing research, and the interfaces we consider are not only mediating, but they also 'add' intelligence to the interaction. Intelligent movement-based interfaces, being able to know and learn about their users, should also be able to provide means to keep their users engaged in the interaction. Issues that will be discussed in this chapter are 'flow' and 'immersion' for movement-based interfaces and we look at the possible role of interaction synchrony to measure and support engagement.

Introduction

Nowadays, when we talk about human-computer interaction, it is not about the mouse and the keyboard anymore. Clearly, mouse and keyboard are useful and needed for many useful and mundane tasks, but they do not provide natural and non-intrusive interaction between humans and the environments in which they live and work. The environments in which humans live are now becoming equipped with sensors that collect data about what is going on in the environments and are

A. Nijholt (✉), B. van Dijk, D. Reidsma, and D. Heylen
Human Media Interaction, University of Twente, PO Box 217, 7500 AE
Enschede, The Netherlands
e-mail: anijholt@cs.utwente.nl; bvdijk@cs.utwente.nl; dennisr@cs.utwente.nl

M. Pasch
Faculty of Informatics, University of Lugano, Via Buffi 13, 6900 Lugano, Switzerland
e-mail: marco.pasch@usi.ch

D. England (ed.), *Whole Body Interaction*, Human-Computer Interaction Series,
DOI 10.1007/978-0-85729-433-3_9, © Springer-Verlag London Limited 2011

backed up by computers that integrate and interpret this data. Hence, we have environments that can observe their human inhabitants, can interpret what they know, want and do, and re-actively and pro-actively support them in their activities. In these ambient intelligence environments there is an inhabitant (often called a user), but more importantly, this 'user' is one of the many 'agents' that are modeled in such environments. Human inhabitants, (semi-) autonomous human-like agents (virtual humans, robots), and 'intelligent devices' such as furniture and other natural and obvious devices (pets, TV, pda's ...) with embedded artificial intelligence will be considered part of these environments.

User interfaces have been introduced that offer, elicit and stimulate bodily activity for recreational and health purposes. Obviously, there are other applications that can be informed and guided by bodily activity information and that can be controlled by such information. For example, in a smart, sensor-equipped, home environment bodily activity can be employed to control devices, or the smart home environment might anticipate our activities and behave in a pro-active and anticipatory supporting way. Although in home environments there exists freedom concerning when and how to perform tasks, there are regular patterns of bodily activity and therefore activities can be predicted and anomalies can be detected.

Whole Body Movement Interfaces

In game or entertainment environments the 'user' may take part in events that require bodily interaction with sensor-equipped environments. This can be a home environment, but it can be a city environment as well. For example, in a home environment we can have a user use an exercise bicycle or a treadmill to navigate or play a game in a 'Second Life'-like environment. Clearly, we can inform the user about performance in the past (allowing him or her to compete with him- or herself) and we can inform the user about the performance of other users. In an urban game, mobile devices may be used to inform the users about activities they have to perform or about activities of their partners or opponents in the game. The game can require the gamer to walk, run, or perform other activities, in order to compete or cooperate with others involved in the game. Other types of these so-called exertion interfaces have been designed. Some characteristic examples will be discussed later in this paper.

In this chapter we assume that these entertainment and exertion interfaces will be anywhere: in home, office, sports, fitness, and medical environments, and also in public spaces. The motivation to use them can differ. For example, we can look at exertion exercises to improve health conditions, sports performance, or (therapeutic) physical rehabilitation. Often these interfaces are promoted from the point of view of fighting obesity. But, we want to look at exertion interfaces that are designed to provide fun and that engage a user in a game and entertainment experience, and in which considerations about health, physical performance, and rehabilitation are by-products.

Whether such interfaces are designed for fun or for health and well-being purposes, they need to engage the user in the interaction in order to be successful. This view has led to new interesting research in which rather than the efficiency of interaction the quality of interaction is investigated. Can we make an interface affective or persuasive, can we make the interaction intuitive and rewarding, and can we define and measure interaction experience and involvement? Two concepts that seem to be particularly interesting from the point of view of whole body interaction and exertion interfaces are 'flow' and 'immersion'. The concept of flow was introduced by Mihaly Csikszentmihalyi [12] to describe a mental state of 'optimal experience', a state induced by focused and successful activity. These concepts have been studied in the context of work, sports, education, art and music, and games.

In game design measuring experiences and mental states in order to improve the design of an interaction or to real-time adapt the interface and the application to the user has become a flourishing research area. Questionnaires have been developed to measure the emotional experiences of users. Rather than having self-reports that can help in improving the design it would be useful to have ways and sensors to automatically measure these experiences. And, preferably, be able to do so in an unobtrusive way. These topics will be discussed in this chapter.

About This Chapter

The main aim of this chapter is to provide a review of the issues that need to be considered for entertainment and exertion interface design. We want to embed this interface design in the frameworks that have been suggested for game design, where, as mentioned, we look in particular at flow and engagement issues.

The organization of this chapter is as follows. In section "Exertion and entertainment interfaces" we discuss some existing exertion interfaces. A short state-of-the-art survey is presented, where we look at entertainment and exertion interfaces that allow direct and mediated interaction. Section "Intelligent exertion interfaces" of this chapter is on 'intelligence' in exertion interfaces. That is, how does the interface perceive and interpret the exertion activities of the user? Obviously, in general this requires interpretation of multi-modal input signals; in particular we look at audio-visual signals and the interpretation of these signals in order to provide the user with relevant (and stimulating) feedback. We discuss flow and immersion in general and in particular in interfaces that aim at whole-body interaction. In section "Joint and coordinated activities in exertion interaction" we discuss interactional synchrony and its role in measuring the quality of whole body interaction. It is argued that this interactional synchrony has a role in measuring and maintaining flow and immersion in whole body interaction. This chapter ends with section "Conclusions" in which we have some notes on future research and conclusions.

Exertion and Entertainment Interfaces

Interfaces that require body movement as input also require some physical effort from the user. In particular exertion interfaces are designed in order to elicit exertion. Exertion can be fun, social and rewarding. As an example, marathons are organized all over the world. In 2009 more than 40,000 people finished the New York City marathon. Similar events take place in almost any capital of the world. 'Fun', 'social', 'rewarding' are keywords for designing exertion interfaces. Improvement of well-being, health conditions, and useful or entertaining physical skills are other effects of exertion interfaces.

The notion of exertion interfaces was introduced by Florian (Floyd) Müller in his 'sports over a distance' research [30]. he introduced many examples of 'exergames' where people had to play a physical game such as football, tennis or hockey against a remote player and both players' actions are detected and displayed on some kind of shared video wall. But clearly, exertion interfaces do not necessarily require a remote player whose actions are mediated and visualized by the exertion interface. The interface can challenge the user to jump, to move his arms, his legs and use all kinds of body movements to earn points or have another satisfying experience. Rather than having a human opponent it is also possible to design an exergame that requires one or more human opponents, but where the human opponents are played by virtual humans or characters that have the required skills to play these roles.

Looking back, accepting these points of view, we can say that already in the early 1980s we can recognize examples of exergaming, e.g., the Atari Puffer exercise bike or games with foot operated pads, that resemble the now popular Nintendo balance board. Pressure sensors and accelerometers have been used to detect activities and embed them in playful interactions with visual challenges and feedback on a computer screen.

We distinguish three ways of looking at exertion interfaces:

1. adding game elements to computer mediated physical exercises for health, well-being, and rehabilitation,
2. adding exertion elements to existing games or variants of existing games, and, nowadays more obvious,
3. have an integrated approach where game and exertion experience are designed in an interface that has sensors and sensor intelligence to detect and interpret the activities of the exergamer in a game aware, context aware and person aware way.

It is important that in these cases exertion activities and game elements are coupled. Game elements seduce and motivate users to engage in physical activity [54]. In the past only the first two viewpoints became visible in exergaming research. Currently, as will be discussed in more detail in section "Intelligent exertion interfaces" of this chapter, because of the availability of all kinds of sensor hardware and software the third viewpoint has entered the domain of game, entertainment, and exergaming interface research.

However, starting with the past and the first mentioned viewpoint, an obvious way to obtain an exertion interface is to connect existing exercise devices (treadmills, rowing machines, exercise bikes) to an activity in a 3D virtual environment or in a game environment. The exercise device can be used to control a game, or to navigate in an interesting virtual environment (e.g., a beautiful landscape, or a Second Life city-like environment). In the virtual environment we can introduce challenges, competition and social interaction with other users. A well-known early example is the Virku (Virtual Fitness Centre) research project [28], where a traditional exercise bike is used to explore interesting surroundings and where environmental sounds are added to these surroundings to increase the presence of the user. And, not too difficult to realize, when a user cycles uphill it will take more effort and when going downhill less effort. In a similar project [17] but more recent project it was investigated whether an increase in presence (by making the environment more realistic) led to an increase in motivation. It turned out that the users not only reported more interest and enjoyment, but they also pedaled faster, without realizing they put more effort in.

Looking at the second mentioned viewpoint, we can mention that existing popular video games are sometimes exported to the physical world. Probably the first computer game that was exported from a 3D virtual world to the physical world was the classic arcade Pacman game. Researchers of the Mixed Reality Lab in Singapore introduced this game at the campus of their university. Students were equipped with wearable computers, head sets and sensing mechanisms and then could play the role of one of the Ghosts or Pacman while running around on the campus [9].

A more recent floor-sensor controlled game, where an existing game is provided with an exertion interface is a 'space invaders' game, again developed by the Mixed Reality Lab in Singapore [22]. In this game the elderly and children play together and have to follow patterns that light up on the game floor, but they are also able to trigger bombs and rockets that force other players to jump out of the way and use other sub panels on the floor. The game has been designed in such a way that the elderly have more time to evade bombs and rockets than the children.

There are more examples where popular video games are translated into games that have to be played in real-life situations and where rather than PC game engines games are controlled by 'performance' engines that control, using scripts, the physical environment and activities that can take place in these environments.

In contrast to the idea of connecting exercise devices to a game or entertainment environment, or introducing game elements into an environment for performing physical exercises, we can also look at interfaces where ideas about exertion, games, and entertainment, and the use of (intelligent) sensors are there from the beginning of the design. One early example, the Nautilus game [47], can illustrate this. In this game a group of players have to work together and control the game (displayed on a big screen, sound effects and light effects) with the group's center of mass, speed and direction of movements that are detected by floor sensors.

One of the best known exertion interfaces is 'sports over a distance', where players from different sites have to hit a wall with a ball [30]. The position on the wall and the force with which the ball hits the wall are mediated and made visible for opponents. A player can earn points by 'breaking' tiles on the wall and can profit from weak but not yet broken tiles that are left by his or her opponent. 'Sports over a distance' can be called a networked exertion interface. The same authors have introduced other networked exertion interfaces. For example, air hockey, table tennis, and, more recently, 'shadow boxing over a distance' [29]. In the latter application computer vision is used to extract the players' silhouettes that are displayed on a screen. Players can hit their opponents in the game, that is, they can hit the silhouettes of their opponents. Pressure sensors behind the textile 'screen' measure the position and the impact of the hits and keep track of the score.

In these latter applications entertainment, including entertaining social interaction, has been the main reason to build these interfaces. Improving a particular skill in sports (e.g. baseball [23] or Tai Chi [49]) or improving fitness (aerobics [13] or physiotherapy [1]) have also been main reasons to introduce exertion interfaces. With the growing interest in exertion interfaces designing for social and physical play has become a flourishing research area [2, 7, 11, 24, 32, 45]. Obviously, as will be discussed in the next sections, we need to know how users experience the systems we design and implement. We will return to this (and some of these papers) in section "Intelligent exertion interfaces".

Finally, we need to mention the commercially available exertion interfaces. From the success of Dance Dance Revolution, Sony's EyeToy [46] applications and the Wii Sports (tennis, golf, baseball, boxing and bowling), that allow the player to control the game through natural movements, we now may expect to see more advanced exertion interfaces in the future that do not require a controller like the Wii remote control. These advanced systems will use more sensors that allow, among other things, audio-visual processing and interpretation of the user's activities and affective state. Recently Microsoft also launched an Xbox 360 add-on Kinect (earlier called project NATAL) [16] that uses a sensor device to track whole body gestures, facial recognition and to record spoken comments. Clearly, these commercially available systems still lack many capabilities that are required when we want systems to understand, to anticipate and to provide (adaptive) feedback to gaming or exercising activities of the user.

Intelligent Exertion Interfaces

Intelligent exertion interfaces detect a user's activity and the (possibly continuously) changing environment in which the user operates. That allows them to provide real-time feedback that displays understanding of what the user is doing and experiencing. This makes the difference between many of the current exertion interfaces and the advanced and intelligent interfaces that we see appear in research prototypes of exertion interfaces. In addition, dependent on the application, in intelligent exertion interfaces user feedback should be persuasive, motivating, and rewarding.

Game design requires designing game experience. We need to be aware which issues play a role in experience, how we can adapt them to a particular user during the game, and, in particular for our kind of research, what role does the physical activity have in the game experience.

The relationship between body movement and engagement experience in computer games is studied in [3], where experimental results showed that an increase in body movements resulted in an increase in the player's engagement level. Here it is suggested to use the experience of the player itself as an input to the game. One point in particular is what the user can tell us or the interface about his or her experiences. In this study the gamer's engagement level was assessed with a questionnaire. According to Mueller and Bianchi-Berthouze [31] questionnaires and interviews that are conducted after the gaming action should take into account that the exertion activity demanded physical effort of the participants. This will affect the evaluation task, since players might be out of breath and they are probably in an altered emotional state. Moreover questionnaires and interviews for evaluating user experience are inadequate in capturing a user state during the game. Videotaping playing sessions and coding verbal and non-verbal behaviors that can be analyzed statistically can give valuable information about the player's experience to game designers. But for the automatic adaptation of the game or exertion environment during interaction, to improve the experience, we need automatic detection of the user's experience.

More Advanced Sensing of User and Activities

As mentioned above, in order to design and implement successful exertion interfaces that know about the experience of the users, we need exertion environments that can detect, measure, and interpret physical activity. In the ball and shadow-boxing games of 'sports over a distance' [29, 30], for example, there is no direct sensing of body movements or physiological information. 'Only' the result of the exertion (force, location) is measured and mediated. In contrast – without necessarily leading to a 'better' interface – there is also an interactive boxing interface, where the 'punch' is recognized using gesture recognition with computer vision [15, 39]. In [42] we introduced a virtual dancer that interacts with a human dancer. Pressure sensors, computer vision and audio analysis are used to detect the gestures and movements of the human dancer and to have real-time analysis of the music that is played. The results of the detection are used to generate the animations of the virtual dancer. The virtual dancer can decide to follow the human dancer but she can also take the initiative, introduce new dance movements and do some unexpected things to surprise the human dancer.

Hence, there exist exertion interfaces with direct sensing of bodily activity (body movements, gestures, bodily and facial expressions, dynamic aspects of expression, etc.) and of speech activity that accompanies bodily activity (effort and pain utterances, laughs, prosodic aspects of speech utterances...). Among the sensors are cameras and microphones that allow visual and audio processing of a user's activity. They can provide information about posture and position changes (tracking bodies and faces of individuals) and, among other things, frequency and expressiveness of movements. Other sensors in exertion interfaces can detect touch, pressure or proximity.

Sensing user's activity in ambient entertainment environments is discussed in [36]. Rather than using questionnaires we discuss how in the near future information obtained with computer vision and other sensors can help a movement-based interface to consider experience related issues such as personality, mood, and also pain, fatigue, frustration, irritation, etc.

One step further is to take into account physiological information obtained from the user. This information can be used both to guide the interaction and to measure the user experience [40, 41]. A continuous evaluation method to model the user's emotional state from physiological data is presented in [26]. It is also suggested to use this modeled emotion to dynamically adapt the play environment to keep users engaged. In the FUGA research project [19], among other things, the goal was to find game experience measures that are based on psychophysiological recordings and brain imaging techniques. In [53] the authors explore the relation between behavioral measures (movement of the upper body measured by an accelerometer, changes in sitting position measured by a pressure sensitive chair, force with which players made each mouse click) and people's self-reported emotional experience, measured by questionnaires: the Self Assessment Manikin (SAM) [4] and an in game version of the Game Experience Questionnaire [20]

Clearly, BCI (Brain-Computer Interfacing) may be an extra source from which an interface can learn about the way the user experiences the interaction (besides using it to control the game as we can expect in the future [38]). In [34] Nacke et al. use psychophysiological measurements (electroencephalography-EEG) in studies of affective player-game interaction to understand emotional and cognitive player experiences. In [35] they present the results of a study that assessed game-play experience with subjective and objective measures. Their research shows that EEG measurements can be used for studying affective responses to player-game interaction.

Flow and Immersion in Games

In the previous section we looked at game experience and sensors and questionnaires to measure game experience. When modeling game experience the two issues that often arise are 'flow' and 'immersion'. We will discuss these two issues in the next sections.

The theory of flow was introduced by Csikszentmihalyi [12]:

> a sense that one's skills are adequate to cope with the challenges at hand, in a goal-directed, rule-bound action system that provides clear rules as to how well one is performing. Concentration is so intense that there is no attention left over to think about anything irrelevant, or to worry about problems. Self-consciousness disappears, and the sense of timing becomes distorted. An activity that produces such experiences is so gratifying that people are willing to do it for its own sake, with little concern for what they will get out of it...

Eight (sometimes nine or ten) elements or features of this definition have been distinguished and generally it is assumed that these elements should be present in a game. They are: challenging activity that can be completed, facilitation of concentration, clear goals, immediate feedback, deep and effortless involvement, sense of control over one's actions, disappearing concern for the self, and finally, altered sense of duration of time. All these features can be found as prescriptions in present-day game design literature [48], sometimes using more refined features (agency, rewards, narrative…) and they play a role in game experience evaluation. Until now, they have hardly been explicitly considered in the design of movement-based interfaces for exertion and entertainment. A similar observation can be made for the concept of 'immersion'. Immersion ([33], p. 98) has been described as:

> The experience of being transported to an elaborately simulated place is pleasurable in itself, regardless of the fantasy content. We refer to this experience as immersion. Immersion is a metaphorical term derived from the physical experience of being submerged in water. We seek the same feeling from a psychologically immersive experience that we do from a plunge in the ocean or swimming pool: the sensation of being surrounded by a completely other reality, as different as water is from air that takes over all of our attention our whole perceptual apparatus…

Despite the rather vague nature of the conception there are several approaches to model immersion in a gaming context. Brown and Cairns [5] interview gamers regarding their experiences during gameplay and find three levels of immersion, labeled engagement, engrossment, and total immersion. For each level there exist barriers that have to be overcome to reach the level. Figure 9.1 clarifies the relation between levels and barriers.

To reach engagement, the first level of immersion, access must be provided. This refers to the gamers' preferences and game controls. The gamer must also be willing to invest time, effort, and attention. Bad game construction is the barrier to engrossment, which in Brown and Cairns' terms refers to visuals, tasks, and plot.

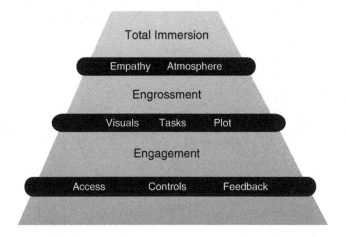

Fig. 9.1 Three levels of immersion from Brown and Cairns [5]; own depiction

Brown and Cairns point out that at this stage the gamers have already invested emotionally into the game and this makes them continue gaming. Total immersion is the final level and it is described as being cut off from the world to an extent where the game is all that matters. Barriers to total immersion are a lack of empathy with game characters or a lack of feeling the atmosphere of the game. In a follow-up study, Cheng and Cairns [8] investigate the stability of immersion. Here, they attempt to deliberately break the immersion of subjects and find that already low levels of immersion make subjects ignore drastic changes in the games' behavior.

A totally different approach to immersion is reported by Ermi and Mäyrä [14]. Looking into different qualities of immersion they interview gaming children and their non-gaming parents. This way they identify three different types of immersion: sensory, challenge-based, and imaginative (SCI), from which they built their SCI-model, which is shown in Fig. 9.2.

Sensory immersion refers to sensory information during gaming. Large screens and powerful sound are given as examples where sensory information of the real world is overpowered and the gamer entirely focuses on the game. Challenge-based immersion is described as most powerful when a balance between the abilities of the player and the challenge of the game is achieved and as such seems to correspond to the flow concept mentioned earlier. Finally, imaginative immersion happens when the player gets absorbed with the story line and identifies with the game characters.

Presence is another term that appears in the literature to describe the gaming experience. The term originates from studies into virtual reality and is often defined as "the feeling of being there" [18]. Cairns and colleagues [6] argue that presence

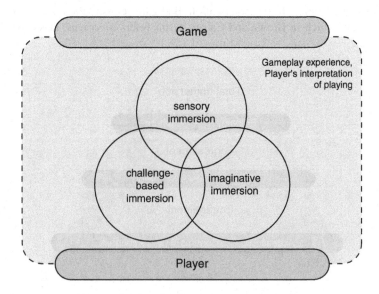

Fig. 9.2 Three types of immersion from Ermi and Mäyrä [14]; simplified

in virtual reality context corresponds to immersion in a gaming context. Similarly, Ermi and Mäyrä prefer the term immersion as "it more clearly connotes the mental processes involved in gameplay" ([14], p. 19). Most scholars seem to agree with this view and see immersion as the appropriate term when speaking of user experience in a gaming context.

Csikszentmihalyi's views on flow as well as the two models based on immersion allow an assessment of the user experience during gameplay. What lacks in these models is an understanding of how body movements or physical activity during gameplay influences the gaming experience. To get a better understanding of the magnitude of the influence that physical activity can have, the following section looks at the experience of physical activity during sports and games.

Flow and Immersion in Exertion Interfaces

The Experience of Physical Activity. What motivates people to engage in physical activity? This section gives an overview of theories of enjoyment of physical activity. But it appears reasonable to first disentangle different types of activity, i.e. play, game, sport, and exercise, before focusing on motivation and enjoyment and clarify their relationship. Figure 9.3 illustrates that relationship.

Play can be defined as "behaviour for the purpose of fun and enjoyment with no utilitarian or abstract goal in mind" (Shaw et al. [44], p. 2). Shaw and colleagues list four reasons why people play: First, play serves relaxation and recuperative purposes. Second, play can be used to reduce surplus energy. Third, play is an opportunity to practice and rehearse skills. Finally, play can be important to reduce anxiety by confronting one's fears in a safe environment.

Play becomes game when competition is involved in the activity. Hence, they define game as "any form of playful competition whose outcome is determined by

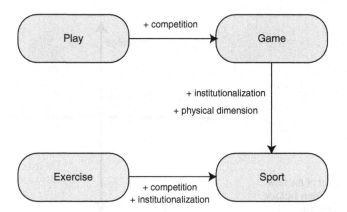

Fig. 9.3 Types of physical activities

physical skill, strategy or chance" and give the following example to illustrate the difference: If one is playing ping pong for fun without keeping score it is play. Once score is kept it is game.

Sport is then defined as "institutionalized competitive play involving physical skill, strategy and chance". The two criteria that distinguish sport from game are institutionalization and physical dimension. Four forms of institutionalization are given: First, sport involves a high degree of organization, in terms of governing bodies, leagues, and sponsors. Another form is technological development, which refers to equipment, clothing, and facilities. Ceremonies and rituals add a symbolic dimension to sport. Finally, sport includes educational aspects that are represented by coaches or written manuals. Apart from institutionalization, a physical dimension is required for sport. This does not necessarily require fitness. For instance, dart can still be seen as sport, while bridge hardly qualifies as sport and suits better into the definition of game. Exercise finally is defined as "any form of physical activity carried out for the purpose of health or fitness" [44].

It should be noted that some activities do not fall into one of the categories and can be rather seen as hybrids in this framework. Still, the framework is helpful to get a clearer view on different types of activities and their specific characteristics.

Jackson and Csikszentmihalyi [21] apply Csikszentmihalyi's theory of flow to the sport domain. They relate the components of flow to aspects an athlete should consider in sport. With the limitation of being intended for a broad audience as a guide to better sport experiences, it still gives some valuable insights into the study of sport experiences.

Figure 9.4 shows how flow can only happen when the challenge at hand is matched by a person's skills. When the challenge is too low boredom occurs, if the skills are insufficient a person might experience anxiety. Both low challenge and low skills result in a state of apathy. Only when both the challenge is demanding and

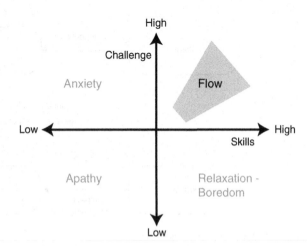

Fig. 9.4 Model of the flow state (Adapted from Jackson and Csikszentmihalyi [21], p. 37)

the skills are high enough to measure to the task the state of flow can be reached. In this context it should be noted that not an objective measurable challenge is decisive for the experience, but rather how a person subjectively estimates the challenge. The same holds for skills: A person might objectively have sufficient skills for a task, but if for some reason the person has only little confidence in his abilities then anxiety or apathy are bound to set in.

State of the Art of Physical Activity in Games. While we have no models of the gaming experience including body movements at present, there are several initial investigations into the area, which are presented in the following.

The only attempt for a model of body movements in video games so far is described by Sinclair and colleagues [45]. They focus on physically intense games, such as exergames, that promote the improvement of fitness levels along with extensive use. Their Dual Flow model is based on Csikszentmihalyi's flow theory (Fig. 9.5). It encompasses the two dimensions attractiveness and effectiveness.

Attractiveness here is modeled by the standard model of Csikszentmihalyi's flow theory. This model calls for a balance between a gamer's perceived skills and the perceived challenge he is facing. Thus, it can be seen as the mental side of the dual flow model. Effectiveness is modeled as the physical side, calling for a balance between fitness, which is defined as the body's skill in tolerating exercise and intensity, which is defined as the challenge of the exercise of the body.

The left side of Fig. 9.5 corresponds to the standard flow model and its four quadrants that are presented in Fig. 9.4. To achieve a state of flow, which Sinclair and colleagues translate into the attractiveness of movement-based video game, a balance between the perceived skills of a gamer and the perceived challenge must be established. Four quadrants are also used to illustrate the physical side of their dual flow model. Here, a state of flow sets in if the fitness of the gamer matches the intensity of the exercise that is experienced in the game. This leads to an improvement

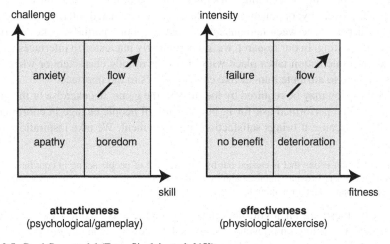

Fig. 9.5 Dual flow model (From Sinclair et al. [45])

in the gamer's fitness. Whereas when the intensity surpasses the fitness level of the gamer, failure occurs and the gamer cannot continue. Deterioration sets in when the fitness level of the gamer greatly outmatches the intensity, where the fitness levels will drop. If both fitness level and intensity are low, there is simply no benefit to the use of the game.

In non movement-based games there only has to be match between skills and challenge. Sinclair and colleagues point out that in commercial development projects this is achieved through extensive testing, which leads to fixed levels of challenge. They claim that in movement-based games this fixed matching is less effective:

> Tuning each successive level of an exergame to achieve a balance of player skill, level of general fitness, and current physical tiredness becomes problematic.

While it is relatively safe to assume that in traditional games the gamer's skills increase parallel to playing time and difficulty level, this is more complicated for movement-based games. Here, the daily form of the gamers can vary significantly. As a solution they envision games that monitor the gamer's current skill level and modify the difficulty level accordingly:

> Rather than just the simple feedback of clearly indicating success or failure to the player, feedback from the player relating to fatigue, exercise level, and boredom should be used to infer the player's current physical state and adjust the level of challenge accordingly. ([45], p. 294)

Joint and Coordinated Activities in Exertion Interaction

Exertion interfaces emphasize the conscious use of bodily activity (jogging, dancing, playing music, sports, physical exercises, fitness, etc.) in coordination and sometimes in competition with other human users (friends, community or team members, accidental passers-by, opponents, etc.). Real-time coordinated interaction between human partners or between humans and virtual or robotic partners makes exertion interfaces exciting. In our research we are particularly interested in interfaces where the exertion interaction takes place with virtual or robotic characters or where the users are able to attribute human-like characteristics to the interface.

Coordination may be required by the rules of the game, the exercise or the tasks that have to be performed ask for it, but most of all people engage in coordinated interaction because it brings satisfaction and enjoyment. We take inspiration from Clark [10]:

> A joint action is one that is carried out by an ensemble of people acting in coordination with each other. As some simple examples, think of two people waltzing, paddling a canoe, playing a piano duet, or making love.

Clearly, these are all joyful and engaging interactions. While Clark uses this observation to explore and develop theories of coordinated language use, we think it can be a useful observation when designing and evaluating exertion interfaces.

For users of exertion interfaces the interaction supporting feedback and the interaction experience are important.

We have studied face to face conversations, multi-party interaction, interactions between a virtual and a human dancer [42], a virtual conductor and a human orchestra [51], and a physiotherapist and her student [43] from the point of view of coordinated interaction [37]. Underlying the joint activities are rules and scripts. To learn these and to put them into practice requires social intelligence, guided by empathy, moods and emotions. Despite many research results from social and behavioral sciences, computational models of joint activities are hardly available. This makes it difficult to design interfaces that aim at providing a similar interactional experience between real humans and virtual humans or robots, as is provided in a real-life human-human exertion activity, as in dancing, paddling, playing quatremains, and making love. Endowing the computer with a human-like appearance strengthens the expectation that the computer will take part in joint activities in human-like ways. Hence, there is a need for computational modeling of human joint activities. We replace one of the human partners in a joint exertion activity by a computer (i.e., a robot or a virtual human). Hence, we need to model joint exertion interaction in order to have the computer behave in a natural and engaging way.

In addition to rules that underlie joint activity there can be a need to align the interaction to external events over which the interaction partners do not necessarily have control. E.g., if we have a human and a virtual dancer then their moves have to be aligned with the music. Similarly, a virtual conductor and his human orchestra follow the score; a virtual aerobics trainer and human student have to align their movements to some kind of rhythm, often supported by upbeat music.

In our present research we investigate ways to measure engagement by looking at the degree of coordination between the activities of a human and a virtual partner in exertion and other entertainment interfaces [37]. In this research, supported by [27, 50, 52], we investigate how to make entertainment interactions more engaging by looking at interaction synchrony. In these and other papers the relation is investigated between synchrony and the quality of the interaction, as it is perceived by the interaction partners. The idea is that on the one hand we aim at disturbing this synchrony in order to introduce new challenges, and on the other hand we aim at convergence towards coordinated anticipatory interaction between humans and artificial partners and their environment. Evidence that this approach will be successful is not yet available. Moreover, there are so many different types of exertion and movement-based entertainment interfaces that a comprehensive hypothesis about the role of interaction synchrony can not be expected to be given.

Design of experience and flow now receives much attention. Most research however is still about ways to characterize complex concepts such as experience, immersion, engagement, and flow. Exceptions are becoming available. For example, when we see the mentioning of 'altered sense of duration of time' in the description of flow, then indeed we can interview gamers about the time they think they have spent during a game and compare their perceived time spent with the actual time that has been measured. Interesting hypotheses related to our point of view on the role of interaction synchrony can be found in [6]. There the authors hypothesize that when players are immersed in a game their eye and body movements are different from those in a non-immersed situation. Obviously, again, there are many types of games and for video games where the gamer controls a game using mouse and keyboard or a joystick we have a quite different situation when the gamer is using a Wii remote control or a Wii Fit or no remote control at all, like in Kinect. The development of controllers designed to allow or impose natural body movements changes the nature of gaming into a more social activity [25] and leads to increased engagement that is moreover qualitatively different from the engagement experienced in games controlled by mouse, keyboard or joystick [3].

In our 'implicit' hypothesis on interactional synchrony we explicitly link this difference to the synchronization that is or is not present between gamer and game events. Notice that the main characteristic of 'flow' is the balance between challenges and skills. We can look at this as being able, as a gamer, to maintain a perfect coordination between eye, finger, and body movements on the one hand, and game/ exercise events on the other hand.

Conclusions

We surveyed characteristics of movement-based and exertion interfaces, i.e. interfaces that require and stimulate bodily activity. We discussed recent and future research in this area by zooming in on sensor technology, intelligence and well-known game design and game experience principles. We argued that for future development of interesting exertion (sports and entertainment) interfaces it is useful to embed this research in game design and game experience research. In particular we looked at sensor technology that can not only be used to design interesting exergames, but that can also be used to measure the experience of users. We surveyed the literature on flow and immersion and looked at the modest attempts to model these concepts in movement-based interfaces. In addition we looked at a possible role for coordinated interaction research in the design and the evaluation of exertion interfaces.

Acknowledgments This research has been supported by the Dutch National GATE project, funded by the Netherlands Organization for Scientific Research (NWO) and the Netherlands ICT Research and Innovation Authority (ICT Regie).

References

1. Babu, S., Zanbaka, C., Jackson, J., Chung, T.-O., Lok, B., Shin, M.C., Hodges, L.F.: Virtual human physiotherapist framework for personalized training and rehabilitation. In: Graphics Interface 2005, Victoria (2005)
2. Benford, S., Schnadelbach, H., Koleva, B., Gaver, B., Schmidt, A., Boucher, A., Steed, A., Anastasi, R., Greenhalgh, C., Rodden, T., Gellersen, H.: Sensible, sensible and desirable: a framework for designing physical interfaces. Technical Report Equator-03-003 (2003)

3. Bianchi-Berthouze, N., Kim, W.W., Patel, D.: Does body movement engage you more in digital game play? And why? In: Proceedings of Affective Computing and Intelligent Interaction 2007. Lecture Notes in Computer Science, vol. 4738, pp. 102–113. Springer, Heidelberg (2007)
4. Bradley, M.M., Lang, P.J.: Measuring emotion: the self-assessment manikin and the semantic differential. J. Behav. Ther. Exp. Psychiatry 25(1), 49–59 (1994)
5. Brown, E., Cairns, P.: A grounded investigation of game immersion. In: Proceedings CHI 2004, pp. 1297–1300. Vienna (2004)
6. Cairns, P., Cox, A., Berthouze, N., Dhoparee, S., Jennett, C.: Quantifying the experience of immersion in games. In: Cognitive Science of Games and Gameplay, Workshop at Cognitive Science, Vancouver (2006)
7. Campbell, T., Fogarty, J.: Applying game design to everyday fitness applications. In: ACM CHI 2007 Workshop on Exertion Interfaces, San Jose (2007)
8. Cheng, K., Cairns, P. A.: Behaviour, realism and immersion in games. In: Proceedings CHI 2005, pp. 1272–1275. Portland (2005)
9. Cheok, A.D., Goh, K.H., Liu, W., Farbiz, F., Fong, S.W., Teo, S.L., Li, Y., Yang, X.: Human Pacman: a mobile, wide-area entertainment system based on physical, social, and ubiquitous computing. Personal Ubiquit. Comput. 8, 71–81 (2004)
10. Clark, H.: Using Language. Cambridge University Press, Cambridge (1996)
11. Consolvo, S., Everitt, K., Smith, I., Landay, J.A.: Design requirements for technologies that encourage physical activity. In: ACM Conference on Human Factors in Computing Systems (CHI 2006), pp. 457–466. Vancouver (2006)
12. Csikszentmihalyi, M.: Flow: the psychology of optimal experience. Harper & Row, New York (1990)
13. Davis, J.W., Bobick, A.F.: Virtual PAT: A Virtual Personal Aerobics Trainer. Technical Report: 436. MIT Media Laboratory (1998)
14. Ermi, L., Mäyrä, F.: Fundamental components of the gameplay experience: analysing immersion. In: de Castell, S., de Jenson, J. (eds.) Changing views: worlds in play, Selected Papers DiGRA Conference, pp. 15–27. Vancouver (2005)
15. Höysniemi, J., Aula, A., Auvinen, P., Hännikäinen, J., Hämäläinen, P.: Shadow boxer: a physically interactive fitness game. In: Third Nordic Conference on Human-Computer inter-action (NordiCHI 2004), vol. 82, pp. 389–392. ACM, New York (2004)
16. Microsoft Kinect, http://www.xbox.com/en-US/kinect. Accessed Oct 2010
17. IJsselsteijn, W., Kort, Y., de Westerink, J., Jager, M., de Bonants, R.: Fun and sports: Enhancing the home fitness experience. In: Rauterberg M. (ed.) ICEC 2004. Lecture Notes in Artificial Intelligence, vol. 3166, pp. 46–56. Springer, Heidelberg (2004)
18. IJsselsteijn, W., Riva, G.: Being there: the experience of presence in mediated environments. In: Riva, G., Davide, F., IJsselsteijn, W. (eds.) Being There: Concepts, Effects and Measurements of User Presence in Synthetic Environments, pp. 3–16. IOS Press, Amsterdam (2003)
19. IJsselsteijn, W.A., van den Hoogen, W.M., Klimmt, C., de Kort, Y.A.W., Lindley, C., Mathiak, K., Poels, K., Ravaja, N., Turpeinen, M., Vorderer, P.: Measuring the experience of digital game enjoyment. In: Spink, E.J., Ballintijn, M.R., Bogers, N.D., Grieco, F., Loijens, L.W.S., Noldus, L.P.J.J., Smit, G., Zimmerman, P.H. (eds.), Proceedings of Measuring Behavior 2008, pp. 88–89. Maastricht (2008)
20. de Kort, Y.A.W., IJsselsteijn, W.A., Poels, K.: Digital games as social presence technology: development of the social presence in gaming questionnaire, PRESENCE 2007 Proceedings (Barcelona, Spain, 25–27 Oct 2007), pp. 195–203
21. Jackson, S.A., Csikszentmihalyi, M.: Flow in Sports: The Keys to Optimal Experiences and Performances. Human Kinetics, Leeds (1999)
22. Khoo, E.T., Cheok, A.D.: Age invaders: inter-generational mixed reality family game. Int. J. Virtual. Real. 5(2), 45–50 (2006)
23. Komura, T., Kuroda, A., Shinagawa, Y.: NiceMeetVR: facing professional baseball pitchers in the virtual batting cage. In: ACM Symposium on Applied Computing, pp. 1060–1065. Madrid (2002)

24. Larssen, A.T., Robertson, T., Loke, L., Edwards, J.: Special issue on movement-based interaction. Personal Ubiquit. Comput. **11**(8), 607–701 (2004)
25. Lindley, S., Le Couteur, J., Bianchi-Berthouze, N.: Stirring up experience through movement in game play: effects on engagement and social behaviour. In: ACM Conference on Human Factors in Computing Systems (CHI 2008), pp. 511–514. Florence (2008)
26. Mandryk, R.L., Atkins, M.S., Inkpen, K.M.: A continuous and objective evaluation of emotional experience with interactive play environments. In: ACM Conference on Human Factors in Computing Systems (CHI 2006), pp. 1027–1036. Montreal (2006)
27. Michalowski, M.P., Sabanovic, S., Kozima, H.: A dancing robot for rhythmic social interaction. In: Human Robot Interaction 2007, pp. 89–96. Arlington (2007)
28. Mokka, S., Väätänen, A., Heinilä, J., Välkkynen, P.: Fitness computer game with a bodily user interface. In: 2nd International Conference on Entertainment Computing,, pp. 1–3. Pittsburgh (2003)
29. Mueller, F., Agamanolis, S., Gibbs, M.R., Vetere, F.: Remote impact: shadowboxing over a distance. In: CHI 2008 Extended Abstracts on Human Factors in Computing Systems. ACM, New York (2008)
30. Mueller, F., Agamanolis, S., Picard, R.: Exertion interfaces: sports over a distance for social bonding and fun. In: ACM Conference on Human Factors in Computing Systems (CHI 2003), pp. 561–568. Ft. Lauderdale (2003)
31. Müller, F., Bianchi-Berthouze, N.: Evaluating exertion interfaces. In: Bernhaupt, R. (ed.) Evaluating User Experience in Games: Concepts and Methods, pp. 187–207. Springer, London (2010)
32. Müller, F., Vetere, F., Gibbs, M.: Considerations for the design of networked exertion interactions. Int. J. Arts Technol. **3**(4), 374–389 (2010)
33. Murray, J.H.: Hamlet on the Holodeck: The Future of Narrative in Cyberspace. MIT Press, Cambridge (1999)
34. Nacke, L.E.: Wiimote vs. controller: electroencephalographic measurement of affective gameplay interaction. In: Proceedings of FuturePlay 2010, pp. 183–190. Vancouver (2010)
35. Nacke, L.E., Stellmach, S., Lindley, C.: Electroencephalographic assessment of player experience: a pilot study in affective ludology. J. Simulation & Gaming. Published online, August 10, (2010)
36. Nijholt, A.: Playing and Cheating in Ambient Entertainment. In: Ma, L., Rauterberg, M., Nakatsu, R. (eds.) ICEC 2007. Lecture Notes in Computer Science, vol. 4740, pp. 415–420. Springer, Heidelberg (2007)
37. Nijholt, A., Reidsma, D., Welbergen, H., van Akker, H.J.A., op den Ruttkay, Z.M.: Mutually coordinated anticipatory multimodal interaction. In: Esposito, A., et al. (eds.) Nonverbal Features of Human-Human and Human-Machine Interaction. Lecture Notes in Computer Science, vol. 5042, pp. 73–93. Springer, Heidelberg (2008)
38. Nijholt, A., Tan, D.: Playing with your Brain: Brain-Computer Interfaces and Games. In: Bernhaupt, R., Tscheligi, M. (eds.) Proceedings International Conference on Advances in Computer Entertainment Technology, pp. 305–306. ACM, New York (2007)
39. Park, J.Y., Yi, J.H.: Gesture recognition based interactive boxing game. Int. J. Inf. Technol. **12**(7), 36–44 (2006)
40. Picard, R.W., Daily, S.B.: Evaluating affective interactions: Alternatives to asking what users feel. Human factors in computing systems. In: Workshop on Innovative Approaches to Evaluating Affective Interfaces, Portland (2005)
41. Picard, R.W., Vyzas, E., Healey, J.: Toward machine emotional intelligence: Analysis of affective physiological state. IEEE Trans. Pattern Anal. Mach. Intell. **23**(10), 1175–1191 (2001)
42. Reidsma, D., Welbergen, H., van Poppe, R., Bos, P., Nijholt, A.: Towards bi-directional dancing interaction. In: Harper, R., Rauterberg, M., Combetto, M. (eds.) ICEC 2006. Lecture Notes in Computer Science, vol. 4161, pp. 1–12. Springer, Heidelberg (2006)
43. Ruttkay, Z.M., van Welbergen, H.: On the timing of gestures of a virtual Physiotherapist. In: Lanyi, C.S. (ed.) 3rd Central European MM & VR Conference, pp. 219–224. Pannonian University Press, Hungary (2006)

44. Shaw, D., Gorely, T., Corban, R.: Sport and Exercise Psychology. BIOS Scientific Publishers, London (2005)
45. Sinclair, J., Hingston, P., Masek, M.: Considerations for the design of exergames. In: 5th International Conference on Computer Graphics and Interactive Techniques in Australia and Southeast Asia, pp. 289–295. Perth (2007)
46. Sony Eyetoy, http://en.wikipedia.org/wiki/EyeToy. Accessed Oct 2010
47. Strömberg, H., Väätänen, A., Räty, V.: A group game played in interactive virtual space: design and evaluation. Designing Interactive Systems, pp. 56–63. New York (2002)
48. Sweetser, P., Wyeth, P.: Gameflow: a model for evaluating player enjoyment in games. Comput. Entertain. **3**(3), 1–24 (2005)
49. Tan Chua, P., Crivella, R., Daly, B., Hu, N., Schaaf, R., Ventura, D., Camill, T., Hodgins, J., Pausch, R.: Training for physical tasks in virtual environments: Tai Chi. Virtual Reality, pp. 87–94. IEEE, Los Alamitos (2003)
50. Tanaka, F., Suzuki, H.: Dance interaction with QRIO: a case study for non-boring interaction by using an entrainment ensemble model. In: IEEE International Workshop on Robot and Human Interactive Communication (RO-MAN 2004), pp. 419–424. Kurashiki (2004)
51. ter Maat, M., Ebbers, R., Reidsma, D., Nijholt, A.: Beyond the Beat: Modelling Intentions in a Virtual Conductor. In: INTETAIN '08: Proceedings of the 2nd International Conference on INtelligent TEchnologies for Interactive enterTAINment, ACM Digital Library, Cancun (2008)
52. Tomida, T., Ishihara, A., Ueki, A., Tomari, Y., Fukushima, K., Inakage, M.: In: MiXer: the communication entertainment content by using "entrainment phenomenon" and "biofeedback". Advances in Computer Entertainment Technology, pp. 286–287. New York (2007)
53. van den Hoogen, W.M., IJsselsteijn, W.A., de Kort, Y.A.W.: Exploring behavioral expressions of player experience in digital games. In: Nijholt, A., Poppe, R. (eds.), Proceedings of the Workshop on Facial and Bodily Expression for Control and Adaptation of Games, ECAG 2008, pp. 11–19. Amsterdam (2008)
54. Yim, J., Graham, T.C.N.: Using games to increase exercise motivation. In: Proceedings of the 2007 Conference on Future Play (Future Play '07), pp. 166–173. New York (2007)

Chapter 10
Capacitive Sensors for Whole Body Interaction

Raphael Wimmer

Abstract Capacitive proximity sensors can be used to implement a variety of expressive input devices. They are especially suitable for Whole Body Interaction as they are small, robust, flexible, and can be both worn on the body or embedded into the environment. This chapter discusses technical challenges that arise when using capacitive sensors for tracking human motion, namely sensor shielding and ensuring both low latency and high sensitivity. A custom sensor design and an adaptive moving average filter presented here address these challenges. Two user studies evaluated these sensors as input modalities for different computer games. They found evidence that capacitive sensors offer a friendly but challenging behavior, being easy to learn but hard to master.

Introduction

Using the whole expressivity of human body motion for interacting with intelligent environments or computer systems allows for novel applications and action-ladden exertion games. A first step when implementing such an interactive system, is choosing an appropriate hand and body tracking technology. Capacitive sensors offer a cheap, robust, and flexible way of prototyping and implementing sensor systems for Whole Body Interaction. However, their capabilities seem to be unknown to many researchers. This chapter presents principles, properties, and prototypes of capacitive sensing for Whole Body Interaction. It has the following structure: Section "Capacitive Sensing" explains the basic mode of operation of capacitive sensors. Section "RelatedWork" presents existing input devices using capacitive sensors. Section "A Simple Capacitive Sensor" describes a simple capacitive sensor design that can be used for prototyping capacitive-sensing applications. Section "Signal Processing" describes technical challenges for

R. Wimmer (✉)
University of Munich, Amalienstr. 17, 80333 Munich, Germany
e-mail: raphael.wimmer@ifi.lmu.de

D. England (ed.), *Whole Body Interaction*, Human-Computer Interaction Series,
DOI 10.1007/978-0-85729-433-3_10, © Springer-Verlag London Limited 2011

capacitive sensing that are especially relevant for human–computer interaction and describes how these can be approached. Section "Game Controllers Built from Capacitive Sensors" presents learnings from a user study that evaluated different sensor setups as input modalities for computer games. The Conclusion argues why the inherent properties of capacitive sensors make them very well suited for implementing Whole Body Interfaces for games.

Capacitive Sensing

The term capacitance describes how much electrical charge can be stored between two non-connected conductive objects. These form a capacitor. The capacitance depends primarily on the size of the objects, their distance, and the dielectric properties of objects and insulates between them. A small capacitance always exists between an object and its environment.

Capacitive Sensing is a term for a number of different sensing techniques that measure changes in capacitance between a sensor antenna and its surrounding. Smith et al. have characterized three different capacitive sensing techniques: loading mode, transmit mode, and shunt mode [12, 13]. Loading mode is widely used for touch sensors, while transmit mode and shunt mode are often used for capacitive touchscreens. The following sections focus on loading mode capacitive sensing as it is the simplest and most versatile mode. Several physical effects are neglected for clarity.[1] A more thorough description of capacitive sensing can be found in [5, 12, 19].

A loading mode capacitive sensor measures the capacitance between its antenna and the environment, for example by completely charging this capacitor and discharging it. From the time needed to completely discharge the capacitor, its capacitance can be calculated. In practice the charge/discharge-cycle is often implemented as a resonant circuit. The lower the capacitance at the antenna, the higher the frequency of the circuit. The capacitance greatly depends on the distance between antenna and environment. Thus, bringing part of the environment closer to the antenna increases the capacitance between both. This effect can be used to measure the distance between the antenna and an object near it. In particular, such a sensor can determine the proximity of a human body or hand (Fig. 10.1). Using several sensors one can track a hand or body in three dimensions [18]. However, each object near the antenna contributes to the capacitance that can be measured at the antenna. Therefore, it is impossible to determine how many objects are near the antenna, or how close they are. As capacitive sensors can be used to measure the distance between the antenna and a hand, they allow for easy gestural human–computer interaction.

---

[1] For example, in theory objects need a ground connection for the capacitor to work. However, such a ground connection is provided by *capacitive coupling* between the object and the environment. Therefore, in practice a conductive ground connection is not needed.

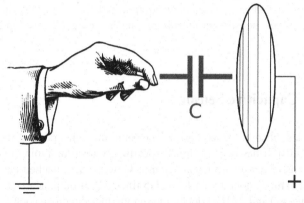

Clipart courtesy FCIT (http://etc.usf.edu/clipart)

Fig. 10.1 Basic principle of capacitive sensing. An antenna and a nearby conductive, grounded object form a capacitor. The capacitance of this capacitor is determined by antenna size, object size, distance between both, and material properties. By measuring the capacitance, movement near the antenna can be detected. This can be used for tracking hand or body movement

Related Work

A variety of sensors are available for tracking human motion. They can be either embedded into the environment or worn by the user. Teixeira et al. conducted a survey of available sensing techniques [16]. One of these are capacitive sensors, sometimes also called electric field sensors. This section provides a short overview of existing research using capacitive sensors for tracking human motion, focusing on novel ways of human–computer interaction.

Probably the first use of capacitive sensors for primitive Whole Body Interaction was in 1907. German physician Max Cremer put a living frog between two capacitor plates. By measuring capacitance changes he could observe the frog's heartbeat [1]. In 1919 Leonid Termen presented the Theremin, a musical instrument using two capacitive sensing antennas for controlling pitch and volume of a tone [2]. The Theremin is played by hand movement near each antenna. It is said to require a great deal of body control as the arms are not mechanically supported and minor trembling of a hand can cause great tone changes. With the Terpsitone, Termen used the same sensing principle for tracking body movement [6]. The sensing circuit is connected to a large metal plate lying on a platform. A dancer on top of the plate would permanently change the capacitance, allowing her to control the pitch of a synthesized tone. Colored lights would light up according to the notes played by the dancer.

Recently, capacitive sensors have been used in a variety of human–computer interfaces. Rekimoto determined hand poses by capturing the wrist shape using a wrist band containing capacitive sensors [9]. Taylor and Bove equipped a baseball with a capacitive sensor matrix which allows to determine how the ball is being held [15]. Valtonen et al. track users by equipping floor tiles with capacitive sensors [17]. By embedding sensors into furniture, one can unobtrusively capture everyday actions [20].

A Simple Capacitive Sensor

The sensor described here (see Fig. 10.2) is an improved version of the one used in CapToolKit [19]. It has been designed specifically for prototyping interactive systems. The sensor measures the capacitance between the attached antenna and the environment. This is done by an LMC555 timer IC. It outputs a signal with a frequency between 0 and 2 MHz, depending on the measured capacitance. The sensor is intended to be connected to a microcontroller that continuously measures the frequency and filters the resulting signal.

A common requirement for a capacitive sensor is that it should only sense objects in a certain directions. Generally, the antenna of a capacitive sensor is omnidirectional. Usually, this is not wanted for two reasons: Firstly, any objects moving near the antenna affect the sensor readings. For example, people passing near an installation using capacitive sensors might interfere with its intended operation. Secondly, antennas that are placed on other objects – like a wall-mounted or a body-worn sensor – get electrically tainted by these objects. This results in decreased sensor range and resolution. A capacitive sensor mounted on a user's chest would be saturated by the capacitance to the chest. Thus, a hand moving near the sensor would only minimally affect the overall capacitance.

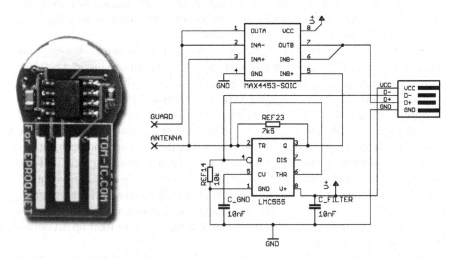

Fig. 10.2 Photo and schematic of a simple capacitive sensor. An LMC555 timer IC converts the capacitance between an antenna and the environment to a high-frequency digital signal. A MAX4453 dual-op amp (on the back of the circuit board) is used to shield the antenna from unwanted capacitive coupling

Therefore, capacitive sensor antennas should be shielded from the environment in one or more directions. However, a grounded electrode – as normally used for shielding electronics – would form a capacitor together with the antenna, even decreasing the sensor's range. Instead, the shield electrode needs to be actively kept at the same electrical potential as the antenna. This has to be done without galvanically connecting both, however. In order to distinguish them from passive shields, such active shields are called *guards* or *guard electrodes*. Commonly, antenna and guard are connected to a sensor chip or microcontroller by cables. This requires the antenna cable to be guarded, too. Our sensor gets directly soldered to both antenna and guard electrode, avoiding cables that would need to be guarded. As the sensor is very small (20 × 10 mm), the antenna/sensor-combination is still easily embeddable. The sensor's connector is compatible to USB-A plugs. This allows to use off-the-shelf USB extension cables for connecting the sensor to the sensing board. These are cheap, capable of transmitting high-frequency signals, and available in a multitude of lengths and types.

Placing sensor and antenna as close together as possible has another advantage: the conversion from (analog) capacitance to (digital) frequency happens as soon as possible. This leaves little room for electric fields and other noise sources to affect the sensor reading. The frequency-encoded signal can be transferred over long distances without degradation.

For coupling antenna electrode and guard electrode, a *voltage follower* circuit can be used [11]. Such a circuit ensures that the voltage at its output is always kept at the same level as its input. Unlike a direct connection, it does not propagate capacitance changes at the output to the input. The MAX4453 integrated circuit (IC) combines two rail-to-rail[2] operational amplifiers (op-amps) in one chip package. One op-amp drives the guard electrode while the other capacitively insulates the sensor's output line. This is necessary to protect the sensor readings from capacitance changes near the microcontroller board or the host PC.

Signal Processing

Capacitive sensors suffer from two sources of errors as illustrated in Fig. 10.3:

Random noise is inherent to all analog sensors. For touch sensing, this noise is usually several factors lower than the capacitance change caused by touching the sensors. For proximity sensing, however, the signal-to-noise ratio (SNR) of a sensor determines its range. With increasing distance between sensor and object, the signal amplitude decreases quadratically. As the noise level stays the same, the SNR quickly decreases. Once the signal level falls below the noise level, the object can no longer be detected. A simple *moving average* filter is very effective

---

[2] Rail-to-Rail means that the output voltage can reach the full range of the input voltage.

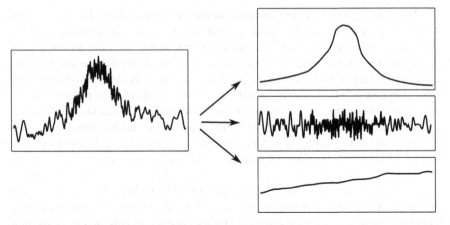

Fig. 10.3 Components of capacitive sensor readings: signal caused by a person passing the sensor (*top right*), random noise of the electrical circuit (*center right*), and drift due to changes in temperature or humidity (*bottom right*)

against such random noise [14]. It attenuates signal components with high frequency (usually noise) and leaves signal components with low frequency (slow movement near the sensor) intact. The filter adds the last n samples obtained from the sensor and divides the sum by n. The lower the SNR, the more samples need to be averaged in order to eliminate random noise. However, the moving average filter inevitably introduces latency, delaying and attenuating the effects of capacitance changes. The more sensitive a sensor needs to be, the more samples need to be averaged, and the greater the latency. However, for human–computer interaction, and especially for computer games, a latency of significantly less than 100 ms is desirable.

Sensor drift is especially problematic for capacitive sensors. These are very susceptible to changes in environmental humidity and temperature. Such gradually changing parameters can hide important events or generate fake events. For example, once started, a sensor might heat up minimally. Such minimal temperature changes lead to increasing sensor readings. These readings can be misinterpreted as a slow movement of an object towards the sensor. Usually the sensor drift is very slow so that it can be clearly distinguished from movement events. However, sometimes the measured capacitance quickly changes due to changes in the environment. For example, a conductive object might have been placed near the sensor. Also, the sensor antenna might have been deformed, resulting in a significantly different sensor reading. Usually, such changes should be filtered out.

CapToolKit [19] aggressively filters out noise while still offering low latency interaction. To this end, we utilize the speed-accuracy tradeoff inherent to human motion: the more precise a movement needs to be, the slower it has to be performed – and vice versa [8]. Therefore, the sensor needs to be *either* fast or sensitive, not both at a time. To this end, the microcontroller that transmits sensor readings to a computer applies an *adaptive moving average* (AMA) filter to the raw sensor data.

The AMA is a moving average filter that adjusts the number of samples used for averaging based on the current signal properties. Initially, the sensor uses a 16 sample buffer for averaging. This almost completely eliminates random noise. Very small movement – resulting in very small capacitance changes – can be reliably tracked in this way. However, this also introduces a latency of several hundred milliseconds. For slow movement this is no problem, for rapid movement such a latency is not acceptable. Therefore, the AMA continuously observes the unfiltered signal. If there is a change in the signal that is much larger than random noise, the filter assumes a large, fast movement nearby the sensor. The filter then immediately reduces the number of samples used for averaging. This decreases latency. The larger the sudden change in the signal, the less averaging will be applied to the signal. Once the signal changes less rapidly, the number of samples used for averaging is increased again.

When no movement is detected, the sensor is automatically recalibrated at regular intervals, compensating for temperature and humidity drift. In order to not mistakenly compensate small movements, the recalibration only takes place if the sensor reading has constantly and evenly risen or fallen for some time.

Game Controllers Built from Capacitive Sensors

We conducted a first user study in order to learn more about the suitability of capacitive sensors for controlling different types of computer games. In this study, 13 participants (6 female, mostly students, on average 25 years old) had to play three different games. The games' concepts and graphics were kept very simple in order to reduce confounding variables and provide a coherent feel across the three games.

The first game, MoveBall, required fine motor skills. Four capacitive sensor strips were placed at on a tabletop, forming a square. A computer screen showed a 2D, top-view arena with a randomly placed ball and a randomly placed hole. By approaching one of the sensors with the hand, the user could move the ball in one of the four directions. In each round it was counted how many times the user could move the ball into the hole within 1 min. The second game, HitBall, required gross motor skills. The user stood on a large sensor plate. Two antennas were placed at arms length to his/her left and right. A red circle appeared randomly at the top, left, or right edge of the screen. Depending on its position the user had to reach out towards the left or right antenna, or jump. In each round it was counted how many times the user "hit" the correct target. The third game, WalkBall (see Fig. 10.4), required simultaneous movements. The sensor layout was the same as with HitBall. The goal was the same as with MoveBall, moving a ball into a hole. The user could move the ball forward by walking in place. By leaning towards the left or right antenna, the user could change the ball's direction. In each round it was counted how many times the user could move the ball into the hole within 1 min.

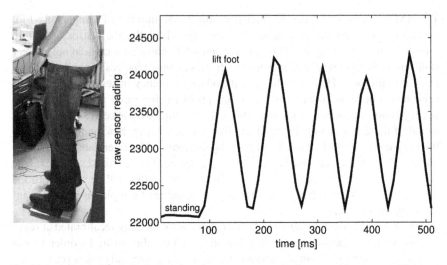

Fig. 10.4 A simple Whole Body Interface that was prototyped using capacitive sensors. The user controls a ball by walking on top of a metal plate that acts as the sensor antenna. The sensor readings allow to determine pace and amplitude of the stride

The order of the games was counterbalanced across the participants. The participants first played each game once using the cursor keys of a keyboard in order to familiarize themselves with the game's concept. Afterwards, they played three rounds of each game, answering a questionnaire between rounds.

There was no statistically significant learning effect regarding the scores for HitBall and WalkBall. However, we observed a learning effect ($p < 0.002$) for MoveBall which exercises fine motor skills. Obviously, simple, gross movements do not require much training – precise control does. Participants didn't generally feel more exerted using capacitive sensor controls for the three simple games than using the keyboard. Only for the HitBall game capacitive sensor controls required significantly higher exertion ($p < 0.05$). Keyboard control was significantly less challenging than capacitive sensor control for all of the simple games. This shows both in higher game scores ($p < 0.01$ for all games) and the answers to the questionnaire: Participants felt more challenged using the capacitive sensor controls (($p < 0.05$, except for WalkBall, where participants felt challenged using the keyboard, too). Despite (or because of) the greater challenge, participants preferred capacitive sensor controls over the keyboard for all three simple games ($p < 0.05$). Capacitive sensor controls were especially preferred for HitBall, which requires rapid physical action.

These findings suggested that capacitive sensors are easy to learn but precise control is challenging. This is in fact a wanted behavior for games.

Myers found "challenge" to be, "the most preferred characteristic of a favorite game" [7]. In his book "A Theory of Fun", game designer Raph Koster describes one key principle of games:

> When you're playing a game, you'll only play it until you master the pattern. Once you've mastered it the game becomes boring. [3]

Thus, a game should be complex and difficult enough to challenge the player. A game controller can support this behavior by being hard to master. On the other hand, it needs to be intuitive and easy to learn. In this context, "learning" can be seen as understanding the basic capabilities and the mapping of the controller, "mastering" as getting the controller to do what the player wants.

To investigate whether capacitive sensors were indeed "easy to learn but hard to master", we conducted a second study with 16 participants (7 female, mostly students, on average 24 years old). Participants had to play a jump'n'run video game, SuperTux. They controlled a small penguin using three capacitive sensors. Two antennas mounted in front of the user controlled left/right movement while an antenna plate on the ground detected when the user was jumping, making the penguing jump, too (see Fig. 10.5). Again, the users first played the game using a keyboard to familiarize themselves with the game. Afterwards, they played using the capacitive sensors. In both cases the users could play as long as they wanted. On average, the game was played for 1.75 min using the keyboard and for 3.94 min using the capacitive sensors. Afterwards, the participants answered a questionnaire.

On five point Likert scale all participants answered that the capacitive sensors reproduced their movements accurately or very accurately. Thirteen of the

Fig. 10.5 In a second study users played a jump'n'run video game using capacitive sensors. By approaching one of the two antennas mounted in front of the user, he/she could move a penguin left or right. When the user jumped, the penguin would jump accordingly

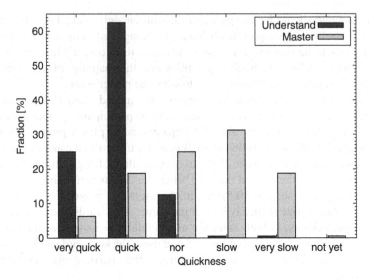

Fig. 10.6 Participants playing a jump'n'run game using capacitive sensors took significantly less time to understand the controls than to master them

Sixteen participants found the capacitive sensor controls to be challenging. Those participants who enjoyed the capacitive sensor controls more than the keyboard (12 of 16) also found them more challenging ($p < 0.01$). We asked participants how long it took them to understand the capacitive sensor controls and how long it took them to actually master them. Learning and mastering were defined as above. Most participants understood the controls quickly or very quickly but mastered it only slowly. Figure 10.6 shows the distributions. Obviously, participants took significantly less time to understand the controls than to master them ($p < 0.001$). Unfortunately, we asked slightly different questions about the keyboard control. Therefore, it is not clear whether this difference also hold true for keyboard control.

We found no significant correlation between how often people play sports and how challenging or exertive they rated the capacitive sensor controls. However, people who play sports at least once a week would like to use capacitive sensor controls again. People who play sports less often are undecided. Using capacitive sensor controls participants enjoyed playing the game at least as much as when using the keyboard. If participants already had played an exertion game before (mostly Wii games) they preferred capacitive sensor controls over the keyboard ($p < 0.001$). They enjoyed these controls more than the keyboard ($p < 0.02$) and would use them again ($p < 0.05$).

Overall, these studies provide some evidence that game controllers using capacitive sensors can add an additional layer of complexity to game. While novice players have little trouble understanding the mapping between their movements and the game's reaction, ample time is needed for actually mastering the controls, giving skilled players an advantage.

Conclusion

Due to some unique properties, capacitive sensors are especially suited for Whole Body Interfaces, especially for game controllers:

Robust hardware. Capacitive sensors have no moving or fragile parts. The sensor itself is a small circuit board that can be hidden almost everywhere. The antenna can be made of different materials, e.g. a sturdy metal plate or a flexible fabric, depending on the application. Thus the sensors can be easily embedded into installments, play objects, or clothes. We have also embedded wireless sensors in small tangible interfaces, using Bluetooth for sending sensor data to a host PC.

Flexible placement and layout. Capacitive sensors are very versatile. The one-dimensional, continuous sensor output can be directly used as an input parameter for a game. The sensitivity and direction of the sensor is determined by electrode size, shape and placement. Sensors can be customized for an application, so that they are sensitive only to specific movements. For example, the force of a punch or touch can be measured by gluing a piece of foam on top of the antenna [4]. The stronger the punch, the more the foam gets compressed, and the closer the user's hand gets to the electrode. Thus, the sensor effectively measures the remaining distance between fist and electrode. The one-dimensional, continuous sensor output can be directly used as an input parameter for a game.

Capacitive sensors may also be used for tracking more complex motion. The capacitive coupling between user and ground continuously changes while walking. By putting a sensor below the user's feet or by attaching a sensor to the user [10], walking motions can be detected and quantified.

Friendly but challenging behavior. As capacitive sensors generate data of very low complexity, they allow for a straightforward mapping from sensor output to input event. A user can quickly grasp the correlation between his/her movements and the system's reaction. Thus the barrier to entry of such an interface can be very low. However, the many influencing factors determining a sensor reading also introduce higher complexity. While new users may quickly learn the basic usage of such an input device, they may needs lots of time in order to master the device. Accidental observations or attempts to fudge the device may open up entirely new game tactics. For example, a user may learn from which direction to approach a sensor in order to remain undetected or effect a higher sensor reading. Requiring extra effort in order to master a game corresponds with many physical game "interfaces", like bats and balls.

In conclusion, capacitive sensors are a simple and versatile sensor type that is especially suited for Whole Body Interaction. Off-the-shelf sensors and simple custom-built sensors allow tracking of body movement, touch, and pressure. Additionally, capacitive sensors can also measure a variety of other properties and actions like finger position, fluid level, or proximity to other objects. Some examples for such interfaces might be: sturdy, foam-covered sensor bars, which the user has to hit at the right places in order to destroy enemies attacking his avatar on the computer screen. Balls may determine, if they are held by one or more persons, or lying on the ground. An game like "Dance Dance Revolution" might not only track feet movement, but the whole body. The filtering techniques described in this chapter can also be applied to other domains where high precision and low latency are required.

Acknowledgement The user studies were planned, conducted, and analyzed by Annette Reiter, a graduate student I supervised.

References

1. Cremer, M.: Ueber die Registrierung mechanischer Vorgänge auf electrischem Wege, speziell mit Hilfe des Saitengalvanometers und Saitenelectrometers. Münch. Med. Wochenschr. **54**, 1629–1630 (1907)
2. Glinsky, A.V.: The theremin in the emergence of electronic music. Ph.D. thesis, New York University, New York (1992)
3. Koster, R.: A Theory of Fun for Game Design. Paraglyph Press (2004)
4. Lee, C.H., Hu, Y., Selker, T.: iSphere: A proximity-based 3D input interface. In: Proceedings of CAAD Futures 2005. http://web.media.mit.edu/~jackylee/publication/209J.pdf (2005)
5. Lion Precision: Capacitive sensor operation and optimization. Tech. rep.http://www.lionprecision. com/tech-library/technotes/cap-0020-%sensor-theory.html (2006)
6. Mason, C.: Terpsitone.A new electronic novelty. Radio Craft **335** (1936)
7. Myers, D.:A q-study of game player aesthetics. Simul.Gaming **21**(4), 375-396 (1990). doi:http://dx.doi.org/10.1177/104687819002100403. http://dx.doi.org/http://dx.doi.org/10. 1177/104687819002100403
8. Plamondon, R., Alimi, A.M.:Speed/accuracy trade-offs in target-directed movements. Behav. Brain Sci. **20**(2), 279–303; discussion 303–349 (1997). http://www.ncbi.nlm.nih.gov/ pubmed/10096999
9. Rekimoto, J.:Gesturewrist and gesturepad:unobtrusive wearable interaction devices. http:// citeseer.ist.psu.edu/rekimoto01gesturewrist.html (2001)
10. Rekimoto, J., Wang, H.: Sensing gamepad: electrostatic potential sensing for enhancing entertainment oriented interactions. In: CHI '04, pp. 1457–1460. ACM Press, New York (2004). doi:http://doi.acm.org/10.1145/985921.986089.   http://dx.doi.org/http://doi.acm. org/10.1145/985921.986089
11. Reverter, F., Li, X., Meijer, G.: Stability and accuracy of active shielding for grounded capacitive sensors. Meas. Sci. Technol. **17**, 2884 (2006)
12. Smith, J.: Electric field imaging. Ph.D. thesis, Massachusetts Institute of Technology (1999). http://web.media.mit.edu/~jrs/phd.pdf
13. Smith, J., White, T., Dodge, C.: Electric field sensing for graphical interfaces. Comput. Graph. Appl. **18**(3), 54-61 (1998). http://www.media.mit.edu/physics/publications/papers/98.02. CGA_Final.pdf
14. Smith, S.: Digital Signal Processing: A Practical Guide for Engineers and Scientists, p. 278f. Newnes (2003)
15. Taylor, B.T., Bove, M.V.: Graspables: grasp-recognition as a user interface. In: In Proceedings CHI'09, pp. 917-926. ACM, New York (2009). doi:10.1145/1518701.1518842. http://dx.doi. org/10.1145/1518701.1518842
16. Teixeira, T., Dublon, G., Savvides, A.: A Survey of Human-Sensing: Methods for Detecting Presence, Count, Location, Track, and Identity

17. Valtonen, M., Maentausta, J., Vanhala, J.: Tiletrack: Capacitive human tracking using floor tiles. In: PERCOM '09: Proceedings of the 2009 IEEE International Conference on Pervasive Computing and Communications, pp. 1–10. IEEE Computer Society, Washington, DC (2009). doi:http://dx.doi.org/10.1109/PERCOM.2009.4912749
18. Wimmer, R., Holleis, P., Kranz, M., Schmidt, A.: Thracker – using capacitive sensing for gesture recognition. ICDCSW **0**, 64 (2006). doi:http://doi.ieeecomputersociety.org/10.1109/ICDCSW.2006.109.   http://dx.doi.org/http://doi.ieeecomputersociety.org/10.1109/ICDCSW.2006.109
19. Wimmer, R., Kranz, M., Boring, S., Schmidt, A.: A capacitive sensing toolkit for pervasive activity detection and recognition. In: PerCom '07 (2007)
20. Wimmer, R., Kranz, M., Boring, S., Schmidt, A.: CapTable and capShelf-unobtrusive activity recognition using networked capacitive sensors. In: Fourth International Conference on Networked Sensing Systems, 2007. INSS'07, pp. 85–88 (2007)

Chapter 11
Towards a Whole Body Sensing Platform for Healthcare Applications

P. Fergus, J. Haggerty, M. Taylor, and L. Bracegirdle

Abstract The barriers between human internal body sensing systems (its biological sensors, networks and analogue data flows) and computer science are on the verge of disappearing. Information, once considered concealed, is becoming more accessible through advances in information and communications technology. This has allowing us to isolate and interface with biological sensors and data sources in the human body. Common examples of this already exist, such as electrocardiograms for detecting heart rate and electroencephalography for identifying regions of electrical activity in the brain. Less obvious examples are more complex, such as the mapping of *c-fibers* found in the peripheral nerves of the somatic sensory system to individual neurons, yet advances are being made. Whole body sensing and the granularity of measurement in this way is timely and if successful is likely to impact all aspects our lives, from entertainment, health, right through to unrivalled scientific understandings of the human condition This chapter considers this idea further and details approaches that have moved us towards this goal. It highlights the challenges faced by researchers in this new discipline and provides the beginnings of one possible whole body sensing platform. The applicability of our own approach is demonstrated through a working prototype system and several case studies.

P. Fergus (✉) and M. Taylor
School of Computing and Mathematical Sciences, Liverpool John Moores University,
Byrom Street, Liverpool L3 3AF, UK
e-mail: P.Fergus@ljmu.ac.uk

J. Haggerty
School of Computing, Science and Engineering, University of Salford,
Greater Manchester M4 4WT, UK

L. Bracegirdle
Newcastle Biomedicine, The Medical School, Newcastle University,
Newcastle Upon Tyne NE2 4HH, UK

D. England (ed.), *Whole Body Interaction*, Human-Computer Interaction Series,
DOI 10.1007/978-0-85729-433-3_11, © Springer-Verlag London Limited 2011

Introduction

The relationship between people and computers has evolved in diverse ways. From simple tasks, like creating documents and emailing each other, a more intimate relationship between technology and people has occurred. Small digital sensing devices are being developed capable of accessing concealed information (ranging from atmospheric temperature to human physiological states and kinematics) by interfacing themselves with everyday objects and biological systems. In similar ways that Web Servers and services are accessed, internet-enabled objects also have the ability to be reached with the help of ubiquitous internet access, via Ethernet, WiFi and 3/4G cellular networks. In this new post-PC world everything, everywhere will be considered a networked device that has sensing, and data processing capabilities. This will make it possible to use concealed information in new and novel ways. For example, whole body sensing will provide a new type of information system that will utilise nervous, muscular, vascular, kinematic and kinetic data, as well as contextual sensing using environmental data. This system will drive applications in entertainment, lifestyle management, health, the environment and energy, amongst others, and they will be clear leaders in this post-PC era.

The major challenge in whole body sensing will be to determine how potentially discontinuous and discrete patterns of data relate to each other. This is important for a number of reasons. First, context and time may affect segments and alter the meaning of data accordingly. Second, there will be variability within data that will differ from those that are static – it is variability that makes the classification process complex. For example, increases in heart rate could produce the same data under many different contexts, for example caused by a sport activity or a fearful situation. Hence context directly influences the classification process and as such it is important to consider the data streams around the area under investigation.

This chapter presents one of the most timely research topics. Whole body sensing will have a significant presence in the post-PC era. This chapter explores some of key challenges faced by researchers posits a working prototype system to demonstrate some of these ideas further.

Networking People and Everyday Objects

The general idea of networking people and everyday objects will be an umbrella idea that comprises many technologies. People and everyday objects will be considered networked devices and they will be embedded within the post-PC era. People, gadgets, sensing, and monitoring technologies will be interfaced, interlinked and internetworked via wireless communications. The following subsections explore some of these ideas in more detail with a focus on research within healthcare, which is one of the most active areas of research in whole body sensing.

Body Sensors

Body sensors are not something new. For example, the first pacemaker was implanted into a human body over 40 years ago. Nonetheless, its success has spurred a great deal of research into how other devices can be used to manage human disability and illness. The most common medical sensors are those designed to extract information from the body [23] to gain and understand information, for example, about a person's physical mass, kinematics, a person's mood [14] and even the behaviour of Alzheimer's patients to roaming [15]. Technology provides the basis for understanding mechanics of behaviours like gait and gestures. Coupled with tangible user interfaces it is possible to support clinical practices and treat medical conditions, such as strokes, ischemic disorders, Parkinson's disease and Huntington's chorea, in new and novel ways. For example, applying algorithms for gesture spotting (the start of a gesture) the beginning and end of a meaningful gesture pattern can be determined. This has been particularly useful in rehabilitation to quantify musculoskeletal movement for the purpose of ongoing monitoring and assessment [9, 16, 24].

Medical implants are now a reality and interest in this area has grown [10]. Cardiac devices, such as cardioverter defibrillators [11] and nerve stimulation (retinal implants, cochlear implants, glaucoma sensors, and intracranial pressure sensor to name a few) [8] have seen mainstream usage within medical facilities. For example, The Health Aims project [8] has utilised strain gauge technologies (a sphincter sensor that is used in urodynamics) to diagnose the cause for urinary incontinence. By placing a microfabricated strain gauge mounted on a catheter, deformities can be monitored in relation to pressure. Similar techniques have been investigated to calculate very slight distortions in an anatomically correct knee were strain gauges are placed on the surface of the Fibular collateral ligament, Anterior cruciate ligament, Posterior cruciate ligament, and the Tibial collateral ligament [7]. Given that 500 million people in the western world are estimated to suffer from illnesses or disabilities, research in this area is timely, and it has the potential impact society as a whole.

Smart Environments

In the post-PC world everyday objects will be networked and the functions they provide will be pervasively distributed and used to create new and innovative healthcare solutions. In support of this Lee et al. [12] point out that realising such a complex integration will result in a ubiquitous heterogeneous overlay containing different protocols, different contexts, location and property independent device control, ad hoc device registration and updating, real-time data processing and alarm management, and high volumes of event traffic.

This would aid the correlation of sensor data received from people and everyday objects to provide additional contextual information, i.e. situation and activity awareness. For example, Surie et al. [22] propose an activity-centred middleware to determine the activity being carried out and the situation the user is in. The HydroSense platform allows all water usage within a home to be monitored, e.g. dishwasher usage, going to the toilet, having a shower and using the sink [5]. The power line infrastructure has also been utilised to monitor activity, i.e. what food is being cooked, and whether they have had coffee or tea [2]. All these provide sources of information about people. Monitoring such activities helps to understand patients and their unique requirements, i.e. the activity levels of obese people, fluid intake of people with diabetes, and the general hygiene of people with mental disabilities.

Measuring Behaviour

Behaviour can be broadly thought of as the action or reaction made by some entity (human, machine, chemical or substance) given some situation, stimuli, or event. Measurement on the other hand relates to the processes and algorithms used to assign a value to some phenomena (action or reaction) using pre-defined rules. The main challenge is to divide behaviour into segments or pieces and to understand how they relate to each other. Furthermore, making distinctions between possibly similar behaviours under different contexts poses further challenges given that this affects segments and alters behaviour accordingly. It is variability within behaviour segments that makes classification difficult [4].

Nonetheless, technology is making it easier to infer the physical and psychological properties of people and understanding the environments and contexts they are by observing simple interactions in the home. For example, floor maps have been used in many healthcare applications to identify people and household artefacts [18]. Through simple triggering mechanisms it is possible to determine a person's location and their mobility patterns, including what household appliances or artefacts they have used. Using voice recognition and learning algorithms control mechanisms can be put in place for people with visual disabilities, where control and collaborative communications between friends, family and healthcare professionals is important. Similar applications have also been used to recognise context [17].

Classification of Behaviour

A whole body sensing platform will provide multiple streamed events obtained from different body and environmental systems. This allows specific episodic manifestations to be monitored, such as cardiac arrhythmia, diabetes mellitus, and drug regime monitoring and assistance to elderly patients. Nonetheless, mapping isolated data streams and their relationships to higher order behaviours is non-trivial.

One area that could potentially help is ontology – the idea of segmenting behaviour into pieces is similar to the definition of concepts and the constituent entities that formalise and guide the mappings between function and behaviour.

The Web Ontology Language (OWL) [19] specification is considered the de-facto specification for describing ontologies. OWL provides a means of defining concepts from elements; the same principles could be used to guide the mapping algorithms needed to link functions with behaviour. Depending on the level of activation, links between segments of behaviour will give rise to higher order concepts, such as dehydration, fear, anxiety, or pain. This provides a means of modelling or formally defining behaviour and its relationship with isolated streamed events. However, Stephens et al. [21] suggest that there is no comprehensive ontology that can solve the problems associated with information processing. Even if such an ontology could be created it would be so eclectic that no one would adhere to it. A common terminology could be used with agreed semantics. However this solution is highly improbable. Different terminologies could be used and explicit translations mapped to a global ontology, yet this is difficult and as a result highly unlikely.

Yet despite the difficulties faced it is worth exploring this idea further. Whilst it may be difficult to map complex behaviours, many forms of basic stimuli could be used to invoke general behaviours and these would act as building blocks for research into the classification of more complex behaviour that could be used as a crude classification mechanism. Through adaptation models classifications are dynamically defined based on commonalities between streamed data events from the whole patient population. For example, pictures, sounds and video clips could be dynamically categorised under specific groups. In parallel, monitoring facial supercilli muscle activity or skin conductance and heart rate could all be classed as generalised emotional states and whilst the stimulus may differ there may be sufficient commonality to help in classification [1].

An interesting research area that is heavily focused on the formal representation and understanding of data streams is Stream Reasoning. The key challenge is to reason over rapidly changing data using different levels of abstraction that allow streams to be integrated and used in the classification of higher order behaviour [3]. The research agenda is timely and fundamentally important as an increasing number of data streams are sent over public networks.

Whole Body Sensing Platform

Many aspects of whole body sensing have been proposed as is evident in the literature presented above, yet a consistent and unified platform for achieving this in an open and flexible way is yet to be fully realised. This section describes how our previous work in networked appliances might be extended to achieve this and to thus incorporate whole body sensing services [13].

Physiological, Inertial and Environmental Sensing Service

The proposed whole body sensing services posited in this chapter build on our networked appliances service utilisation framework. This framework allows device functionality to be abstracted and deployed as network services. Interconnected devices are free to utilise these services and given that all functionality is viewed as a collection of these services, compositions are automatically created based on shared characteristics.

Sensors are connected together within a peer-to-peer overlay network and each of the functions they provide, such as ECG, EMG, EEG and respiration, are abstracted as network services, as illustrated in Fig. 11.1. There are three categories of sensors, bio-sensors, motion-sensors and environmental sensors. The data streams they produce are processed by the whole body sensing services where digital signal processing algorithms are applied for data filtering, including time-series and domain frequency analysis, amongst other pluggable bio-signal algorithms, such as drift detection, ECG beat detection and ECG QRS detection. The ability to include any signal processing algorithms makes the framework flexible, extensible and open.

The whole body sensing services extend the service interoperability and semantic matching framework service provided by the networked appliance service utilisation framework and this allows functionality and services to be semantically described. The multi-stream composition mechanism allows specific types of services to be discovered, such as temperature, to test geographically specific areas or heart rate to test the level of fear or mood amongst individuals in particular areas or regions. Alternatively, different service types can be grouped into compositions – this is

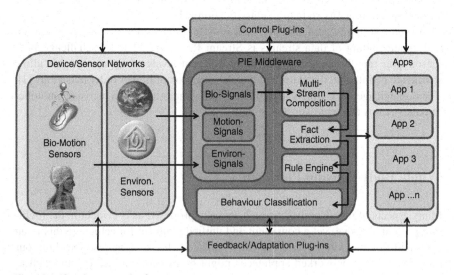

Fig. 11.1 Overlay network of sensors

particularly useful when the context around an individual service is required, i.e. the reasons why a person's heart rate has increased.

Stream compositions feed directly into the fact extraction algorithms and this allows classifications or markers to be automatically isolated from irrelevant or noisy data. Markers become know facts about information in isolated or composition data streams, for example, the QRS complex found in ECG signals.

Facts provide the basis for more detailed or higher level intelligence using rule engines that operate on these facts. This helps provide an understanding about facts, their relationships between each other and the contexts in which they occur. For example, it is possible to predict different types of heart disease from facts about the QRS complex, i.e. a shortened or prolonged QT interval often relates to Hypercalcemia, flattened or inverted T waves indicate the onset of acute Myocardial Infraction and Prominent U waves indicate Hypokalemia. Analysis of a single individual helps detect the existence of such diseases; looking at groups of individuals allows mean averages about a population to be analysed for specific heart conditions. This information, used in conjunction with other facts (obtained from data streams), may provide contextual information about why this is happening.

The rule engine provides a foundation on which classification can occur, i.e. the patient's heart rate shows Prominent U waves and in turn has Hypokalemia. Behaviour classifications emerge as a direct result of the real-time emergence of facts or markers, their relationships with each other and the contexts under which they occur. Obviously any changes within these layers affects the final classification, i.e. if the context changes but the facts remain the same then this is likely be classified in some other way. For example, increases in heart rate as a result of someone breaking into your home or being attacked, whilst producing the same or similar facts would produce a different classification to say a person who has just completed a 6 mile run.

For a more detailed discussion on the underlying framework that supports the whole body sensing services the reader is referred to [13]. In the following section some case studies are presented to demonstrate the use of the whole body sensing services in working prototypes that have been developed.

Case Studies

In this section several case studies are presented to demonstrate possible uses for a whole body sensing platform. Different devices and wireless communication protocols have be incorporated within the framework. Interoperability between different devices and protocols is achieved using intermediary Bluetooth services wrapped around peer services provided by our peer-to-peer network (JXTA) [6]. For example, the SunSPOT sensors [20] used in the case studies are based on 802.15.4 communications and this required a Bluetooth wrapper service to allow the accelerometer and analogue functions to be abstracted as services and included in the networked appliance service utilisation framework. More detailed discussions about the peer-to-peer network can be found in [13].

Physiotherapy

Fitting sensors to the body to collect and analyse motion data has generated a great deal of interest across different disciplines, i.e. entertainment, sport and health. In healthcare it has allowed the effectiveness of treatments, for example, physiotherapy, to be quantified. This has made assessment and treatment more precise providing a historical data trail, which helps inform progress and further treatment regimes. In the first case study a prototype system has been used to provide patients suffering from arthritic hips and knee pain with aquatic exercise routines.

SunSPOT sensors are attached to a patient's leg as illustrated in Fig. 11.2 and they are asked to lift their leg up and down between 25° and 45° angles with the leg straight. The legs position is measured every millisecond and data values, for the purpose of illustration, have been converted into 3D coordinates and used to animate a 3D model as can be seen in Fig. 11.2.

Sample results obtained from a physiotherapy session can be seen in Fig. 11.3. Data along the *x* axis demonstrates the total time taken in a specific therapy session; and the speed in which the leg was moved; the *y* axis shows the position of the leg at different time intervals. The leg position at position three on the graph shows that the leg has been has been lifted to a 45° angle and 0 means the leg has been returned to a standing position.

In Fig. 11.3 the graph illustrates a number of curves which in turn represent the leg moving in an up and down position. Using these values physicians are able to determine how accurate the therapy has been performed. Graphs can be easily overlaid on top of each other to see the level of improvement and used to tailor future therapy techniques and make compensatory changes.

Fig. 11.2 Right leg lifting exercises

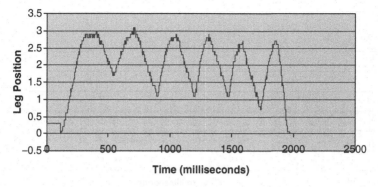

Fig. 11.3 Arthritic hip and knee pain therapy sessions

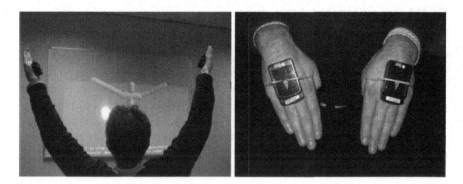

Fig. 11.4 Arm lift lower back therapy

In the second case study lower back therapies are demonstrated using the same type of SunSPOT sensor attached to the patient's arms as illustrated in Fig. 11.4. The patient is asked to lift their arms up and extend them as illustrated in Fig. 11.4. At the same time the patient is asked to breath in and out and hold the arms up for a time duration between 7 and 10 s. This exercise is repeated a number of times. During this therapy the arms should be moved slowly and kept steady.

The results from the therapy session are illustrated in Fig. 11.5. During the exercise routine in this session the position of the arms was measured every millisecond. Again the acceleration data is used to drive the 3D model. The *x* axis demonstrates the total time taken for the session and the movements. On the *y* axis the position of the arm at different time intervals can be seen. In Fig. 11.5 the arm position at position four shows that the arms are completely straight (180°). Position 0 means that the arms are at the patient's side. In this session the patient's arms are held up between 7 and 8 s.

All data is saved in a data store and this helps to record specific readings for all therapy sessions undertaken by the patient. This provides value to physiotherapists

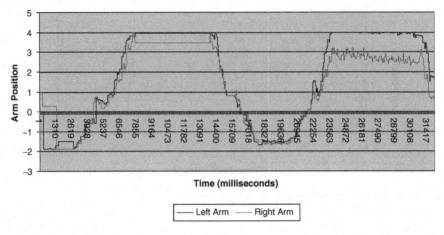

Fig. 11.5 Arm and lower back therapy sessions

who currently have limited mechanisms to collect quantitative data. Currently, they are required to rely on the subjective opinions and assessments made by the physician. This is further complicated by the fact that such opinions may differ given that patients could be assessed by different therapists. Whilst, experienced physicians make a good diagnosis, our system aims to enhance the diagnosis to quantify the true performance of the patient over time and this may help tailor future assessments and treatments.

Arthritis and Progressive Deterioration

There is a need to provide a greater level of granularity during the measurement processes. This is particularly true when assessing and treating smaller body parts, such as the hand. In our third case study the arthritic hand has been considered to monitor progressive deterioration. To meet the requirements for hand and finger digit movements the 5DT Data Glove has been used as illustrated in Fig. 11.6.

The Java SunSPOT application utilises the 5DT Data Glove services to request all data from the gloves sensors. This results in a continuous stream of data from the glove and via the home sensor network this data is streamed to another laptop and SunSPOT-base station configuration to control a 3D representation of the patient's hand as illustrated in Fig. 11.6.

As with the two previous case studies data can be collected, stored and used to historically assess the patient's condition, i.e. the effects of treatment, medication and progressive deterioration. There is little quantitative data relating to the assessment of arthritis in current systems, thus will provide a way to capture data and use it to influence or guide future decisions on treatment and medication.

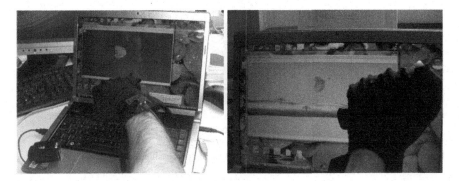

Fig. 11.6 5DT data glove process

Fine Measurement Sensing for Progressive Deterioration

The 5DT data glove provides an interesting way for measuring more precise movement as apposed to approximate not actual movement, provided by acce-lerometer and gyroscope technology. It is particularly useful to detect things that go wrong at its earliest occurrence. The next case study investigates this idea further using strain gauges attached to the musculoskeletal system to detect the onset of progressive deterioration and to intervene early enough to prevent permanent damage.

For this case study a custom strain gauge devices have been developed and appropriate circuitry for signal processing (filtering noise and amplifying signals). The strain gauge and its circuitry are connected to the analogue inputs of the SunSPOT to allow data to be wirelessly transmitted (again 802.15.4, was wrapped around Bluetooth services which in turn was wrapped around peer services in our peer-to-peer network). The prototype mimics a fully working sensing device for the detection of slight movement in body regions, such as joints, i.e. wrists, elbows and knees, for the purpose of prevention and medical treatment.

Figure 11.7 (a) illustrates the strain gauge applicator; (b) the signal pro-cessing circuitry; and finally (c) the strain gauge connected to the free-range SunSPOT.

A flexible anatomically correct artificial knee was used to test the devices sensitivity to slight movement as illustrated in Fig. 11.8. The strain gauge applicator monitors the movements of the Quadriceps tendon, the Patella and the Patellar tendon (ligament). The left hand diagram shows the artificial knee in a rest position with the strain gauge sensor fitted to the surface of the Quadriceps tendon. The strain gauge is not at a zero output position and a form of substitution is performed using an 'offset adjustment'. This is achieved by adjusting the potentiometers (connected in series with the strain gauge sensors). This is useful to accommodate different subjects and their own specific characteristics.

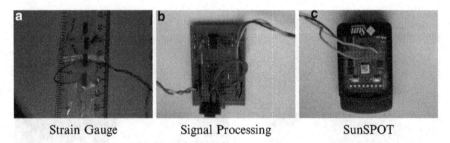

Strain Gauge   Signal Processing   SunSPOT

Fig. 11.7 Prototype system. (**a**) Strain gauge. (**b**) Signal processing. (**c**) SunSPOT

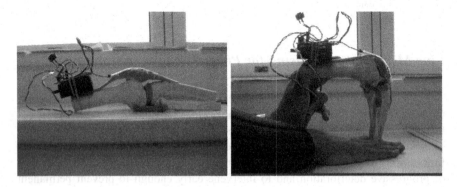

Fig. 11.8 Strain gauge arrangement attached to the artificial knee

The applicator could just as easily be applied to the Lateral collateral ligament, the Medial Collateral ligament or the Anterior cruciate ligament. Using this model the knee can be flexed as a normal knee would (illustrated in the right hand diagram of Fig. 11.8) and then allowed to return to its resting position. For the purpose of the demonstration the knee was flexed five times to show the real-time data readings collected from the strain gauge sensor. This can be seen in Fig. 11.9.

From the graph it is possible to observe that the patient's knee has managed to achieve constant bend amplitudes over a period of five consecutive exercises, with a rest period of approximately 5 s between each set. Although the graph is uncalibrated and generic values are used at this point, it is possible to convert the x and y values to units of time and degrees respectively due to the linear characteristics of the strain gauges performance.

The applicator is designed to be fitted with different body structures and capabilities. Using an offset facility a *Null* position can be calibrated once the applicator has been fitted. This provides the therapist with a starting point of reference. This *Null* or datum position can be set very easily by the therapist for individual patients. This allows the same reference point to be set every time and removes the possibility of errors and inconsistencies from affecting the results.

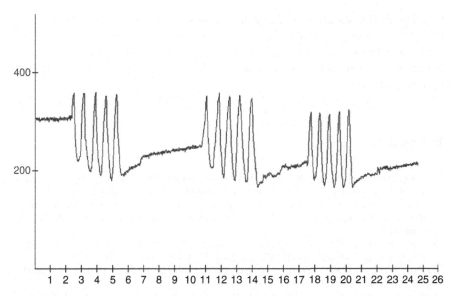

Fig. 11.9 Real-time data stream from artificial knee flexions

Conclusions and Future Work

The ongoing development of wireless technologies has allowed the physical size of wireless micro-electro-mechanical systems to be produced much smaller in size and lighter in use. This has opened up new opportunities that enable their application to be more widespread than previously thought. This chapter has argued that one high impacting domain is healthcare where wireless communications and sensing technologies are regarded as fundamentally important in supporting the development of better healthcare services. This is evident in gait analysis and physiological computing systems where sensors attached to the body help to understand the human condition and deliver better healthcare services. For example, whole body sensing can be used to measure the effectiveness physiotherapy has on a person suffering from cerebral palsy and strain gauge technology is now beginning to provide more fine grained information about the inner workings of muscles, tendons, ligaments and cartilage. The aim of this chapter is to explore these ideas further and to outline a possible whole body sensing platform. We have successfully demonstrated the applicability of our approach using a number of working prototype systems and these are presented in the form of case studies.

This provides the basis for our whole body sensing platform and a great deal of work is still required. Current research strands include better motion capture capabilities using XSens and its application to other research strands, i.e. fall detection and prevention, mood analysis, cystic-fibrosis and asthma adherence through exercise amongst others. A second strand of research currently under development focuses on physiological computing using the NeXus bio-feedback technology.

Currently, all data streams from the XSens and NeXus sensors have been incorporated into the framework (they exist in the peer-to-peer network as services). Yet appropriate digital signal processing and displacement algorithms are still under investigation. Furthermore, additional work is required at the semantic layer to provide stream reasoning services.

References

1. Arroyo-Palacious, J., Romano, D.M.: Towards a standardization in the use of physiological signals for affective recognition systems. In: Measuring Behaviour, Maastricht (2008)
2. Bauer, G., Stockinger, K., Lukowicz.: Recognizing the use-mode of kitchen appliances from their current consumption. In: 4th European Conference on Smart Sensing and Context, Guildford (2009)
3. Della Valle, E., Ceri, S., van Harmelen, F., Fensel, D.: It's a streaming world! Reasoning upon rapidly changing information. IEEE Intell. Syst. **24**, 83–89 (2009)
4. Fentress, J.C.: Streams and patterns in behaviour as challenges for future technologies. Behav. Res. Meth. **41**, 765–771 (2008)
5. Froehlich, J.E., Larson, E., Campbell, T., Haggerty, C., Fogarty, J., Patel, S.N.: HydroSense: infrastructure-mediated single-point sensing of whole-home water activity. In: 11th International Conference on Ubiquitous Computing, Orlando (2009)
6. Gong, L.: JXTA: a network programming environment. IEEE Internet Comput. **5**, 88–95 (2001)
7. Hanley, P.: Development of a patient monitoring system using IEEE 802.15.4 enabled SunSPOT sensors and utilising add-on strain gauge devices. In: School of Computing and Mathematical Sciences, vol. MSc. Liverpool John Moores University, Liverpool (2010)
8. Hodgins, D., Bertsch, A., Post, N.: Healthy aims: developing new medical implants and diagnostic equipment. IEEE Pervas. Comput **7**, 14–21 (2009)
9. Jovanov, E., Milenkovic, A., Otto, C., de Groen, P.C.: A wireless body area network of intelligent motion sensors for computer assisted physical rehabilitation. J. Neuroeng. Rehabil. **2**, 6 (2005)
10. Kailas, A., Ingram, M.A.: Wireless communications technology in telehealth systems. In: 1st International Conference on Wireless Communications, Vehicular Technology, Information Theory and Aerospace & Electronic Systems Technology, Aalborg Congress and Culture Centre, Aalborg, Denmark (2009)
11. Lazarus, A.: Remote, wireless, ambulatory monitoring of implantable pacemakers, cardio-verter defibrillators, and cardiac resynchronization therapy systems: analysis of a worldwide database. Pacing Clin. Electrophysiol. **30**, S2–S12 (2007)
12. Lee, M., Kang, S.: Multimedia room gateway for integration and management of distributed medical devices. In: Workshop on High Confidence Medical Device Software and Systems (HCMDSS), University of Pennsylvania, Philadelphia (2005)
13. Merabti, M., Fergus, P., Abuelma'atti, O., Yu, H., Judice, C.: Managing distributed networked appliances in home networks. Proc. IEEE J. **96**, 166–185 (2008)
14. Michalak, J., Troje, N.F., Fischer, J., Vollmar, P., Heidenreich, T., Schulte, D.: Embodiment of sadness and depression – gait patterns associated with dysphoric mood. Psychosom. Med. **71**, 580–587 (2009)
15. Moore, D.H., Algase, D.L., Powell-Cope, G.: A framework for managing wandering and preventing elopement. Am. J. Alzheimers. Dis **24**, 208–219 (2009)
16. Mundermann, L., Corazza, S., Andriacchi, T.P.: The evolution of methods for the capture of human movement leading to markerless motion capture for biomechanical applications. J. Neuroeng. Rehabil. **3** (2006)

17. Bagci, P.J.F., Trumler, W., Ungerer, T., Vintan, L.: Global state context prediction techniques applied to a smart office building. In: Communication Networks and Distributed Systems Modelling and Simulation Conference, San Diego (2004)
18. Sanchez, D., Tentori, M., Favela, J.: Activity recognition for the smart hospital. IEEE Intell. Syst. **23**, 50–57 (2008)
19. Smith, M.K., Welty, C., McGuinness, D.L.: OWL Web ontology language guide, http://www.w3.org/TR/2003/CR-owl-guide-20030818/(2003). Accessed Oct 2010
20. Smith, R.B.: SPOTWorld and the Sun SPOT. In: 6th Symposium on Information Processing in Sensor Networks, Cambridge (2007)
21. Stephens, L.M., Huhns, M.N.: Consensus ontologies – reconciling the semantics of web pages and agents. IEEE Internet Comput. **5**, 92–95 (2001)
22. Surie, D., Laguionie, O., Pederson, T.: Wireless sensor networking of everyday objects in a smart home environment. In: 4th IEEE Conference on Intelligent Sensors, Sensor Networks and Information Processing, Sydney (2008)
23. Terry, M.: The personal health dashboard: consumer electronics is growing in the health and wellness market. Telemed. J. E. Health. **15**, 642–645 (2009)
24. Zhou, H., Hu, H.: Human motion tracking for rehabilitation – a survey. Biomed. Signal Process. Control **3**, 1–18 (2007)

Chapter 12
Feasibility of Using a Head-Mounted Camera to Capture Dynamic Facial Expressions During Body Movement

Elizabeth A. Crane, M. Melissa Gross, and Barbara L. Fredrickson

Abstract In this study, we tested the feasibility of capturing video of facial expressions while concurrently capturing motion capture and video of bodily expressions. To collect facial expression data, we used a custom designed head-mount for a video camera that provided images for facial expression microanalysis but did not limit freedom of movement. We assessed the effect of the head-mount on emotion elicitation, emotion recognition, qualitative aspects of body movement, and quantitative aspects of body movement. The results indicate that while the head-mount may slightly constrain arm movement, wearing the head-mounted camera during motion capture is a valid method for collecting facial and bodily data.

Introduction

Many studies have documented that emotions can produce measurable changes in expressive modalities, including the face [1, 11, 22], voice [3, 4, 13], and body [2, 9, 20, 21, 26]. Recent advances in computing provide the opportunity to integrate expressive behavior into computer applications. A critical limitation for integrating signals from the face and body is that current methods for

E.A. Crane (✉)
Department of Biologic and Materials Sciences, School of Dentistry,
University of Michigan, Ann Arbor, MI 48109, USA
e-mail: bcrane@umich.edu

M.M. Gross
Department of Movement Science, School of Kinesiology, University of Michigan,
Ann Arbor, MI 48109-2214, USA
e-mail: mgross@umich.edu

B.L. Fredrickson
Department of Psychology, Davie Hall, University of North Carolina at Chapel Hill,
Chapel Hill, NC, USA
e-mail: blf@email.unc.edu

D. England (ed.), *Whole Body Interaction*, Human-Computer Interaction Series,
DOI 10.1007/978-0-85729-433-3_12, © Springer-Verlag London Limited 2011

capturing facial video limit whole body movement. Indeed, in one of the first studies to assess multimodal expressive patterns and the relationship with emotion, the authors acknowledge the importance of the behaviors studied and conclude that their results may be limited by the behaviors in their analysis [23]. Therefore, methodology to simultaneously capture signals from multiple modalities that allows freedom of movement is needed so that whole body expression is not constrained by the technology used to capture the signals. The primary objective of this study was to overcome this technical constraint by testing the feasibility of capturing video of the face during a movement task in which a subject changes location.

Applications that incorporate expressive behavior have typically captured face video by placing a stationary camera directly in front of the participant (e.g., [25, 27]). However, for applications that require the participant to change location or engage in tasks that take their face away from the camera, one camera is not sufficient to capture a continuous and unobstructed frontal view. The ability to move freely is an important aspect of whole body interaction and ultimately should not be constrained due to technical limitations. Although multiple cameras placed around the application space could provide a continuous view, the video image of the face would have to be assembled from multiple cameras with differing angles and distances, thereby affecting face size or shading. Such a compromised view of the face impairs the ability to use well-established methods, such as the Facial Action Coding System (FACS) [12], to document and characterize the expressive facial behaviors. Even with the introduction of automated FACS coding and facial expression detection systems (see [8]), a continuous view of the face is needed for these systems to function optimally.

An alternative to using multiple, stationary cameras is to fix a single camera to the subject's head so that a continuous and unobstructed video of the face can be captured. However, wearing a head-mounted camera could potentially interfere with the production of expressive behavior by affecting emotion elicitation, emotion recognition, or whole body movements. If the method for capturing the expressive stimuli interferes with the expressive behavior, then the multimodal signals captured may not accurately represent target emotions. Therefore, methods for capturing expressive stimuli are valid only if they do not interfere with expressive behavior. Because the effectiveness of whole-body-interaction applications that incorporate expressive signals depends on capturing as natural behaviors as possible, it is necessary to have methods for capturing the signals that do not interfere with the expressive behavior.

In this study, face video was collected simultaneously with whole-body video and motion capture data to qualitatively and quantitatively assess body movements. To determine whether wearing a head-mounted camera interfered with expressive behavior, this study was divided into four parts assessing the effect of the head-mount on (1) emotion elicitation, (2) emotion recognition, (3) qualitative aspects of body movement, and (4) quantitative aspects of body movement.

Part 1: Emotion Elicitation

The first aim was to test whether wearing a head-mounted camera to record facial expressions affected emotion elicitation during a movement task in which a subject changes location. Walking was studied because it is a well-documented movement task in biomechanics, it is an emotionally neutral task, it requires subjects to change location, and emotions are recognizable in walking [15, 20]. To address this aim, we tested (1) whether the proportion of movement trials in which the target emotions were felt was different between head-mount (HM) and non-HM groups, and (2) whether the self-reported intensities of the target emotions were different between the groups.

Participants

Walkers were recruited from the University of Michigan undergraduate student population and gave informed consent before participating. Walkers (n = 42, 52% female) ranged in age from 18–32 years (20.1 ± 2.7 year.). All participants were able-bodied and no special skills were required. They were randomly assigned to the non-HM (n = 21, 57% female) and HM groups (n = 21, 48% female). The difference in gender distribution was not significant ($X_{(1)}^2 = 0.4$, p = 0.54).

Head-Mounted Camera

To capture a consistent image of the face during movement, a head mount was custom designed in our laboratory to support a small video camera (Adventure Cam II, Viosport). The camera weighed 80 g, was 76 mm in length by 22 mm in diameter, and had a resolution of 380 TV Lines. The camera rested on the head mount approximately 30.5 cm from the face and was adjusted to ensure that the participant's field of view was not obstructed and that a full view of the face was captured (Fig. 12.1).

Procedure

Walkers completed an autobiographical memories worksheet [17, 19]. They described times in their own life when they felt two negative emotions (anger and sad), two positive emotions (joy and content), and neutral emotion. Walkers wore a motion capture suit and 31 light-weight spherical markers (2 cm diameter) were placed over specific anatomical landmarks. They walked 5 m at a self-selected pace after recalling a memory from their worksheet. Side-view video and 3-D motion

Fig. 12.1 Head mount apparatus used to support video camera for recording facial expression. The adjustable mount for the camera is located at the tip of the *horizontal* strut. The right photo is the face view captured from the head-mounted camera

capture data were recorded, and face-view video was additionally recorded for the HM group.

Participants performed three walking trials of each memory in a block; memory order was randomized. To determine if the target emotion was felt, walkers completed a self-report questionnaire after each trial to indicate what they felt while walking. After each emotion block, walkers indicated which trial was their best trial for that memory.

Measures

Subjective experience of emotion was assessed using a self-report questionnaire to report emotion intensity [14, 18]. The questionnaire included the four target emotions and four non-target, distracter emotions (awe, disgust, fear, and surprise). Walkers rated the intensity that they felt each emotion using a five-item Likert scale (0 = not at all; 1 = a little bit; 2 = moderately; 3 = a great deal; 4 = extremely).

A binary variable was created to code the target emotion as felt or not felt. The variable was coded as "felt" when the self-reported intensity score for the target emotion was greater than or equal to two ("moderately"). Because an item for neutral was not included on the questionnaire, a neutral trial was considered "felt" if all eight items on the questionnaire were scored less than two.

Data Analysis

210 walking trials (5 emotions × 42 walkers) were selected for evaluation. For analysis details see supplementary materials. To be selected, a trial needed to have (1) usable kinematic data, and (2) usable side-view video and face-view video (if applicable). A generalized linear mixed model with random walker effects was used to model the probability of the binary response variable (felt emotion) with a

logit link. Fixed effects of group, emotion, walker gender, and walker age, and the interactions between group – emotion and group – gender were tested. Fixed effects were significant if the absolute value of the t-ratio of the estimate to its standard error was greater than two. Approximate likelihood ratio tests were used to determine if the interaction effects were significant: effects with a p-value greater than .05 were removed from the model.

Results

Proportions of Felt Trials

There were no significant differences in the proportion of trials coded as felt between the HM and non-HM groups for each emotion. The difference between groups for each emotion, except neutral, was less than 5% and the emotions were coded as felt in more than 95% of the trials in each group. Our success in eliciting neutral trials was less effective, however, and the criterion for felt neutral trials was met in only 68% of the trials. In the majority of "failed" neutral trials, walkers reported feeling either content or anxious at a moderate level. Although the average percentage of felt neutral trials tended to be greater for walkers wearing the head-mounted camera (non-HM = 60%, HM = 76.2%), the difference was not significant.

Fixed effects of emotion, walker gender, and walker age did not significantly effect felt emotion. Likewise, there were no interaction effects for group and emotion or group and gender.

Intensities of Felt Emotions

There were no significant differences in the distributions of the self-reported intensity scores between the HM and non-HM groups for any of the target emotions. The largest difference in reported intensities between groups was for content in which the HM group had a greater percentage of the highest intensity scores (76.2% vs. 57.1%) but the difference was not significant.

Part 2: Emotion Recognition

The second aim was to determine whether the head-mounted camera worn by the walkers affected emotion recognition by observers. Therefore, we tested whether observer recognition of emotion in the body movements of the walkers differed between HM and non-HM groups.

Participants

Observers (n=60, 48% female) ranged in age from 18–30 years (20.9±2.7 year). They provided informed consent prior to beginning the study. No special skills were required. However, observers were excluded if they had participated as a walker.

Video Clips

Side-view video clips from the 210 trials were shown to the observers to determine if the target emotion was recognizable in the body movements of the walkers. The walkers' faces were blurred and the movement clips were looped three times.

Procedure

Observers were randomly assigned to one of two groups with 30 observers in each group so that a single observer did not see more than 110 clips. The video clips were shown in one of three different randomized sequences. Observers selected one of ten emotions that they thought the walker experienced during the trial. The forced choice items included the same four target emotions and four non-target emotions as before, as well as neutral/no emotion and none of the above.

Measures

The total number of emotion observations for each group for each emotion was 630 (21 walkers × 30 observations for each clip). Each emotion observation was coded as recognized if the observed emotion agreed with the target emotion.

Data Analysis

A generalized linear mixed model with crossed random effects of walkers and observers was used to model the probability of the binary response variable (recognized emotion) with a logit link. The analysis was performed separately for each emotion and the model included fixed effects of head-mount group, walker gender, observer gender, walker age, observer age, video sequence and observer group. Fixed effects were determined as significant if the absolute value of the t-ratio of the estimate to its standard error was greater than two. To check for random observer effects, a likelihood ratio test was used to determine if the variance of the random observer effect was significantly greater than zero.

Results

Recognition

Recognized emotion was not significantly different between the HM and non-HM groups. The differences in the number of observations that were recognized between the two groups were small, ranging from 19 observations for sad (3% of the total observations) to four observations for neutral (0.06% of total).

Additional Measures

Fixed effects of head-mount group, walker gender, observer gender, walker age, observer age, video sequence and observer group were not significant for any emotion. Random observer effects were observed, however, indicating that the observer effects should remain in our statistical model.

Part 3: Effort-Shape Analysis

The third aim was to determine if wearing the head-mounted camera affected qualitative characteristics of the walkers' body movements. In this part of the study, we used an Effort-Shape analysis to assess the qualitative characteristics of the body movements and we tested whether Effort-Shape scores differed between the groups.

The same video clips and procedures used in the recognition study were used in this study. However, observers completed a six-item Effort-Shape questionnaire after viewing each video clip. Two questionnaire items were related to the shape of the body (i.e., torso shape and limb shape), and four items were related to the effort quality during the movement (i.e., space, time, energy, flow).

Participants

Observers (n = 60, 52% female) ranged in age from 19–30 years (22.0 ± 2.6 year). No special skills were required. However, participants were excluded if they participated in as a walker or in the recognition study.

Measures

The observers rated the qualities using a five-item Likert scale (1 = left-anchor quality; 5 = right-anchor quality). The anchor points represented opposite qualities for each Effort-Shape factor. They were shown a bar with a gray-scale gradient from white on the left to black on the right. The gradient bar had five evenly spaced points from which they could select. Observers were instructed to think of the scale as a continuum rather than five discrete points on a scale.

Data Analysis

A linear mixed model with crossed random walker and observer effects was used to model means on the response variables (i.e., Effort-Shape scores) for each emotion. The model included fixed effects of walker gender, observer gender, walker age, observer age, video sequence, and observer group. Fixed effects were determined as significant if the absolute value of the t-ratio of the estimate to its standard error was greater than two. To check for random observer effects, a likelihood ratio test was used to determine if the variance of the random observer effects was significantly greater than zero.

Results

Effect of HM

In general, wearing the head-mounted camera did not affect qualitative characteristics of body movements. 93% of all mean differences for the Effort-Shape scores between groups were 0.4 or less and 57% were 0.2 or less. The head-mount did, however, have statistically significant emotion-specific effects on limb shape and time qualities. For content and neutral emotions, the mean limb shape scores were 0.46 and 0.45 less in the HM group, shifting the limb shape quality towards "close to the body". For neutral emotion, the mean time score was 0.35 less in HM group shifting the time quality towards "slow, sustained, leisurely". Overall, all differences between groups were less than 0.5 on a five point scale but we do not know if this relatively small difference should be interpreted as a meaningful, expressive difference in movement quality.

Additional Measures

While observer group and observer age did not have any significant motion-specific effects for any of the Effort-Shape qualities, all other measures (i.e., sequence, walker gender, walker age, and observer gender) had at least one significant emotion specific effect for at least one of the Effort-Shape qualities. In these cases, mean differences were 0.30 or less ($t > 2$) with some differences as small as 0.08

(t = 2.099). These differences were accounted for by including these measures in all our statistical analyses.

Part 4: Kinematic Analysis

The fourth aim was to determine whether wearing the head-mounted camera affected the quantitative aspects of body movement. We tested whether there were significant differences in gait cycle descriptors or joint angular kinematics between HM groups.

Kinematic Data

Motion capture data from trials selected for analysis were included in the kinematic analysis if the target emotion was both felt and recognized (138 of 210 trials; non-HM trials: n = 66, 50% female; HM trials: n = 72 trials, 49% female). One gait cycle (i.e., when the left heel strikes (toe-off) to the next left heel strike (toe-off)) was selected for analysis for each walking trial. Joint angles were calculated for the neck, trunk, shoulder, elbow, wrist, hip, knee, and ankle for each walking trial using C-Motion Visual 3D software package.

Measures

Gait cycle descriptors included cycle duration (time to complete a gait cycle), normalized stride length (distance traveled in one gait cycle normalized by walker height), and normalized gait velocity (m/s, normalized by walker height). Joint angular kinematic measures included the mean angle and range of motion of each joint during the gait cycle.

Data Analysis

A linear mixed model with random walker effects was used to model means on the response variables (i.e., gait cycle descriptors and joint angular kinematic measures) for each emotion. The model included fixed effects of emotion, group, walker gender, and the interaction between group – emotion. Fixed effects were determined as significant if the absolute value of the t-ratio of the estimate to its standard error was greater than two. To check for significant interaction effects, a likelihood ratio test (LRT) was used; only significant interactions (p > 0.05) were included in the model.

Results

Gait Cycle Descriptors

Wearing the head-mounted camera did not affect any of the gait cycle descriptors nor were there any significant interaction effects between wearing the head-mount and emotion. However, the fixed effect of walker gender was significant for cycle duration ($t = 2.699$) and there were significant differences among emotions (independent of head-mount) for cycle duration and normalized gait velocity.

Joint Angular Kinematics

Wearing the head-mounted camera affected elbow range of motion in anger and content. The elbow flexed $10.3°$ (22.6%) and $12.8°$ (32.3%) less in anger and content, respectively.

Significant gender effects were also observed for some angular measures. To understand these effects we ran a post hoc analysis to determine if there was an interaction between gender and wearing the head-mounted camera. The mean angle of shoulder flexion was reduced less in males ($1.2°$) than in females ($10.2°$) when wearing the HM. However, significant gender effects, independent of wearing the head-mounted camera, were also observed for the mean angles of elbow and hip flexion. Finally, there were significant differences among emotions (independent of head-mount) for most joint angular measures studied.

Discussion

This study evaluated the feasibility of collecting facial and bodily expression data concurrently using a head-mounted video camera and motion capture technology. We tested four aspects of emotion expression that could have been affected by wearing a head-mounted camera, including self-report of emotion, observer recognition of emotion, observer assessment of qualitative aspects of the walkers' body movements, and the quantitative aspects of body movements assessed with a kinematic analysis. We found that wearing a head-mounted camera did not affect emotion elicitation or recognition in regard to self-report and observer recognition of emotion.

Some aspects of the walkers' body movements, assessed either qualitatively or quantitatively, were slightly affected by wearing the head-mounted camera for some emotions. The small differences in movement characteristics associated with wearing the HM are consistent with what might be expected from wearing such a device. The limb shape quality differences corresponded to joint angular differences, particularly in the shoulder and elbow. These results suggest that when wearing the head-mounted camera the walkers held their arms slightly closer to their torso (particularly in females) and they did not move as much at the elbow. This more constrained upper body position is consistent with what we might expect from walkers wearing an unfamiliar device on their head. We conclude that adding a warm up session to help the walkers become more comfortable wearing the head-mounted camera may mitigate these small effects. Additionally, with rapid advances in technology we can also expect that cameras will decrease in both size and weight, thereby reducing this effect.

In the context of whole body interaction, the important point is that capturing expressive signals from the face in conjunction with the body can be done without constraining movement or significantly affecting a participants feelings or expressions. This is critical for applications that require monitoring of both facial and bodily expression. To date, most applications have focused either on the face or the body. Two methods for characterizing bodily expression that have been used in gaming, animation, or human–computer interaction applications are Effort-Shape/Laban analysis [6, 7, 24] and motion capture data [10, 16], both of which were evaluated in the present study. While Effort and Shape have been used to simulate natural looking behavior in animated characters [6, 7], Isbister and DiMauro (see Chap. 6 in this book) used Effort qualities to assess movement mechanics of players during active gaming. They found that in the context of gaming, full body movement was more engaging for participants' resulting in an experience qualified by participants as more fun. This finding demonstrates the potential advantages of using signals from the whole body in a new generation of applications. Beyond the body, however, multimodal signals also provide important nonverbal cues [5, 23]. Thus, a next step is to begin integrating face and body into whole body interaction applications.

Conclusions

Overall, we recommend wearing the head-mounted camera as a valid method during concurrent collection of facial and bodily data. While we recognize that the head-mount may slightly constrain arm movement, the benefits to capturing multimodal data are significant enough that we recommend these methods for future whole body interaction applications.

References

1. Ambadar, Z., Schooler, J.W., Cohn, J.F.: Deciphering the enigmatic face. The importance of facial dynamics in interpreting subtle facial expressions. Psychol. Sci. **16**, 403–410 (2005)
2. Atkinson, A.P., Dittrich, W.H., Gemmell, A.J., Young, A.W.: Emotion perception from dynamic and static body expressions in point-light and full-light displays. Perception **33**, 717–746 (2004)
3. Bachorowski, J.-A.: Vocal expression and perception of emotion. Curr. Dir. Psychol. Sci. **8**, 53–57 (1999)
4. Banse, R., Scherer, K.R.: Acoustic profiles in vocal emotion expression. J. Pers. Soc. Psychol. **70**, 614–636 (1996)

5. Castellano, G. Kessous, L., Caridakis, G.: Emotion recognition through multiple modalities: face, body gesture, speech. In: Peter C., Beale R. (eds.) Affect and Emotion in Human–Computer Interaction, vol. 4868. Springer, Heidelberg (2008)
6. Chi, D.M.: A motion control scheme for animating expressive arm movements. University of Pennsylvania (1999)
7. Chi, D., Costa, M., Zhao, L., Badler, N.: The EMOTE model for effort and shape. In: Proceedings of the 27th annual conference on Computer Graphics and Interactive Techniques, pp. 173–182 (2000)
8. Cohn, J.F., Kanade, T.: Use of automated facial image analysis for measurement of emotion expression. In: Coan, J.A., Allen, J.J.B. (eds.) Handbook of Emotion Elicitation and Assessment, pp. 222–238. Oxford University Press, Oxford (2007)
9. Coulson, M.: Attributing emotion to static body postures: recognition accuracy confusions, and viewpoint dependence. J. Nonverbal Behav. **28**, 117–139 (2004)
10. De Silva, P.R.: Therapeutic tool for develop child nonverbal communication skills through interactive game. In: International Conference on Computational Intelligence for Modelling Control and Automation and International Conference on Intelligent Agents Web Technologies and International Commerce (CIMCA'06), pp. 33–33 (2006)
11. Ekman, P.: Facial expression and emotion. Am. Psychol. **48**, 384–392 (1993)
12. Ekman, P., Friesen, W.V.: The facial action coding system. Consulting Psychologists Press, Palo Alto (1978)
13. Ellgring, H., Scherer, K.: Vocal indicators of mood change in depression. J. Nonverbal Behav. **20**, 83–110 (1996)
14. Gray, E.K., Watson, D.: Assessing positive and negative affect via self-report. In: Coan, J.A., Allen, J.J.B. (eds.) Handbook of Emotion Elicitation and Assessment, pp. 171–183. Oxford University Press, Oxford (2007)
15. Janssen, D., Schöllhorn, W., Lubienetzki, J., Fölling, K., Kokenge, H., Davids, K.: Recognition of emotions in gait patterns by means of artificial neural nets. J. Nonverbal Behav. **32**, 79–92 (2008)
16. Karg, M., Hnlenz, K., Buss, M.: Recognition of affect based on gait patterns, part B: cybernetics. IEEE Trans. Syst. Man Cybern. **40**, 1050–1061 (2010)
17. Labouvie-Vief, G., Lumley, M.A., Jain, E., Heinze, H.: Age and gender differences in cardiac reactivity and subjective emotion responses to emotional autobiographical memories. Emotion **3**, 115–126 (2003)
18. Larsen, R.J., Fredrickson, B.L.: Measurement issues in emotion research. In: Kahneman, D., Diener, E., Schwarz, N. (eds.) Well-Being: The Foundations of Hedonic Psychology. Russell Sage, New York (1999)
19. Levenson, R., Cartensen, L., Friesen, W., Ekman, P.: Emotion, physiology and expression in old age. Psychol. Aging **6**, 28–35 (1991)
20. Montepare, J., Goldstein, S.B., Clausen, A.: The identification of emotions from gait information. J. Nonverbal Behav. **11**, 33–42 (1987)
21. Pollick, F.E., Paterson, H.M., Bruderlin, A., Sanford, A.J.: Perceiving affect from arm movement. Cognition **82**, B51–B61 (2001)
22. Scherer, K., Ellgring, H.: Are facial expressions of emotion produced by categorical affect programs or dynamically driven by appraisal? Emotion **7**, 113–130 (2007)
23. Scherer, K., Ellgring, H.: Multimodal expression of emotion: affect programs or componential appraisal patterns? Emotion **7**, 158–171 (2007)
24. Torresani, L., Hackney, P., Bregler, C.: Learning motion style synthesis from perceptual observations. In: Conference Proceedings of Neural Information Processing Systems, Vancouver (2007)
25. Vural, E., Cetin, M., Ercil, A., Littlewort, G. Bartlett, M., Movellan, J.: Drowsy driver detection through facial movement analysis. In: ICCV Workshop on Human Computer Interaction Rio de Janeiro, Brazil (2007)
26. Wallbott, H.G.: Bodily expression of emotion. Eur. J. Soc. Psychol. **28**, 879–896 (1998)
27. Zhan, C., Li, W., Ogunbona, P., Safaei, F.: A real-time facial expression recognition system for online games. Int. J. Comput. Game. Technol. **2008**, 7 (2008)

Chapter 13
Body Gestures for Office Desk Scenarios

**Radu-Daniel Vatavu, Ovidiu-Ciprian Ungurean,
and Stefan-Gheorghe Pentiuc**

Abstract Gestures have been used in interfaces within a large variety of scenarios: from mobile users that interact with their smart phones by using touch gestures up to the most recent game technology that acquires 3D movements of the whole player's body. Different contexts lead to different acquisition technologies, gesture vocabularies, and applications. We discuss in this chapter gesture-based interfaces for office desk scenarios by taking into account the constraints of the workspace that limit the available range of body motions. The focus is therefore on hands and head movements captured using non invasive computer vision techniques. We review existing works in order to spot common findings and designs for such a working scenario as well as to understand how gestures can fit into the everyday office desk environment. Several application scenarios are discussed by considering criteria such as the intuitiveness, ease-of-use, and the similarity of proposed interactions with real-world actions.

Introduction

Over the past decades, we have witnessed a growth of interest from both the research and industry communities for technologies, devices, and techniques that would make natural interactions accessible and reachable to an increasingly large audience of consumers. This enthusiastic interest led to technological advances which made natural interaction stand out as a new field of research with great opportunities to offer. As a result, many technologies are available today for capturing and recognizing body motions at various rates and resolutions [2, 8, 13, 16, 19, 20, 25, 28, 29]. Such interfaces designed to recognize the natural body movements and interpret the gestures of their users are being perceived as *ideal* by general media as they resemble and imitate everyday interactions. However, important

R.-D. Vatavu (✉), O.-C. Ungurean, and S.-G. Pentiuc
University Stefan cel Mare of Suceava, 720229 Suceava, Romania
e-mail: vatavu@eed.usv.ro; ungurean.ovidiu@gmail.com; pentiuc@eed.usv.ro

D. England (ed.), *Whole Body Interaction*, Human-Computer Interaction Series,
DOI 10.1007/978-0-85729-433-3_13, © Springer-Verlag London Limited 2011

questions must be raised and properly addressed on how such technology should be implemented and used in order to compete with the mouse and keyboard input devices on the same comparison term of efficiency.

This chapter is organized around today's most predominant scenario for interacting with computers: home and office environments with desktop PCs equipped with standard mice and keyboards. We are definitely seeing many computing trends today that are moving away from this rather static scenario. Personal computing on smart mobile devices is just one example of changing users' computing habits in an irreversible manner [9] leading towards a more complex-to-define ubiquitous computing. In order to support such transition, advanced systems that can sense, acquire, and interpret complex data and movement patterns have already proved to function well [16, 19]. While these changes in computing habits are highly visible today, the fact remains that desktop PCs with standard interfacing equipments still represent the most commonly encountered computing scenario. We therefore investigate in this chapter techniques which are meant to enhance interaction at the desktop. The goal of this pursuit is not to completely and definitely replace the mouse and keyboard but rather to enhance the interactions achieved using these input devices. The greater motivation is to design fluent, intuitive, and easy to use interfaces as development objectives of natural interaction.

Understanding Current Interaction Practices at the Office Desk: Ergonomics and Input Devices vs. Natural Interaction

Several limitations and constraints arise when trying to use body motions interactions for office desk scenarios. They are induced by the working position which reduces considerably the motions that can be captured and used efficiently. Directly put, the seated position limits body motions to gestures performed by head and hands in the immediate space above the desk. It is important to insist on the fact that all the interaction takes place from the seated position: the users are seated on their chairs in front of their desks looking at the computer monitors. We therefore continue our discussion with observations that come from research in ergonomics where vast materials do exist that address seating and desk postures; we look at the available interaction devices that are already present in the desk scenario such as mice and keyboards and report on research that tries to combine them with gestures; and, we finally address the advantages but also mention the current limitations of the non-intrusive technology of video processing.

Desk Ergonomics

The ergonomic aspects of the user's working position have been very much dealt with in the specialized literature with results that suggest correct body postures and office equipments placement [7, 34] but that also inform the design of ergonomic office furniture [21].

While looking at the ergonomic research, it is interesting to note that the simple act of sitting involves both micro body movements for maintaining balance and position changes as well as macro movements which involve the arms and legs. Seating for long periods of time is not natural as stress and tension affect the body and particularly the lumbar area and the back spine. With this respect,

> the only truly effective way to maintain a seated posture for extended durations is to continuously cycle through a range of natural, centered and healthful positions

as concluded by Lueder [14]. This observation is particularly interesting to gesture-based interaction at the office desk as it motivates, at some different level than before, the introduction of gestures into the interface. However, particular attention must be adopted so that the design would incorporate gestures that are indeed easy to use, easy to perform and that do not give rise to execution stress (Nielsen et al. [17] describe procedures for identifying gestures that would have such desiderates).

Ergonomics equally deals with designing for safety hence any inclusion of gesture movements that may affect the balance of the seating position needs be dealt with carefully. For example, active involvement during a video game could require the use of large amplitude arm or head movements with the attention primarily directed to the game rather to one's real environment. Such safety issues need to be considered seriously – see for example the Health and Safety Precautions that accompany the Wii Remote.[1] They deal with play area precautions (as there should be a safely amount of room around the player), motion sickness, and repetitive motion injuries among others.

Gestures vs. Mouse and Keyboard

Due to their extensive and exclusive use, the mouse and keyboard make gestures appear as occasional and complementary forms of interaction, at least for the moment. And this considering the fact that the design of the computer mouse has remained practically unchanged since its invention more than 40 years ago [6]. With the current interaction metaphors that include pointing, windows, and menus, it is very hard to change the existing software in order to accommodate for gesture input which comes with its own interaction techniques as well. It seems more plausible therefore that a combination between mouse, keyboard, and gestures is more likely to appear as an intermediate step. With this respect, previous works have been considering combining the mouse design with gesture-based commands in the form of enhanced mice. The 4DOF Rockin' Mouse of Balakrishnan et al. [1] that allows tilting or the 6DOF VideoMouse of Hinckley et al. [8] incorporating a video camera are such examples. Villar et al. [29] introduced several input devices that

---

[1] http://www.nintendo.com/consumer/wiisafety.jsp

combine the standard mouse with multi-touch sensing in order to augment traditional pointer-based interactions. They implement and discuss multiple prototypes in order to investigate on touch sensing strategies, form factors, and interactive opportunities.

Within the same idea of combining existing devices with gesture commands, Dietz et al. [5] introduced a pressure sensitive keyboard that is able to sense the force level of each key. The authors suggest application opportunities in gaming, emotional instant messaging, and enhanced typing. The Touch-Display-Keyboard of Block et al. [2] combines a traditional keyboard with touch-sensing and graphics display on each key. The authors propose and demonstrate new interaction techniques that accommodate the new enhanced keyboard.

Gestures as Commands

When discussing interactive gestures, a clear distinction must be made between gestures and commands where gestures resemble real-world actions and movements that maintain their exact meaning and signification during interaction with the computer (i.e. they are *natural*) while gesture commands are mainly used as shortcuts (they are *artificially created*). Vatavu and Pentiuc [26] investigated the various forms and representations that gesture commands posses at various levels for human–computer interaction by performing an analysis on postures and motions. The authors provide a classification of commands into four distinct categories with regards to their structural pattern or, equivalently, the amount of posture/motion information needed for performing the command: static simple, static generalized, dynamic simple, and dynamic generalized commands. The classification builds from a single posture to a complex command including both dynamics and varying postures.

Computer Vision at the Desk

Computer vision has developed from its early days into an accessible technology that gives good results in practice. Important advances have been reported with respect to image processing techniques while the increase of desktop computing power allowed many algorithms to become real-time. There are still important challenges the community is facing such as perfect segmentation, robust tracking, understanding contexts, and, on top of all, performing all these complex computations in real time. However, many algorithms exist that work reasonably well for interactive purposes at real time rates. Web cameras are available for purchasing at low prices which greatly expanded the use of computer vision techniques outside their specific community. Cameras are usually installed on the top of the computer monitor facing users for instant messaging and video chat applications but this scenario has also been exploited for gesture-based interaction [22]. Video cameras may be installed face down in order to capture the movements of the hands above the desk [27, 28, 31]. They were also hidden inside the desk transforming its surface into an interactive computing medium [4, 30, 32].

The great advantages of using video-based processing are represented by flexibility and unobtrusiveness of the interaction: users are not being required to wear additional equipments or devices for their motions to be captured. However, several drawbacks are present when using vision technology with the most challenging ones being the dependency on the environment such as lighting conditions and noise motions next to high computing demands. It is important to stress that, when used wisely and appropriately (i.e. focus on the scenario), computer vision will give very good results. We further investigate aspects on capturing hand and head movements with focus on the most commonly used techniques in vision processing.

Capturing Hands and Head Movements

The desktop scenario allows hands and head movements to be exploited at their maximum capacity. As in the real world, hands are used to point and manipulate objects. Considering the specific camera installations, hands are captured while moving in the horizontal plane of the keyboard and in the vertical plane in front of the screen. The users' hands can be detected and tracked with algorithms that use color processing such as skin filtering [10] or by tracking key-features [12]. Mixed approaches usually improve the robustness of the acquisition process. There are cases when tracking the color of the skin fails hence the scenario must be controlled more rigorously. With this respect, colored gloves have been employed in order to attain better segmentation results [33]. However, as is the case of virtual reality sensor gloves, they trade user comfort for acquisition precision and robustness.

Many interaction possibilities are available once the hands are being accurately captured and tracked. The simplest scenario is to use the dominant hand as the cursor while specific gestures or postures simulate mouse click events [31]. More complex interactions can be designed by employing both hands which work together in order to perform objects manipulations similar to actions in the real world [28]. When comparing hands-based interaction for pointing and manipulation with the techniques designed for mouse input, a definite advantage is represented by the extra degrees of freedom of five fingers per hand as well as the benefit of having two manipulation points over the single interaction point provided by the mouse [28, 31]. However, these extra degrees of freedom require special interaction techniques to be designed.

Head movements have been exploited in natural interfaces for indicating viewing direction with great opportunity demonstrated for video games. Detecting the movements of the head may be achieved using simple threshold-based rules on the directional axis once the user's face has been detected. Techniques based on motion flow analysis have also been found popular in order to detect such changes in head movement direction [3]. The common application is to map these movements to the cursor [18] or to include them into specific controlling metaphors such as changing the camera view in a FPS game [22].

Applying Natural Interaction to Practical Scenarios: Interacting with Gestures from the Desk

We continue by discussing several interactive opportunities that are immediately available for hands and head movements. Some of them have proved their success in the literature or commercial applications (especially head tracking for gaming) while others are in still need of improvements with regards to acquisition accuracy, robustness, or interaction metaphors before they achieve desired levels of task performance.

Simple techniques can be used in order to achieve interactions that feel natural. For example, GUI objects can be manipulated using two hand postures (*point* and *pinch*) that, when combined, allow for a wide range of interactions. Even more, postures can be mixed with hand motions in order to add extra meaning (e.g. command parameters) to the users' inputs [24, 27, 28]. It is important to note that the main goal is not to replace the mouse and keyboard but to make use of complementary interactions that would feel right (natural) for some tasks. For example, an object can be naturally rotated using two hands which control its main axis of rotation. This manipulation operation is more intuitive in both perceived experience as well as input parameters (the relative angle between the hands corresponds to the angle by which the object is rotated). The same principle can be applied for resizing the object but with a stretch in imagination when comparing the operation to the real world. However, gestures may not be appropriate to control other parameters such as the object color, texture, or other settings (e.g. what gestures could be designed for changing the color of an object?) for which the keyboard is perfect to enter text and numbers. Wilson et al. [31] demonstrated the use of pinch gestures with a novel detection technique for the pinch posture that allows various manipulations to be performed using one or two hands. Also, Malik and Laszlo [15] demonstrated in their Visual Touchpad several one and two-handed multi-finger interaction techniques.

Head rotations can be easily mapped to cursor movements in order to control the four NESW directions. Tilting the head to either left or right is another event that can be detected rather easily and which can be used to simulate left and right clicks [18]. Lee [13] introduced innovatory ways for performing head tracking by using the Wii Remote and the IR video camera it contains. After attaching two IR LEDs to a pair of goggles, the remote may be used in order to track the user's motions in three dimensions. Tracking head movements has been found to support enhanced gaming experiences [22]. The perceived realism of the game is considerably increased as the viewpoint of the scene follows the movements of the user's head.

Besides head motions, eyes tracking has been used for pointing tasks although stability issues and inaccuracies are still present. However, special interaction techniques have been developed in order to better control the cursor trajectories [20, 36]. It is interesting to note here that nose tracking has been explored as well [35].

For some interactive tasks, gesture commands are either not appropriate or are not providing enough *naturalness* by themselves. This is generally caused by the lack of haptic feedback of free hand interaction in opposition to what actually happens in the real-world (even if the same hand postures are being used to replicate real-world interactions, actual tangible manipulations are missing in free hand movements). For this purpose, interaction at the desk can be further enhanced beyond gesture commands by employing various objects. Such objects are detected on the surface of the desk and can be transformed into virtual graphical elements for which the behavior depends on the context of use. Graphic user elements can become tangible while the intermediate objects create the mapping between real and virtual. This concept was demonstrated for computer games by allowing users to control the context of the action [27]. Techniques such as background subtraction combined with motion tracking and color processing can be used to detect where such objects are located and how did they move. Also, objects can be identified and recognized by using visual markers [11]. In the same idea of tangibles, Van Laerhoven et al. [23] demonstrate various interaction tasks using a custom designed sensing cube.

Hands and head motions prove suited for several office desk tasks. What can be found from practical experiences is that simplifying the scene as much as possible assures good accuracies of computer vision algorithms. The littlest thing to do is to assure a minimum contrast between the desk and the skin color. If the desk does not permit it, black mouse pads usually suffice to create a contrast which is a more than enough for threshold based algorithms to segment the hand reasonably well. We also found that there is no need for a wide range of hand postures to be recognized: most interactions can be achieved using postures such as *point* (the index finger is stretched) and *pinch* (the index and thumb fingers touching). The way hands position themselves one with respect to the other as well as the distance between the hands should be exploited in order to add parameters when performing gesture commands. We found users to accommodate rather easily with head movements. They appreciated the techniques as easy to use after practice. However, in many cases they reported fatigue when required to perform precision movements after a long period of usage. Using direct head commands (vs. monitoring head activity) is a matter of concern with respect to fatigue and such motions should be carefully considered.

Conclusions

The chapter presented an exploration of gesture-based interfaces by clearly delimiting the usage scenario: interactions that are appropriate for office desks. We conducted an investigation on hands and head movements as they were found to work in the literature and presented practical lessons that were learned while developing such systems. An important lesson is that the scenario of use must be carefully analyzed so that it can be exploited by the application designer. With this respect, intuitive gestures that do not come to replace but rather to complement the interactions performed via the mouse and keyboard have been proposed and application opportunities discussed. It is worthwhile exploring further the possibilities that desk scenarios expose for gesture-based interfaces. Also, it may be interesting to understand how the inclusion of gestures into the interface may impact the ergonomic aspects of desk work.

Video demonstrations of various interaction techniques such as object manipulation, motion gesture recognition, head tracking, and head motion detection as well as application studies are available for viewing and download at http://www.eed. usv.ro/~vatavu.

Acknowledgments This paper was supported by the project "Progress and development through post-doctoral research and innovation in engineering and applied sciences- PRiDE - Contract no. POSDRU/89/1.5/S/57083", project co-funded from European Social Fund through Sectorial Operational Program Human Resources 2007–2013.

References

1. Balakrishnan, R., Baudel, T., Kurtenbach, G., Fitzmaurice, G.: The rockin' mouse: integral 3D manipulation on a plane. In: Pemberton, S. (ed.) Proceedings of the SIGCHI Conference on Human Factors in Computing Systems, Atlanta, 22–27 March 1997, CHI '97, pp. 311–318. ACM, New York (1997)
2. Block, F., Gellersen, H., Villar, N.: Touch-display keyboards: transforming keyboards into interactive surfaces. In: Proceedings of the 28th International Conference on Human Factors in Computing Systems, Atlanta, 10–15 April 2010, CHI '10, pp. 1145–1154. ACM, New York (2010)
3. Bradski, G.R., Davis, J.W.: Motion segmentation and pose recognition with motion history gradients. Mach. Vis. Appl. **13**, 174–184 (2002)
4. Cao, X., Wilson, A., Balakrishnan, R., Hinckley, K., Hudson, S.: Shapetouch: leveraging contact shape on interactive surfaces. In: Proceedings of the 3rd IEEE International Workshop on Horizontal Interactive Human-Computer Systems (Tabletop 2008), Amsterdam, 1–3 October 2008
5. Dietz, P.H., Eidelson, B., Westhues, J., Bathiche, S.: A practical pressure sensitive computer keyboard. In: Proceedings of the 22nd Annual ACM Symposium on User Interface Software and Technology, Victoria 04–07 October 2009, UIST '09. ACM,(2009)
6. Engelbart, D.C., William, K.: English, a research center for augmenting human intellect. In: AFIPS conference proceedings of the 1968 Fall Joint Computer Conference, San Francisco, December 1968, Vol. 33, pp. 395–410 (1968). http://sloan.stanford.edu/mousesite/Archive/ ResearchCenter1968/ResearchCenter1968.html
7. Grandjean, E.: Ergonomics In Computerized Offices. Taylor & Francis, London (1987)
8. Hinckley, K., Sinclair, M., Hanson, E., Szeliski, R., Conway, M.: The videomouse: a camera-based multi-degree-of-freedom input device. In: Proceedings of the 12th annual ACM symposium on User Interface Software and Technology, Asheville, 07–10 November 1999, UIST '99, pp. 103–112. ACM, New York (1999)
9. Hong, S., Thong, J.Y., Moon, J., Tam, K.: Understanding the behavior of mobile data services consumers. Inf. Syst. Front. **10**(4), 431–445 (2008)

10. Jones, M.J., Rehg, J.M.: Statistical color models with application to skin detection. Technical Report 98/11, Cambridge Research Laboratory (1998)
11. Kato, H., Billinghurst, M.: Developing AR applications with ARToolKit. In: Proceedings of the 3rd IEEE/ACM International Symposium on Mixed and Augmented Reality (ISMAR'04), 02–05 November 2004, p. 305. IEEE Computer Society, Washington, DC (2004)
12. Kolsch, M., Turk, M.: Fast 2d hand tracking with flocks of features and multi-cue integration. In: Proceedings of the IEEE Workshop on Real-Time Vision for Human–Computer Interaction. IEEE Computer Society Conference on Computer Vision and Pattern Recognition, IEEE (2004)
13. Lee, J.C.: Hacking the nintendo wii remote. IEEE Pervasive Comput. **7**(3), 39–45 (2008)
14. Lueder, R.: Ergonomics of seated movement. A review of the scientific literature. Humanics ErgoSystems, Inc. http://www.allsteeloffice.com/NR/rdonlyres/7D516676-DEBB-4203-8D5D-BAF337556B46/0/SUM_Ergo_Review_RaniLueder.pdf (2008)
15. Malik, S., Laszlo, J.: Visual touchpad: a two-handed gestural input device. In: Proceedings of the 6th International Conference on Multimodal Interfaces, State College, 13–15 October 2004, ICMI '04, pp. 289–296. ACM, New York (2004)
16. Moeslund, T.B., Hilton, A., Krüger, V.: A survey of advances in vision-based human motion capture and analysis. Comput. Vis. Image Underst. **104**(2), 90–126 (2006)
17. Nielsen, M., Storring, M., Moeslund, T.B., Granum, E.: A procedure for developing intuitive and ergonomic gesture interfaces for HCI. In: Proceedings of GW'2003: Gesture-Based Communication in Human–Computer Interaction. Lecture Notes in Computer Science, vol. 2915, pp. 409–420. Springer, Berlin (2003)
18. Pentiuc, S.G., Vatavu, R.D., Ungurean, C.O., Cerlinca, T.I.: Techniques for interacting by gestures with information systems. In: Proceedings of the European Conference on the Use of Modern Information and Communication Technologies (ECUMICT '08), Gent, 14–18 March 2008
19. Poppe, R.: Vision-based human motion analysis: an overview. Comput. Vis. Image Underst. **108**(1–2), 4–18 (2007)
20. Porta, M., Ravarelli, A., Spagnoli, G.: ceCursor, a contextual eye cursor for general pointing in windows environments. In: Proceedings of the 2010 Symposium on Eye-Tracking Research & Applications, Austin, 22–24 March 2010, ETRA '10. ACM, New York (2010)
21. Springer, T.: The future of ergonomic office seating. Knoll Workplace Research, Knoll Inc. http://www.knoll.com/research/downloads/wp_future_ergonomic_seating.pdf (2010)
22. Ungurean, C.O., Pentiuc, S.G., Vatavu, R.D.: Use your head: an interface for computer games using head gestures. In: Proceedings of the 8th International Gesture Workshop (GW'09), Gesture in Embodied Communication and Human–Computer Interaction, Bielefeld (2009)
23. Van Laerhoven, K., Villar, N., Schmidt, A., Kortuem, G., Gellersen, H.: Using an autonomous cube for basic navigation and input. In: Proceedings of the 5th International Conference on Multimodal interfaces (ICMI '03), Vancouver, 05–07 November 2003, pp. 203–210. ACM, New York (2003)
24. Vatavu, R.D., Grisoni, L., Pentiuc, S.G.: Gesture recognition based on elastic deformation energies. In: Dias, M.S., Gibet, S., Wanderley, M.M. Bastos, R. (eds) Gesture-Based Human–Computer Interaction and Simulation, Lecture Notes in Computer Science, vol. 5085, pp. 1–12. Springer, Berlin (2009)
25. Vatavu, R.D., Grisoni, L., Pentiuc, S.G.: Multiscale detection of gesture patterns in continuous motion trajectories. In: Kopp, S., Wachsmuth, I. (eds) Gesture in Embodied Communication and Human–Computer Interaction, Lecture Notes in Computer Science, vol. 5934, pp. 85–97. Springer, Berlin/Heidelberg (2010)
26. Vatavu, R.D., Pentiuc, S.G.: Multi-level representation of gesture as command for human–computer interaction. Comput. Inform. **27**(6), 837–851 (2008). Slovak Academy of Sciences, Bratislava
27. Vatavu, R.D., Pentiuc, S.G., Cerlinca, T.I.: Bringing context into play: supporting game interaction through real-time context acquisition. In: Proceedings of the Workshop on Multimodal Interfaces in Semantic Interaction at ICMI 2007 (WMISI'07), Nagoya, 15 November 2007, pp. 3–8. ACM, New York (2007)

28. Vatavu R.D., Pentiuc, S.G., Chaillou, C., Grisoni, L., Degrande, S.: Visual recognition of hand postures for interacting with virtual environments. In: Proceedings of the 8th International Conference on Development and Application Systems (DAS'06), Suceava, , pp. 477–482 (2006)
29. Villar, N., Izadi, S., Rosenfeld, D., Benko, H., Helmes, J., Westhues, J., Hodges, S., Ofek, E., Butler, A., Cao, X., Chen, B.: Mouse 2.0: multi-touch meets the mouse. In: Proceedings of the 22nd Annual ACM Symposium on User Interface Software and Technology, Victoria, 04–07 October 2009, UIST '09, pp. 33–42. ACM, New York (2009)
30. Wigdor, D., Leigh, D., Forlines, C., Shipman, S., Barnwell, J., Balakrishnan, R., Shen, C.: Under the table interaction. In: Proceedings of the 19th Annual ACM Symposium on User Interface Software and Technology (UIST '06), Montreux, 15–18 October 2006, pp. 259–268. ACM, New York (2006)
31. Wilson, A.: Robust vision-based detection of pinching for one and two-handed gesture input. In: Proceedings of the 19th Symposium on User Interface Software and Technology (UIST '06), Montreux, 15–18 October 2006, pp. 255–258. ACM Press, New York (2006)
32. Wilson, A. D., Izadi, S., Hilliges, O., Garcia-Mendoza, A., Kirk, D.: Bringing physics to the surface. In: Proceedings of the 21st Annual ACM Symposium on User Interface Software and Technology (UIST '08), Monterey, 19–22 October 2008, pp. 67–76. ACM, New York (2008)
33. Wang, R.Y., Popovic', J.: Real-time hand-tracking with a color glove. In: Hoppe, H. (ed.) ACM SIGGRAPH 2009 Papers, New Orleans, 03–07 August 2009, pp. 1–8. ACM, New York (2009)
34. Zhang, L., Helander, M.G., Drury, C.G.: Identifying factors of comfort and discomfort in sitting. Hum. Factors **38**(3), 377–389 (1996)
35. Zhang, L., Zhou, F., Li, W., Yang, X.: Human–computer interaction system based on nose tracking. In: Proceedings of the 12th International Conference on Human–Computer Interaction: Intelligent Multimodal Interaction Environments, Beijing, 22–27 July 2007, Lecture Notes in Computer Science, pp. 769–778. Springer, Berlin (2007)
36. Zhang, X., Ren, X., Zha, H.: Improving eye cursor's stability for eye pointing tasks. In: Proceeding of the Twenty-Sixth Annual SIGCHI Conference on Human Factors in Computing Systems, Florence, 05–10 April 2008, CHI '08, pp. 525–534. ACM, New York (2008)

Chapter 14
Gesture-Based Interfaces: Practical Applications of Gestures in Real World Mobile Settings

Julie Rico, Andrew Crossan, and Stephen Brewster

Abstract In the past, the design of gesture-based interfaces has focused on issues of gesture recognition with consideration of social or practical factors that affect the ability of users to perform gestures on the go largely missing. This work describes two important aspects of gestures design for mobile gesture and body-based interaction. First, this paper discusses the social acceptability of using gesture-based interfaces in the variety of locations where mobile interfaces are used. This includes a discussion of a variety of methods that can be used to evaluate social acceptability early on in the development process. Second, this paper discusses the practical implications of creating gesture recognition using accelerometer based sensing given the challenges of gesturing in mobile situations. This includes a discussion of body-based interactions and the scenarios where these might be used successfully.

Introduction

Although gesture-based interfaces have become a popular topic for research since the success of the "Put-That-There" system in 1980 [1], gestures have not seen successful widespread use. Even though many smart phones now have the capabilities, through accelerometer based sensing, to recognize gestures, users seem unwilling to accept gesture-based interactions outside of the gaming or novelty applications. This paper discusses some reasons for this, including the social acceptability of gesturing in public and the practical implications of using gestures as part of a mobile interface.

J. Rico (✉), A. Crossan, and S. Brewster
Glasgow Interactive Systems Group, School of Computing Science,
University of Glasgow, G12 8QQ Glasgow, UK
e-mail: julie@dcs.gla.ac.uk; ac@dcs.gla.ac.uk; stephen@dcs.gla.ac.uk

D. England (ed.), *Whole Body Interaction*, Human-Computer Interaction Series,
DOI 10.1007/978-0-85729-433-3_14, © Springer-Verlag London Limited 2011

Understanding Gestures

The use of gestures in interfaces has ranged widely from conversational interfaces with speech and gestures used together to interfaces using arbitrary gestures languages. However, when thinking about using gestures as part of an interface, it is important to consider what is being considered as a gesture, and what aspects of the working definition are important to the interface being designed. Although there is no clear or widely accepted definition of 'gesture,' the scope of gestures chosen for an interface has clear implications to the kinds of interactions that interface will facilitate. The following definitions of gesture seek to explore these issues.

Kendon gives a general definition of gestures as voluntary and expressive movements of the body [10]. Kendon's definition of gesture includes what would commonly be thought of as "conversational" gestures, but does not provide guidance in determining which gestures belong to this set. Specifically, this definition fails to address how context, perception, meaning, and relationship to speech affect how an action is identified as a gesture. Kendon does discuss the role that perception plays into determining whether a given action is a gesture [11] even though this isn't included in his definition. Kendon states that individuals are able to understand gestures and identify expressive intent simply by watching how the action is performed. This results in the circular definition that a gesture is simply an action that is considered a gesture by others. This kind of definition is even less helpful than others in determining what is a gesture. In order to narrow down the definition of gesture, Kendon's work only considers those gestures that are used along with speech and are perceived by observers as part of the meaning of the speech. Accidental gestures and fidgeting are not included in his analysis. This difference between the general definition of gestures and the applied definition gesture can be seen in many of the following examples.

Cassell defines gestures as hand movements occur during speech [2] although she criticizes this limited definition. Cassell states that many systems that use gesture recognition focus on "gesture languages" rather than gestures that naturally occur with speech. However, she goes on to state that the communicative elements of gestures that occur with speech are important elements needed to create natural user interfaces. Väänänen and Böhm define gestures as "body movements which are used to convey some kind of information from one person to another" [17]. This definition is then further refined, including that information conveyed by gestures is easily understood by observers yet vague and implicit in nature. For example, an individual might use a gesture alongside the speech "I only want a little bit a milk in my coffee." The gesture will communicate that a small amount of milk is desired, but does not say how much is considered "a little bit" by the speaker. For the purpose of their system, Väänänen and Böhm highlight that gestures used in human computer interfaces must have defined meanings, which is in direct opposition with gestures as they are used in daily life. In order to accommodate the technical restrictions of their gesture-based interface, a limited definition of gestures is used.

For the final system, a set of postures is implemented in place of more fluid or natural gestures. These hand positions included finger pointing, an open palm, and fist. While they are easy to perform movements, they are arbitrary movements and fall short of the original definition that revolved around information exchange.

A major issue with gesture definition is the difference between "conversational gestures" that occur naturally with speech and "gesture languages" that are commonly used in gesture-based systems [19]. Gesture systems such as the general use hand pose recognition system [20] describe a gesture language that can used to define gestures for an interface. These gestures, however, would not fall into the everyday meaning of the term "gesture" but rather a "gesture system." For example, Clara Rockmore's "aerial positions" for playing the Theremin might be considered gestures using one of the above definitions, but this is more like a gesture system in that it is a set of hand positions used in a formally structured manner. These gesture systems might better describe how gestures are used in computing science, but this definition might take away the natural interaction that gestures originally sought to provide [18]. Some researchers argue that gestures cannot be examined without the linguistic context where they occur [12], but multimodal systems have both incorporated speech [1] and used gestures on their own [9]. Since speech plays a significant role in individuals' understanding of gesture meanings [6], using gestures without speech could in some cases remove any natural or cognitive advantages that gestures might have over other forms of communication. Because of this, system designers must carefully evaluate their applied definition of gesture to ensure they are not stripping away the benefits of using gesture.

Gestures and Social Acceptability

Previous work in multimodal interaction has mainly revolved around issues in recognition and detection, as well as advancements in sensing technologies. However, in order to design multimodal interfaces to provide a satisfying and enjoyable experience, interface designers must also consider the social acceptability of using these interfaces in public spaces. This is not simply an issue of "acceptable" or "unacceptable," but a dynamic decision process that occurs in different social contexts at different stages of experience.

Our previous work in understanding social acceptable has utilized a variety of methods, including surveys [15], on-the-street user studies [15], experience prototyping and focus groups [16]. The on-the-street study required participants to perform a set of gestures in both a public outdoor setting and a private indoor setting over three repeated trials. The gestures were selected from a previous survey study to include both highly acceptable and unacceptable gestures. Multiple trials were completed to test the survey results over time, and observe if and how participants' opinions of the gestures changed. The results of this study showed there were significant changes in opinion over time, and also gave insights into the reasons why individuals liked or disliked gestures. The next study involved a survey that incorporated both gesture and voice commands. For the purpose of this survey, a categorization of gestures and voice commands was developed. The survey asked respondents to imagine different situations where they might use a gesture and voice command, giving clear scenarios including the location and audience. The results of this survey showed how gesture and voice ranked, with gestures being more accepted overall than voice commands. This survey also showed the affect that different audiences in the same locations have on social acceptability. This survey was followed by a focus group study, which expanded the gesture and voice lists and used a variety of low-cost prototypes developed for the groups. Participants were also grouped into separate age categories, with groups including participants aged 18–29 and groups including participants age 70–95. The results of this study demonstrated how participants imagined these interfaces working in the real world, and what anxieties they had about using them. This also showed an important difference in the way that older adults approached the gesture and voice commands as compared to the younger adults, resulting in different preferences and different concerns. In each of these studies, the importance of early evaluation and methods for evaluating large sets of gestures at low cost has been emphasized. The importance of gesture selection and evaluation before development can lead to more usable and enjoyable interfaces overall.

Although gestures can provide a rich interaction experience, using gestures in the context of an interface poses challenges. Researchers argue that gestures cannot be examined outside of the context of speech, yet they are used this way in many multimodal interfaces. The gestures commonly used in multimodal interfaces are often sets of arbitrary hand positions designed for the system, rather than something resembling our everyday conversational gestures. While this issue may occur due to technological constraints, it is also due to an incomplete understanding of how users understand and adopt gestures as part of an interface.

Social Acceptability and Gesture-Based Interfaces

Because gesture-based interfaces require users to adopt new and possibly strange behaviors in public spaces, the design of gestures used in these interfaces must take into account the possible meanings that gestures might have when used in this context and the social acceptability of performing that gesture in social settings. This means that designers must understand a variety of factors that influence the way that gestures will be used, including issues of performance, the influence of spectators, and the ways in which technology influences gesturing. These factors each contribute to an overall concept of social acceptability, where the acceptability of a certain action is being constantly evaluated and reevaluated by the performer given continuous feedback from spectators. Thus, social acceptability is not simply a matter of acceptable or unacceptable, but an ongoing decision process.

Performance

Goffman describes every action that takes place in a public setting as a performance [1], and as mobile phones become increasingly integrated into our personal appearance, mobile phone usage becomes a performance. The variety of places where mobile interfaces are used means that performances are constantly changing and being reevaluated. With respect to gesture-based interfaces, the performative aspects of these interactions are accentuated given the often highly visible nature of these interactions. The required performance of a given gestures varies both on the gesture itself and the performer perceptions of that gesture. Evaluations of performance and perceptions of gestures can be done early in the development process through the use of surveys and video prototypes. Our previous work using surveys to evaluate social acceptability based on visual aspects of the gestures and the places they might be used proved a valuable evaluation tool [15].

User Experience and Spectators

Although the exact scope and definition of user experience is still debated, it is clear that an understanding of an individual's thoughts, feelings and reactions to an interface are important factors that designers must consider [13]. With respect to gesture-based interaction, an understanding of the user experience of these interactions is especially important because these interactions often require users to try new and possibly unfamiliar actions. The experience of using an interface develops and changes over time as the user is continually exposed to the interaction and experiences it in different settings with different people. User experience, however, is essentially an individual experience [13]. Although other people and spectators heavily influence the social context where an interaction takes place, the decision to interact and the experience of doing so is a personal and individual experience.

Because mobile phones are commonly used in public settings, the presence of spectators and the performative aspects of multimodal interactions play an important role in user acceptance. Following from Goffman's assertion that all actions done in a public setting are performances [8], the performance of an interaction with a mobile device can range from unconscious, automatic actions to explicit and deliberate performance on a stage. The presence of spectators and their affect on the performers has a major influence on the type of interaction the performer will experience [14]. Because of this, performer and spectator roles should play an important part in the design of multimodal mobile interfaces and the evaluation of social acceptability. Early evaluations involving user experience can be completed using low-cost prototypes in focus group settings [16]. The prototypes used in this study allowed uses to experience different gestures and voice commands without the need for sophisticated systems. The simple prototypes also allowed for a large number of interaction techniques to be tested at once. An on-the-street study also allows for early evaluations of social acceptability that take into account the affects which spectators have an evaluations of social acceptability [15].

Technology and Social Acceptability

When individuals imagine the experience of performing gestures in public places, the role that technology plays in facilitating or obstructing an interaction plays an important role in how acceptable a certain interaction will be. In particular, failure scenarios, even when simply imagined rather than experienced, are enough to make an action unacceptable if the user perceives that these failures are likely to occur or likely to cause embarrassment. For example, our previous work shows that users were concerned that an interface would be unable to successfully recognize inputs, results in repeated and increasingly erratic motions to successfully complete a gesture [16]. While the error could happen to any gesture, errors executing a foot tap versus a shrug would lead to very different behaviors. Users were also concerned about the possibility of false positive recognitions by a system, and those gestures that users felt they were more likely to perform 'by accident' were less acceptable [16]. These issues can be discussed even when sophisticated sensing and technology is not part of a user evaluation. In our previous focus group study, participants brought up these issues and anxieties when presented with a variety of low-tech prototypes that portray the devices and sensors that would be part of an interface [16].

Social Acceptability

Individuals make decisions about the social acceptability of their actions by gathering information about their current surroundings and using their existing knowledge [8]. Appropriate actions are then carried out and feedback is gathered through the reactions of observers. The process of experiencing an interface and determining the social acceptability of performing is an ongoing process that changes over time. The social acceptability of technology usage is not a simple matter of embarrassment or politeness, but a continuous evaluation that is influenced by a variety of factors. The factors that influence these decisions include the performance of the action, the experience the user hopes or expects to take away, and the perceived reactions of spectators. These can be evaluated using methods that can be completed early on in the development process and encourage evaluation of more interaction techniques than traditional user studies.

Body-Based Gesturing

While social acceptability is an important aspect of designing gesture-based interfaces, we must also be aware of the practical and technical implications of using the gestures in the variety of places where mobile interfaces are used. Can we design gesture interfaces that are usable while the user is on the move; on a bus or train or while walking? The gestures should be robust to the noisy input channels that a mobile setting invariably creates, and allow a user to use the interface in a low effort, comfortable and safe manner. When designing interactions for use in a mobile context, we cannot assume that the interactions are the user's primary task. For a user crossing a road or walking down a busy street, the primary goal is to navigate the environment safely, avoiding cars and other pedestrians. Users needs to use their eyes to identify obstacles and safety hazards in the environment and avoid them. To a lesser extent users may also use their auditory sense, although the widespread use of music players while on the move suggests that the auditory sense is secondary to vision when navigating. To design an interface that can be used while on the move, there may be benefit in shifting the feedback away from the mobile device's screen and on to the other senses such as hearing and touch. From the point of view of the user's input into the system, again we must take into account mobile contexts. When away from the desktop and involved in other tasks, users may be encumbered, carrying bags or children or holding onto handles to stabilize themselves while standing on public transport. Interfaces designed to be used while encumbered in this manner could lead to very different ways of interacting with a device.

In almost all interfaces, including current gesture-based interfaces, interactions happen through the device. This could be through finger gestures on a touchscreen, pressing physical buttons on the device, or even by moving or orientating the device in a specific way. By shifting away from device-based interactions towards input techniques where the phone remains in the pocket, it is possible to envisage hands free interaction techniques. By employing a whole body interaction mechanism, we can start to take advantage of other areas of the body to provide fast, low effort interaction for mobile situations. For example, users could interact through wrist rotation, or nodding, pointing or shaking their head. For scenarios where the user may be seated or standing, for example on public transport for example, we might also consider foot tapping. These input channels will be lower bandwidth than the more traditional hand and finger-based interactions, but provide a mechanism to allow common actions to be performed with minimal effort and without the need to remove a phone from a pocket or bag. Here we describe three studies examining body-based interaction as an input technique for mobile interaction. In these studies we examine wrist rotation, head pointing and foot tapping as potential whole body interaction techniques for use while on the move. To allow interaction without removing the phone from a pocket, we use wearable sensor packs for input. The SHAKE is a small lightweight Bluetooth sensor pack that can be attached to different parts of a user to sense movement. It contains a three axis linear accelerometer, gyroscope and magnetometer that can be used for inertial sensing. In general, we can consider the inertial input from the user to be discrete action events or continuous steering control. For discrete action events, a gesture classifier continually monitors the stream of data from one or more sensors and attempts to identify preset patterns, such as movements corresponding to a tap, shake or preset trajectory. Once a pattern is detected and recognised, the appropriate control event is generated in the system. For a continuous control interaction, the user controls actions that happen fluidly over time, for example steering a cursor through a menu. A common continuous control input technique, which has been used for this work, uses orientation estimation of the sensor pack. The orientation of the sensor in one or more axes is used to control the position of a cursor within a workspace.

Testing Body-Based Discrete Action Event Control

We tested foot tapping as a mobile interaction technique. Foot tapping is a common action that a user may perform while listening to music for example so does not require unusual movements. We tested the technique using a menu navigation task over a two level hierarchical menu where the root nodes represent common tasks performed on a mobile device. As well as a visual representation, the menu item name was read out as the user moves over an item using high tempo speech, known as spearcons [18], to present the audio. The menus were cyclical such that the currently selected item loops at the bottom and the top of the menus. The final item for each of the sub-menus was 'back', which returns the user to the top of the root menu. During the experiment, participants were asked to complete a set of menu selection tasks, with each task being prompted using a spearcon through the headphones to select a specific menu item. When the spearcon for the menu item was played, the user would then navigate to and select the menu item requested. To navigate through the menus, users tapped their right foot to move down through the menu and tapped their left foot to make a selection. Taps were detected using a high pass filtered accelerometer signal from a sensor pack attached to each foot. For comparison, both a visual control condition and a pocket condition were also completed. In the visual condition the participants were seated and held the phone in their dominant hand. To navigate they used the up/down keys on the phone keyboard, while a selection was made using the central select key. For the in pocket condition, the participants all wore the same jacket with an inside breast pocket. Before each selection, the phone was placed in the pocket. When prompted, the participants removed the phone from the pocket, and navigated to the appropriate menu item as with the visual condition. Twelve users navigated through the menus using all three conditions in a counterbalanced order.

Detailed statistical analysis of the results can be found in [5]. When examining the overall results, it is clear that as a general mobile input technique, foot tapping by itself cannot be considered superior to the traditional mechanisms. Both the visual condition and the in pocket condition demonstrated higher accuracy and faster selection times than the foot tapping condition. This is hardly surprising given the high number of taps or button presses to reach some of the menu items. Additionally, having access to the visual display of the menu allows the user to scan all the menu items quickly and move to the correct location without having the necessity of listening to each item each in turn. If we examine the trends in the data however, it is possible to see where foot tap could provide some benefit. Linear regression of the data suggests that for less than five taps, foot tap can be faster than removing the device from the pocket. In the case of common or simple menu selections, the benefit of leaving the device in the pocket would add to the benefit of quicker selection times. There are also social scenarios where users might not be willing to remove the device from their pockets. For example, in a crowded area where space is limited or theft is common users may feel more comfortable controlling their devices using foot tapping while keeping the device securing stowed.

Testing Body-Based Continuous Control

In order to apply whole body interaction for continuous control, we investigated two areas of the body to provide non-hand-based control in mobile settings; wrist and head input. To evaluate the feasibility of the techniques we use used a Fitts' Law paradigm [7], a common method of characterising performance in a one dimensional targeting task. In this type of evaluation, participants repeatedly move between two targets of varying widths and separations with movement time and accuracy used as metrics of performance. As these interfaces are designed to be used while mobile, we tested targeting performance both while static and while walking a figure of eight route.

Wrist Rotation

Wrist rotation was sensed using the accelerometer of a SHAKE sensor pack attached to the user's wrist. The forearm was held approximately parallel to ground and rotated in a 90° workspace. For a right handed user, palm facing down corresponded to the left of the workspace, and palm facing left corresponded to the right of the workspace. Participants viewed their interactions on phone screen held in one hand. A visual display was used so that results would not be affected by a potentially poor choice of non-visual interface design. Participants selected targets by pressing a button on the phone. A button press was used so that results would not be affected by a potentially difficult or inaccurate gesture-based selection mechanism. This allowed us to investigate if wrist rotation was effective for input without other factors influencing the results. Twenty-four users performed the study both a static and a walking condition. Detailed statistical analysis can be found in [3].

Results showed that while walking, users were significantly slower to target and significantly less accurate. Figure 14.1. Percentage of correct selections (top) and mean time to select in each condition (bottom). Error bars show one standard deviation.

Figure 14.2 illustrates the effect that changing target width and separation had on participants mean movement time and accuracy while static and mobile. In the static condition, participants achieve a high level of accuracy (~90%) for the targets of 9° of rotation wide and larger. This suggests that participants could successfully target using wrist rotation. The walking condition was however was significantly harder for all participants who were both slower and far less accurate than in the static condition. These results for the walking conditions applied to all target width

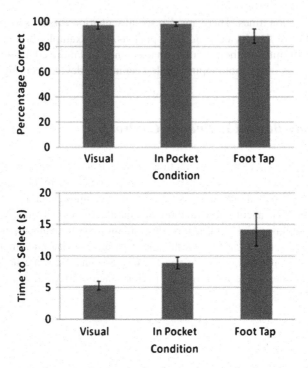

Fig. 14.1 Percentage of correct selections (*top*) and mean time to select in each condition (*bottom*). *Error bars* show one standard deviation

and separation combinations. It is also interesting to note that the accuracy values for this condition are less than 80% in all cases. All participants commented on the difficulty of the task and expressed low confidence in their performance. The accelerometer signal contains both the tilt from the user's targeting, and noise generated by the walking behaviour, which caused the cursor to oscillate in time with the user's walking speed making it difficult to target.

Head Tilt

In order to examine the possibility of continuous control using the body, we also completed a study using head tilt for interaction. In this study, users controlled the cursor by tilting their heads left or right within a range of ±40°. This was estimated through a sensor pack attached to a cap worn by the user. Two different mechanisms were used to control the cursor. In the first, a position control mechanism was used where the position of the cursor changed linearly with respect to the angle of the participant's head tilt. The cursor positions correspond to head positions, where holding your head at a set angle will move the cursor to the corresponding place. The second, a velocity control mechanism was used where the velocity of the cursor

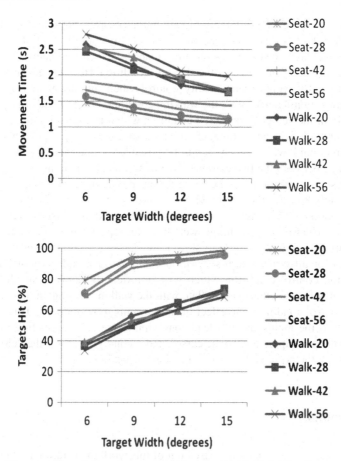

Fig. 14.2 Movement time (*left*) and percentage of targets hit (*right*) for C_{SE} the seated and C_{WA} walking conditions for all width-separation combinations

movement was determined by the angle of head tilt. The greater the tilt, the faster the cursor moves.

For the position control mechanism, the central head position corresponded to the cursor being in the centre of the phone screen. By tilting their heads left, participants could move the cursor left, with the leftmost screen position corresponding to a tilt angle of 40° (and *vice versa* for tilting right). For the velocity control conditions, the velocity of the cursor changed linearly with respect to the head tilt angle with the central head position corresponding to a stationary cursor. Unlike the position control condition, using velocity control allows robustness to be built into the control by using a dead zone as there is no one-to-one mapping between head tilt and cursor position. A dead-zone of ±5° was included to provide some robustness to noise from normal small head movements. Within the dead zone the cursor did not move. Similarly to the wrist rotation study, users interacted both while static and mobile. Detailed statistical results can be found here [4].

There were significant differences found in the accuracy data between the static and mobile conditions using both position and velocity control. Position control did consistently exhibit lower movement time than its velocity counterpart, and was significantly more accurate under the standing condition. However, position control was significantly worse than velocity control when mobile, with performance deteriorating significantly under the walking condition. There is the trade-off with cursor gain in the velocity controlled condition with a low cursor gain giving high accuracy and a longer target time, and high cursor gain giving a potentially faster time to target but lower accuracy. It will be possible for interface designers to shift performance between the two extremes by tuning this gain parameter.

In the static conditions, participants achieved a high level of accuracy, with approximately 80% for the targets with 7° of rotation wide and over 90% accuracy for larger targets. This suggests that participants could successfully target using head tilting. The walking conditions were however reported to be far more difficult for all participants who were both slower and far less accurate than in all other conditions for all target width-separation combinations, and particularly so for the position control condition which was significantly poorer than the others. The tendency for the cursor to oscillate with the walking was again noted. For the velocity control condition, the effect of noise seems to be reduced. This could be due firstly to the inclusion of a dead-zone around the central position making it easier for the participant to stop the cursor, and secondly since it is the velocity that is affected by the noise and not the actual cursor position.

Conclusions

There are many issues that have arisen out of this work in gesture-based interfaces that may also have an effect on practical usage but that have not yet been thoroughly investigated. With respect to social acceptability, factors such as appearance of the performer and cultural context may play a large role in social acceptability. Goffman presents the idea that appearance plays a large role in the types of actions that both performers and observers find acceptable [8]. With respect to gesture-based interfaces, the same may hold true and manifest itself through surprising and unexpected actions and responses from users. Another important issue revolves around the adaptation and appropriation of gesture-based interfaces over time. This includes not only the changes in performance from a sensing and detection point of view but also the motivations and methods that bring about that change. The types of changes in performance that users would create in order to make an interface work practically and socially in different contexts of use is relatively unknown, which makes it difficult for designers and implementers to add the right kind of flexibility and customization to an interface. Because it is important for users to feel comfortable and in control while using an interface, flexibility in personal performance while maintaining accuracy could greatly improve the usability of gesture-based interfaces overall.

Overall, this work focuses on practical usage of gestures as part of a mobile interface. We argue that successful design of gesture-based interfaces requires not only a consideration of the social acceptability of gesturing in public, but also a practical consideration of the usability and robustness of using gestures on the move. These issues can and should be addressed at different stages of development, from early conceptualization and prototyping to development, usability testing, and deployment. With a combination of prototyping with divergent interaction techniques, early evaluations of social acceptability, consideration of constraints on vision, hearing, and movement while on the go, the widespread adoption of mobile gesture-based interfaces may soon become a reality.

References

1. Bolt, R.A.: "Put-that-there": voice and gesture at the graphics interface. In: Proceedings of SIGGRAPH 1980, pp. 262–270. ACM Press, New York (1980)
2. Cassell, J.: A framework for gesture generation and interpretation. In: Cipolla, R., Pentland, A. (eds.) Computer Vision in Human–Machine Interaction, pp. 191–215. Cambridge University Press, Cambridge (1998)
3. Crossan, A., Williamson, J., Brewster, S., Murray-Smith, R.: Wrist rotation for interaction in mobile contexts. In: The Proceedings of Mobile HCI 2008. ACM Press, New York
4. Crossan, A., McGill, M., Brewster, S.A., Murray-Smith R.: Head tilting for interaction in mobile contexts. In: Proceedings of Mobile HCI 2009. ACM Press, New York
5. Crossan, A., Ng, A., Brewster, S.: Foot tapping for mobile interaction. In: The Proceedings of BCS HCI, Dundee (2010)
6. Eisenstein, J., Randall, D.: Visual and linguistic information in gesture classification. In: SIGGRAPH: ACM Special Interest Group on Computer Graphics and Interactive Techniques, San Diego. ACM, New York (2007)
7. Fitts, P.M.: The information capacity of the human motor system in controlling the amplitude of movement. J. Exp. Psychol. **47**(6), 381–391 (June 1954)
8. Goffman, E.: The Presentation of Self in Everyday Life. Penguin, London (1990)
9. Jin, Y., Choi, S., et al.: GIA: design of a gesture-based interaction photo album. Pers. Ubiquit. Comput. **8**(3), 227–233 (2004)
10. Kendon, A.: Gesture. Annu. Rev. Anthropol. **26**, 109–128 (1997)
11. Kendon, A.: Current issues in the study of gesture. In: Nespoulous, J.L., Perron, P., Lecour, A.R. (eds.) The Biological Foundations of Gestures. Lawrence Erlbaum Associates, Hillsdale (1986)
12. Kendon, A.: Language and gesture: unity or duality? In: McNeill, D. (ed.) Language and Gesture. Cambridge University Press, Cambridge (2000)
13. Law, E.L., Roto, V., Hassenzahl, M., Vermeeren, A.P., Kort, J.: Understanding, scoping and defining user experience: a survey approach. In: Proceedings of CHI 2009, pp. 719–728. ACM Press, New York (2009)
14. Reeves, S., Benford, S., O'Malley, C., Fraser, M.: Designing the spectator experience. In: Proceedings of CHI 2005, pp. 741–750. ACM Press, New York (2005)
15. Rico, J., Brewster, S.A.: Usable gestures for mobile interfaces: evaluating social acceptability. In: Proceedings of CHI 2010, pp. 887–896. ACM Press, New York (2010)
16. Rico, J., Brewster, S.A.: Gesture and voice prototyping for early evaluations of social acceptability in multimodal interfaces. In Proceedings of ICMI 2010, Beijing. ACM Press, New York
17. Väänänen, K., Böhm, K.: Gesture driven interaction as a human factor in virtual environments – an approach to neural networks. In: Earnshaw, R.A., Gigante, M.A., Jones, H. (eds.) Virtual Reality Systems. Academic, London (1993)

18. Walker, B. N., Nance, A., Lindsay, J.: Spearcons: speech-based earcons improve navigation performance in auditory menus. In: Proceedings of the 12th International Conference on Auditory Display (ICAD2006). Department of Computer Science, Queen Mary, University of London, London, pp. 63–68 (2006)
19. Wexelblat, A.: Research challenges in gesture: open issues and unsolved problems. In: Wachsmuth, I., Fröhlich, M. (eds.) Proceedings of the International Gesture Workshop, 17–19 September 1997. Lecture Notes in Computer Science, vol. 1371, pp. 1–11. Springer, London (1997)
20. Zhenyao, M., Ulrich, N.: Lexical gesture interface. In: Fourth IEEE International Conference on Computer Vision Systems. IEEE (2006)

Chapter 15
Estimation of Interest from Physical Actions Captured by Familiar User Device

Kumiko Fujisawa and Kenro Aihara

Abstract We propose a methodology to estimate a user's interest in documents displayed on a computer screen from his or her physical actions. We introduce the ongoing pilot study's results which showed a possible relationship between face approaches captured by a web camera and the user's interest in the document on the screen. Some studies have shown that physical actions captured through the device can be indicators of the user's interest. Our system uses a common and low impact device. We discuss the future possibilities of our research.

Introduction

Although keyboards and mice are standard input devices for personal computers, many new devices are coming into use. Nintendo Wii's motion-sensitive controller is a popular example of such futuristic input devices. Video capture devices can also be used as means of input whereby people can control PC software, games, or other machines by moving their hands or bodies.

Techniques to detect and analyze body (including faces) movements are becoming more accessible. In particular, face tracking technologies are now used in household electrical goods (e.g., [9, 11, 14]).

In the field of human-computer interaction (HCI), there has been a lot of research on developing new input devices or using devices to detect the user's reaction [4, 15]. These devices and systems tend to be heavy or distracting in some way, and user experiments involving them have had to be conducted under special situations. To capture natural and emotional behavior, preparation of more common situations would be needed.

Our research focuses on how to capture the users' natural behaviors in response to information displayed on the monitor's screen via low impact devices. By using

K. Fujisawa (✉) and K. Aihara
National Institute of Informatics, The Graduate University for Advanced Studies,
Sokendai, 2-1-2 Hitotsubashi, Chiyoda-ku, Tokyo, Japan
e-mail: k_fuji@nii.ac.jp; kenro.aihara@nii.ac.jp

D. England (ed.), *Whole Body Interaction*, Human-Computer Interaction Series,
DOI 10.1007/978-0-85729-433-3_15, © Springer-Verlag London Limited 2011

such devices, we are planning to collect user actions reflecting their interests and put them to practical use in the real learning situations. Therefore, we need light-weight and effective data for estimating the user's interest.

Here, we propose a methodology to estimate the users' interests by using face tracking data captured by a web camera. We describe our preliminary test results showing the potential effectiveness of such a methodology. This is part of our ongoing research on new interactive systems for supporting users in acquiring knowledge.

Previous Work

Research on recognition of user actions by various sensors has attracted the attention of researchers in computer science for a long time, and quite a lot of devices have been developed. Here, we introduce just some of those.

How to Capture User Actions

For a system to be able to capture whole-body movements, users sometimes have to wear sensor devices. For example, Sementile et al. [13] proposed a motion capture system based on marker detection using ARToolkit. The system consists of the markers with patterns which act as reference points for the attainment of the user's articulation coordinates. This system was used to generate humanoid avatars with similar movements to those of the user. Another example is the emotion recognition sensor system (EREC) that detects the user's emotional state [7]. It is composed of a sensor globe, a chest belt, and data collection unit. Eye tracking cameras are often used, and the EMR eye tracker is one example [12]. This system uses a dedicated computer to make a head-mounted camera track the eye motion of the user.

Jacob categorized input devices in terms of the physical aspect of HCI [5, 6]. He addressed hands, foot position, head position, eye gaze and voice to manipulate computer and described the devices with which to be manipulated. Picard and Daily [10] summarized body-based measures of affect and described typical sensor devices that detect action modalities such as facial activity or posture activity. They picked up video, force sensitive resistors, electromyogram electrodes, microphone or electrodes.

Mota and Picard [8] described a system for recognizing naturally occurring postures and associated affective states related to a child's interest level while he or she performed a learning task on a computer. Their main purpose was to identify natural occurring postures in natural learning situations. The device used in that research was composed of pressure sensors set in a chair. They used hidden Markov models to remove noise from data and estimated the relationship between posture and interest. They found evidence to support a relationship between patterns of postural behaviors and affective states associated with interest.

Wakai et al. [16] proposed a technique for quantitatively measuring the change in interest from a portrait measured with a camera. They focused on the pose of eye gaze and the distance to the object. Their system detected eye gazes and posture from the video image, and they succeeded in detecting changes in the direction of the interest when the experiment participants were asked to choose one favorite advertisement from three. To detect the approach posture from the silhouette, they used three cameras set behind each of the advertisements.

We propose a system that uses a familiar web camera to detect a user's face approaching the screen. We intend to use this system to collect natural movements from a large amount of real-life samples. To detect a user's face, we used OpenCV Library [1], which is developed by Intel and freely distributed under the open source BSD license. OpenCV detects face by using a cascade of boosted classifiers based on the Haar-like features. This excels at detecting faces from blurred images and rapidity of detection.

Proposed System

Figure 15.1 shows the basic structure of our prototype system. The web camera (Qcam E3500) mounted on the screen captures the user and the system detects the face of the user. This camera capable of capturing video at maximum 30 fps at a

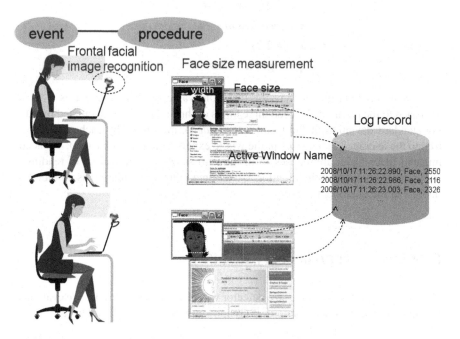

Fig. 15.1 Basic structure of the proposed system

resolution of 640×480 pixels. Harrison and Dey [3] showed that at typical viewing distances, a generic webcam captures a vertical plane approximately 50 cm wide, and a camera with horizontal resolution of 640 pixels allows horizontal movement of 0.8 mm detected.

When frontal face recognition occurs, the log record part records the time, active window name, and URL (only when a browser is active) with face size. The face size is calculated by adding face width and height. The sensor detects the target event from each frame. If the user turned his or her face away from the screen, the system did not record the size.

Detection of the Face Approaches

We propose to estimate user's interest in the target page by accumulating face approach according to the following equations:

$$I(t) = count(t) - count(t - \mathbf{D}t)$$

$$count(t) = \sum_{i=0}^{t/\mathbf{D}t} f(i)$$

$$f(i) = \begin{cases} 1, \text{ if } x > \mathbf{q} \\ 0, \text{ otherwise} \end{cases}$$

$$x = face.height + face.width$$

$$\mathbf{a} = \{1, 2, 3\}$$

$$\mathbf{q} = avg. + \mathbf{a} * stdev.$$

A facial size (x) bigger than the threshold value (θ) was counted as a facial approach to the monitor. We used three kinds of threshold values calculated by adding standard deviation of the facial sizes (*stdev.*), multiplied by each coefficients (α), to the averaged facial sizes in the whole experimental session (*avg.*). We accumulated these facial approaches from the start ($t - \Delta t_i$) to the end (t) of reading a document displayed on the monitor. We assumed this accumulation as an index of interest in the document ($I(t)$).

Pilot Study and Preliminary Results

The implemented frontal face size detector was tested in a pilot study. We evaluated its function and the relationship of body movements to the user's interest.

Fig. 15.2 Participants of the web experiment (*left*; with desktop PC, *right*; with notebook PC)

Participants

Nineteen university undergraduate and graduate students aged from 19 years old to 31 years old (average age of 21.73) participated in our preliminary test (Fig. 15.2). All of them were right-handed. Six of them were without visual correction and the rest wore contacts or eye glasses.

Procedure

Firstly, participants were asked to adjust their monitor and keyboard positions to fit their use. Then they were asked to gaze at the monitor. This was the baseline session and its duration was at least more than 3 min.

In the experimental session, participants were asked to watch and evaluate web pages according to the links on the screen. To distribute the degree of interest on the web page, we prepared ten links to topics on arts, academics, current news, fiction, and commercial goods. Participants were asked to visit all the links shown on the screen and other links if they wanted, and after visiting the link or viewing the new page, they were asked to rate on a scale of 1–10 each page using the following points: degree of "Reading" (from 'did not read' to 'read carefully'), interest (from 'not interesting at all' to 'very interesting'), "Amusingness" (from 'not amusing at all' to 'very amusing'), "Novelty" (from 'not novel at all' to 'very novel'), "Benefit" (from 'not beneficial at all' to 'very beneficial') and "Easiness" (from 'not easy at all' to 'very easy'). The duration of the experiment was around 1 h. The face recognition and motion recognition parts of our system recorded data both in the experimental session and in the baseline session.

Preliminary Results

We used 16 participants' log data for analysis and eliminated three participants' because of a system failure in recording. We analyzed only face approach data at this point. For averaged numbers of approaches at each thresholds, there was no significant difference between male and female (avg. + 1SD; $t(14) = 0.29$, $p = 0.78$, avg. + 2SD; $t(14) = -0.05$, $p = 0.96$, avg. + 3SD; $t(13) = 1.275$, $p = 0.23$). And there was no significant difference between participants with eye correction and without it (avg. + 1SD; $t(14) = 0.32$, $p = 0.76$, avg. + 2SD; $t(14) = 0.80$, $p = 0.44$, avg. + 3SD; $t(13) = 0.03$, $p = 0.97$).

Face approaches were counted on each link page, and Spearman's rank order correlation coefficients between counted number of face approaches and each evaluation value were calculated for three thresholds (Table 15.1).

As for each evaluations, strong and significant correlations were found between "Interest", "Reading" ("Interest" and "Reading"; 0.82**) and "Amusingness" ("Interest" and "Amusingness"; 0.85**). Therefore, these three evaluations were seemed to be strongly related each other.

Significant correlations were found between the face approach frequency and "Reading" (0.32**), "Interest" (0.20*) and "Amusingness" (0.25**) at avg. + 1SD threshold. Results at avg. + 2SD threshold showed similar tendencies. These question items were selectively correlated to the face approach differently from the items of novelty and easiness. At avg. + 3SD threshold, face approach did not show any significant correlations.

There is a possibility that these results was affected by the participant's age. If the participants' ages were much elder (e.g., than 45) and with aged eyes, these results might have shown different tendency. In our experiment, the participants' ages are all under 40 and they had no farsightedness due to old age.

Most participants said that the existence of the camera didn't matter to them (Table 15.2). Even if they had no experience using personal computers with a web camera, they could browse without being concerned. This result showed that the camera on the personal computer was not considered to be out of the ordinary. It supports the purpose of our prototype system.

Conclusion

We described a system to identify the user's interest with an everyday device (a web camera). Although our methodology was very easy to use, the preliminary results showed its possibilities to estimate users' actions reflecting their interest in the target. There was a positive correlation between the face approach frequencies acquired by the system and the degree to which the user had actually read the page and the degree of amusement they felt while viewing the web page. In our experiment, most participants reported that the existence of this camera did not bother their activity of exploring the web.

Table 15.1 Coefficient of correlation between counted numbers of approaches at each thresholds and each evaluation values

		Reading	Interest	Amusingness	Novelty	Benefits	Easiness	Avg+1SD	Avg+2SD	Avg+3SD
Reading	Coefficient of correlation	1.00	0.82 (**)	0.74 (**)	0.16 (*)	0.49 (**)	0.55 (**)	0.32 (**)	0.22 (*)	0.08
	N	219.00	219.00	218.00	219.00	219.00	217.00	152.00	109.00	69.00
Interest	Coefficient of correlation	0.82 (**)	1.00	0.85 (**)	0.11	0.50 (**)	0.57 (**)	0.20 (*)	0.21 (*)	0.02
	N	219.00	219.00	218.00	219.00	219.00	217.00	152.00	109.00	69.00
Amusingness	Coefficient of correlation	0.74 (**)	0.85 (**)	1.00	0.12	0.49 (**)	0.52 (**)	0.25 (**)	0.26 (**)	0.07
	N	218.00	218.00	231.00	231.00	231.00	230.00	164.00	112.00	69.00
Novelty	Coefficient of correlation	0.16 (*)	0.11	0.12	1.00	0.33 (**)	-0.06	0.00	0.06	-0.05
	N	219.00	219.00	231.00	231.00	231.00	230.00	163.00	111.00	68.00
Benefits	Coefficient of correlation	0.49 (**)	0.50 (**)	0.49 (**)	0.33 (**)	1.00	0.03	0.18 (*)	0.16	0.13
	N	219.00	219.00	231.00	232.00	232.00	230.00	164.00	112.00	69.00
Easiness	Coefficient of correlation	0.55 (**)	0.57 (**)	0.52 (**)	-0.06	0.03	1.00	0.06	0.17	-0.01
	N	217.00	230.00	230.00	230.00	230.00	231.00	163.00	111.00	68.00

**Significant correlation at 1% level
*Significant correlation at 5% level

Table 15.2 Questions and answers about the web camera

	Did you care about the camera on the screen?	Have you ever seen a camera like this?	Have you ever used PC with a camera like this?
Yes	2	11	5
No	14	5	11

Analyzing the whole body movement with dedicated equipment continues to have a very important role in the future because our experiment is an application based on the relation revealed by past experiments. On the other hand, experimental analyses using real-world equipment in real situations are becoming to be important now that there is a growing variety of input devices. Developing an application for an actual environment will soon be an important issue.

This technique might be able to be applied to various fields although it is necessary to set the threshold for judging face approach according to circumstances. The degree of reading showed positive correlation, and this seemed to indicate the possibility of utilizing our technique for user profiling in systems that make recommendations. In this field, to estimate the user's interest in the website, researchers use duration, mouse movement, or eye gaze. If our system proves to be valid in future experiments, it may be a useful system for estimating users' actions on the web.

Moreover, it was very important that this amount of face approaches were also correlated to the degree of amusingness. The degree of reading might reflect the reader's interest in some cases, but in other cases this might reflect his/her incomprehension. Our technique has a possibility to detect reading with positive emotions. These emotions are some of the basis of the spontaneous motivation and help people learn in educational environment [2]. Therefore, this technique can be applied in the PC rooms at school or the e-Learning systems to detect in which field the learners are interested.

The results of our experiments are still being examined. Movements and utterances are also possible candidates to be used to estimate user interest or profile user actions in relation to a target. Moreover, we should compare our technique and other techniques being used as indicators of the interest (like reading time or access frequency), and examine its characteristics. We plan to apply this in the real learning situation and conduct some experiments at elementary school. To achieve real-time processing in a real educational environment, we will also examine how to improve image processing performance.

References

1. Dr. Bradski, G.R., Kaehler, A.: Learning Opencv, 1st edn. O'Reilly Media Inc, Sebastopol (2008)
2. Deci, E.L., Flaste, R.: Why We Do What We Do -The Dynamics of Personal Autonomy. Putnam Pub Group, New York (1995)

3. Harrison, C., Dey, A.K.: Lean and zoom: proximity-aware user interface and content magnification. In: Proceeding of the twenty-sixth annual SIGCHI conference on Human Factors in Computing Systems (CHI'08), pp. 507–510. ACM, New York (2008)

4. Hijikata, Y.: User profiling technique for information recommendation and information filtering. J. Jpn. Soc. Artif. Int. **19**, 365–372 (1996)

5. Jacob, R.J.K.: Human-computer interaction: input devices. ACM Computing Surveys, pp. 177–179. ACM, New York(1996a)

6. Jacob, R.J.K.: The future of input devices. ACM Comput. Surv. **28**(4es), 138 (1996)

7. Kaiser, R., Oertel, K.: Emotions in HCI: an affective e-learning system. In: Proceedings of the HCSNet workshop on Use of Vision in Human-Computer Interaction, pp. 105–106. Australian Computer Society, Canberra (2006)

8. Mota, S., Picard, R.W.: Automated posture analysis for detecting learner's interest level. In: Computer Vision and Pattern Recognition Workshop. IEEE Computer Society. 49, Los Alamitos (2003)

9. Nikon. Nikon | Imaging products | The birth of the COOLPIX design. (2010) Retrieved 1 Oct 2010, from http://imaging.nikon.com/products/imaging/technology/scene/31/

10. Picard, R.W., Bryant, D.S.: Evaluating affective interactions: alternatives to asking what users feel. In: CHI workshop on Evaluating Affective Interfaces: Innovative Approaches. ACM (2005)

11. Polaroid Polaroid t1235: 12MP Touchscreen Digital Camera - t Series. (2010). Retrieved 1 Oct 2010, from http://www.polaroid.com/product/0/0/t1235/_/t1235%3A_12MP_Touchscreen_Digital_Camera

12. Prendinger, H., Ma, C.,, Yingzi, J.N., Arturo, I.M.: Understanding the effect of life-like interface agents through users' eye movements. In: ICMI'05: Proceedings of the 7th international conference on Multimodal Interfaces.pp. 108–115. ACM, Toronto (2005)

13. Sementille, A.C., Lourenço, L.E., Brega, J.R.F., Rodello, I. A motion capture system using passive markers.In: VRCAI '04: Proceedings of the 2004 ACM SIGGRAPH international conference on Virtual Reality Continuum and its Applications in Industry. pp. 440–447. ACM, New York (2004)

14. SONY: Cyber-shot® W230 Digital Camera. (2010). Retrieved 1 Oct 2010, from http://www.sonystyle.com/webapp/wcs/stores/servlet/ProductDisplay?storeId=10151&catalogId=10551&langId=−1&productId=8198552921665775588

15. Viola, P., Jones, M.: Rapid object detection using a boosted cascade of simple features. In: Computer Vision and Pattern Recognition. pp. I-511–I-518 IEEE. (2001)

16. Wakai, Y., Sumi, K., Matsuyama, T.: Estimation of human interest level in choosing from video sequence. In: The Actual Use of Vision Technology (2005)

Chapter 16
Towards a Framework for Whole Body Interaction with Geospatial Data

Florian Daiber, Johannes Schöning, and Antonio Krüger

Abstract Since 6,000 years humans have used maps to navigate through space and solve other spatial tasks. Nearly at all times maps were drawn or printed on a piece of paper (or on material like stone or papyrus) of a certain size. Nowadays maps can be displayed on a wide range of electronic devices starting from small screen mobile devices or highly interactive large multi-touch screens. Due to common computer power Geographic Information Systems (GIS) are allowing a rich set of operations on spatial data. However, most GIS require a high degree of expertise from its users, making them difficult to be operated by laymen. In this work we discuss the possibilities of navigating maps using physical (whole body) gestures to easily perform typical basic spatial tasks within GIS (e.g. pan-, zoom- and selection-operations). We studied multi-modal interaction with large- and mid-scale displays by using multi-touch, foot and gaze input. We are interested in understanding how non-expert users interact with such multi-touch surfaces. Therefore, we provide a categorization and a framework of multi-touch hand gestures for interacting with GIS. The combination of multi-touch gestures with a small set of foot gestures to solve geospatial tasks leads to an extended framework for multi-touch and foot input. In an additional step this framework is extended again with eye gaze input.

Introduction and Motivation

Multi-touch has great potential for exploring complex content in an easy and natural manner and multi-touch interaction with computationally enhanced surfaces has received considerable attention in the last years. The geospatial domain provides a rich testbed for multi-touch applications because the command and control of geographic space (at different scales) as well as the selection, modification and

F. Daiber (✉), J. Schöning, and A. Krüger
German Research Institute for Artificial Intelligence (DFKI), Innovative Retail Lab,
Campus D3_2, Stuhlsatzenhausweg 3, 66123 Saarbrücken, Germany
e-mail: flowdie@wwu.de; j.schoening@wwu.de; kruegera@wwu.de

D. England (ed.), *Whole Body Interaction*, Human-Computer Interaction Series,
DOI 10.1007/978-0-85729-433-3_16, © Springer-Verlag London Limited 2011

annotation of geospatial data are complicated tasks and have a high potential to benefit from novel interaction paradigms [23]. One important observation of previous studies [7, 16, 17] shows that users initially preferred simple gestures, that are already known from Windows-Icons-Menus-Pointer (WIMP) systems with mouse input. After experiencing the potential of multi-touch users tended towards more advanced physical gesturing [26], but these gestures were often single hand gestures or gestures, where the non-dominant hand just sets a frame of reference that determines the navigation mode while the dominant hand specifies the amount of movement.

So far, the combination of hand and foot input has gained only little attention [18]. This combination has a couple of advantages and helps to rethink the use of the dominant and non-dominant hand. Foot gestures can be used to provide continuous input for a spatial navigation task, which in some cases is difficult to operate with the hands in a natural way. While hand gestures are good for precise input it is difficult to input continuous data with one or two hands for a longer period of time. For example, panning a map for a larger distance on a multi-touch wall through repeated "wiping"-gestures may lead to ergonomic problems (arm fatigue). In contrast foot interaction can provide continuous input by just pushing the body weight over the respective foot. Since the feet are used to navigate in real space such a foot gesture has the potential advantage of being more intuitive since it borrows from a striking metaphor.

Humans use their eyes to interact with others in communication every day. Even in human-computer interaction eye gaze interaction is getting more and more popular. It is well suited as additional input modality when both hands are needed for bi-manual interaction. The majority of eye gaze interaction techniques lies on pointing and selection tasks. Pointing and selection of geographical objects (features) to gather detailed feature information or to manipulate features are basic tasks in GIS. Thus the integration of eye gaze to interact with geographical data is an obvious step.

The following section places this paper in the context of the related work in the variety of fields that provide the basis for this research. In the third section the three key parts of a conceptual framework for multi-touch interaction with spatial data is proposed. In section "Framework Extension for Multi-modal Interaction with Geospatial Data" the framework extensions for foot gestures and eye gaze are discussed. Section "Implementation" gives a short overview on the implementation. This paper concludes with a discussion of the results and ideas for future work.

Related Work

Mouse and keyboard are still the main devices used to navigate, explore and interact with GIS,even though they are not optimal devices for this purpose. Since 1999 several hardware solutions exist that allow the realization of GIS with multi-touch input on surfaces of different sizes. The webpage of Buxton [2] gives a comprehensive overview on the history of multi-touch surfaces and interaction. With today's technology it is now possible to apply the basic advantages of bi-manual interaction [3, 5] to the domain of spatial data interaction. Also the selection of relevant data, the configuration of adequate data presentation techniques, and the input or manipulation of data are central tasks in a GIS (as in any interactive system) [11]. Much work is done on the definition of frameworks and taxonomies for such gesture-based multi-touch input. Wu et al. defined the principle of Gesture Registration, Relaxation and Reuse [30]. Wobbrock et al. investigated user defined gestures and developed a taxonomy of gestures for surface computing [27].

Even though multi-touch interaction gained a lot of attention in the last few years the interaction possibilities of feet were not considered as much. Various researchers have done relevant work in the area of foot input for interactive systems. Pearson and Weiser identified appropriate topologies for foot movement and present several designs for realising them in [14]. They showed in an exploratory study [15] that novices could learn to select fairly small targets using a mole. Pakkanen and Raisamo [13] highlight alternative methods for manipulating graphical user interfaces with a foot and show the appropriateness of foot interaction for non-accurate spatial tasks. In his research on 3D-input devices Zhai established the distinction in rate controlled and position controlled forms of input. While position controlled input depends on where the user directly maps to, rate controlled input means that the user's input is related to the speed of the cursor movement [31]. Thus multi-touch input can be assumed to be predominantly position controlled while foot input is rate controlled.

Eye gaze interaction is very natural because humans habitually use their eyes for communication with each other. Eye movements are very fast and require little effort [20]. With the development of inexpensive, unobtrusive desktop and wearable eye tracking solutions this technology has become very popular in human-computer interaction. Since the eyes are primarily for perceiving information eye gaze interaction is not suited for explicit input, e.g. eye-blinking to activate buttons, etc. [1]. However eye gaze can be used to track the user's attention. In particular it can be determined where the user is looking at. One crucial aspect of gaze interaction is the so called *midas touch* that stands for accidental interaction with everything the user is looking at [8]. Nevertheless eye gaze interaction could serve as an additional input mode when the user needs both hand for other task [19]. Kumar and Winograd [10] investigated gaze-input based scrolling techniques including a technique for map panning with gaze. Other application examples for eye tracking are video game control [20], 3D interaction in virtual environments [21] and text processing [1]. Holman [6] investigates interaction techniques for gaze-aware tabletops mainly focusing on co-located collaboration tasks.

Multi-Touch Interaction

In contrast to the more general work of Wu et al. [30] and Wobbrock et al. [27], a conceptual framework for multi-touch interaction with spatial data is presented in this section. The framework consists of three key parts (physical interactions, interaction primitives and interaction space) and defines the commands and controls that are needed to manipulate the interaction space (at different scales).

Physical Multi-Touch Interactions

As a first step towards the multi-touch framework, a set of simple physical interaction patterns for multi-touch input is derived (see Fig. 16.1 inspired by [26, 29]).

These physical gestures can be classified in two dimensions: uni- vs. bimanual and finger vs. hand gestures. For the latter there are three classes of these patterns: simple fingertip (F), palm-of-the-hand (H) and edge-of-the-hand (EH) input. Unimanual gestures are simple single hand gestures (gestures with the suffix 1 and 2). Bimanual gestures are simple two handed gestures (3–5) as well as the combination of unimanual gestures (one's and two's) that result in more complex two handed gestures. Gestures F1–F5 are based on one or two single-finger touches. Interacting via one or two whole hands is performed with gestures H1–H5. The main idea behind the F and H interaction classes is the direct manipulation of region shaped objects. To interact with linelike objects and to frame or cut objects, the edge of the hand provides another class of gestures (EH). Each interaction class contains the following gestures: single pointing touch (1), single moving touch (2) (not only limited to linear movement), two touches moving in the same direction (3), two touches moving in opposite directions (4), moving of two touches in a rotational manner (5).

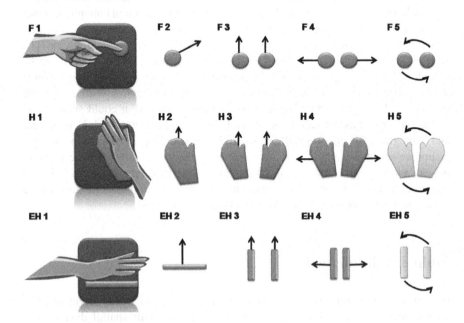

Fig. 16.1 Set of physical multi-touch gestures

Interaction Primitives and Interaction Space

A set of interaction primitives for interaction with geospatial data is defined. These commands and controls (such as pointing or zooming [23]) are needed to manipulate the geographic interaction space (at different scales) as well as to select, modify and annotate geo-objects. The tasks are pointing, zooming, panning, rotating, tilting and cutting as described in [23].

The interaction space contains a set of graphical views and representations for spatial objects. The view (spherical globe and plain map view), spatial objects (features), symbols and layers can be manipulated using the interaction primitives, e.g. zooming, panning, and rotating the view, manipulate feature symbolization, or showing/hiding layers or features.

Framework for Multi-Touch Interaction with Geospatial Data

To get a better understanding of the relationship between gestures and geospatial operations, 12 participants (five female and seven male) were asked to fill out the matrix with one or more physical interaction primitives or a combination of primitives of their choice. Five participants were employees of our Institute, four graduate students outside of the subject area of geoinformatics and three cartographers from a GIS company who completed the subject pool. The participants were asked to fill out the interaction matrix with either (1) one or more physical interaction possibilities, (2) an indication that a cell makes no sense (e.g. zooming a point object), or (3) combinations of primitives, e.g. pointing with two fingers (F1+F1). They completed 149 different matrix cells, which include 12 proposed combined interactions. The preferred gestures got an average of 3.59 votes.

Comparing simple gestures (e.g. F1, H1) against more complex ones (e.g. F5, H1 + F2), the participants predominantly tended to prefer simple gestures, i.e. they tried to use the point-gesture (click) first and subsequently did something with the selected object. 52% of all interactions (66% as in the conceptual framework (CF)) were physical F gestures (see Fig. 16.2), 11% all (10% in CF) were H gestures, 17% of all (17% in CF) were EH gestures and 26% of all (7% CF) were combined gestures. Comparing one handed against two handed gestures, participants tended to prefer both hands (45% all, 44% in CF) instead of just one hand (55% all, 56% in CF). Note that not all possible gestures are used in the framework, because we started the framework with basic interactions and not more complex spatial interactions like buffering, intersecting two or more layers and so on. Interestingly, the participant outside of the subject area had nearly 80% of his/her proposed gestures as simple one handed F gestures.

The participants assigned physical gestures for the interaction primitives to the interaction space. An interaction style was inserted in the framework (see Table 16.1) if three participants agreed on the same interaction primitive. In the resulting framework the rows represent the interaction primitives (a selection of

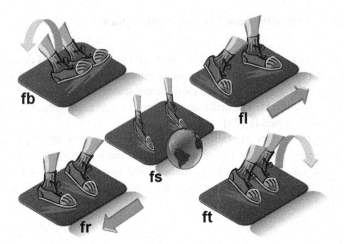

Fig. 16.2 Physical foot gestures

Table 16.1 Framework for physical multi-touch interaction with geospatial data

	World		(Geo-)objects			Symbols		
	Globe	Plain	Point	Line		Polygon	Point-Symbols	Labels	Layer
Point	F1	F1	F1	EH1	H1	F1	F1	F1
Zoom	F4	F4	–	F4	F4	F4	F4	(F4)
Pan	H2	H2	F2	EH2	H2	F2	F2	–
Rotate	F5	F5	–	F5	F5	F5	F5	–
Tilt	H1 + F2,	H1 + H2	–	–	–	F6	–	–
	H1 + H2							
Cut				EH1, EH3	EH1, EH3			–

the most common that are needed for geospatial tasks) and the columns of the table the interaction space (view, features, symbols and layers).

The interaction (selection and manipulation) with geo-objects can be distingui-shed according to their geometric properties: point, line, and polygon. Interestingly, the geometric property of the interaction is reflected in the physical nature of the proposed multi-touch interaction. For example, single point-like objects are referred to with a single pointing gesture (F1), while rotation of a globe or panning of a 2D map is more likely to be performed by a wiping-style gesture (H2). The selection of geo-objects can be improved by referencing their geometric properties. For example, the selection of a street on a map could be more precisely performed by moving a finger along that street (F2) instead of just pointing to it. This helps to reduce the ambiguity of the gesture as pointed out in [24].

Please note that not all of the primitive gestures of Fig. 16.1 are listed in Table 16.1. For example the two-hand gesture (EH4 and H4) seems of no use. However we believe that if we look at more complex operations such as intersecting two poly-gons, these operations will become useful. Of course, this has to be investigated further in future work.

Framework Extension for Multi-Modal Interaction with GeospatialData

Even though multi-touch interaction gained a lot of attention in the last years the question remains how physical multi-touch gestures in combination with other modalities can be used in spatial applications. This section describes two extensions of the multi-touch framework presented above.

Multi-Touch and Foot Interaction

In a second cycle a set of simple physical foot interaction patterns that can be performed by the user standing on a Wii Balance Board (see Fig. 16.2a) are developed. Up to now five different patterns (named with lower case letters) can be investigated: fb = "stand on ball of feet", ft = "stand on tippy-toes", fr = "balance center on the right", fl = "balance center on the left", fs = "stand on sides of feet". Most of the gestures are self-explaining. For example ft means that the user is moving the balance point forward and just stands on tiptoes. fs denotes an action (user standing on sidefeets) people often perform while they are waiting (see Fig. 16.2).

Gaze Interaction

As another modalitity it will be interesting to investigate how to integrate the user's gaze information in spatial applications. This section describes the extension of the multi-touch framework presented above with the focus on gaze input. Eye gaze interaction allows hands-free interaction and therefore it is best suited for bimanual multi-touch interaction as an additional input. Related work shows that gaze interaction is well suited for selection tasks and selection of spatial objects is a crucial task in geospatial applications. Thus our extended framework for gaze interaction will mainly focus on this part of the interaction space.

In a first iteration the following physical interactions are proposed to extend the basic framework with gaze input (see Table 16.2). Eye pointing on a specific location

Table 16.2   Framework extensions for foot and eye gaze interactions

	World		(Geo-)objects		
	Globe	Plain	Point	Line	Polygon
Point	F1, GP	F1, GP	F1, GP	EH1, GM	H1
Zoom	F4, F4 + GP	F4, F4 + GP	–	F4	F4
Pan	H2, fr, fl, GP	H2, fr, fl, GP	F2, fr, fl	EH2, fr, fl	H2, fr, fl
Rotate	F5	F5	–	F5	F5
Tilt	ft, fb	ft, fb	–	–	–
Cut				EH1, EH3	EH1, EH3

of the screen (denoted as "GP"). This can be used to highlight a point of interest or retrieve further information about objects (feature info). Another potential use is panning through looking at the horizon or the edges of the map to initiate "scrolling" [10]. Gaze motion (denoted as "GM") can be used to retrieve information about objects of a certain geometrical form (e.g. line-objects). Furthermore, the combination of gaze and touch additionally offers novel and intuitive interactions, e.g. the user stares at a location where he or she wants to zoom in.

Initial tests show that gaze-based pointing works quite well to display additional information (e.g. displaying latitude/longitude-coordinates of the position the user is looking at). The display of detailed information of a specific object the user is focusing on was also found an interesting feature. This part of the framework has to be investigated more in detail. As other related work has shown the eye gaze pointing technique performs well for geospatial data. The usability of the eye gaze motion technique still remains an open issue and has to be studied in future work.

Extended Framework for Foot and Eye Gaze Interaction

While interaction primitives and the interaction space stay nearly the same (see section "Interaction Primitives and Interaction Space") some interaction primitives can be now (additionally or exclusively) controlled by feet and eye gaze.

The proposed interaction styles for various selection and manipulation tasks are summarized in Table 16.2. The table is organized as described in section "Framework for Multi-touch Interaction with Geospatial Data" but now filled up with physical hand, foot gestures and/or gaze input to interact with geoobjects. For example panning can be accomplished by using the physical multi-touch interaction "H2" or the foot interactions "fr", "fl" and pointing by using eye gaze.

Implementation

Various low-cost multi-touch surfaces at different scales were used as display and touch input devices. All of them utilize the principles of Frustrated Total Internal Reflection (FTIR) [4]. The Wii Balance Board [25] served as foot input device. It is wirelessly connected via Bluetooth and GlovePie[1] and used to stream the sensor data from the Wii Balance Board to the application. A *tobii* X60 Eye Tracker [22] is used for eye tracking. The image processing and blob tracking is done by the Java multi-touch library [12] developed at the *Deutsche Telekom Laboratories*. The library provides the touches as a server using the TUIO-protocol [9]. A virtual globe application based on the NASA World Wind Java SDK [28] was used as testbed.

---

[1] http://carl.kenner.googlepages.com/glovepie

Fig. 16.3 User is interacting with both hands and feet with a virtual globe. The user is interacting with a large size multi-touch wall while standing on a Wii balance board

To evaluate the multi-touch and foot framework the subjects stand on the Wii Balance Board in front of a large (1.8×2.2 m) multi-touch wall (see Fig. 16.3). An initial study that compares multi-touch to multi-touch and foot interaction shows that the users can easily perform this simple foot interactions on the balance board and liked the additional modality [18].

Conclusion and Future Work

In this paper different approaches are discussed on how to navigate and interact with spatial data using various modalities. In the first step multi-touch gestures to navigate and manipulate spatial data are derived from a usability inspection test. Based on the results of the multi-touch framework a first concept and implementation of the combination of multi-touch hand and foot interaction is provided. Users are able to interact with geospatial data in a natural and intuitive manner. Thus whole body interaction with geospatial data has great potential for this domain as well as human–computer-interaction in general. Nevertheless in future work various topics need to be investigated more in detail.

The combination of direct, position controlled (hand) with indirect, rate controlled (feet) input was proposed and evaluated in an initial user study. Hand gestures are well suited for rather precise input. Foot interactions in contrast have a couple of advantages over hand interactions on a surface providing an intuitive and less exhausting modality for continuous input. In a more general way foot interaction provides an orthogonal horizontal interaction plane that indirectly maps to the touch surface. There is a need for further investigation of the interplay between both planes for spatial tasks, but this certainly has a huge potential for interaction with spatial data or even for more abstract visualization that uses a 3D-space to organize data.

Interaction designers should be aware to not degrade multi-touch to single touch, while using the non-dominant hand only for switching between different modes. This paper shows how additional modalities can overcome this problem and let users interact more intuitively and presumably even faster. This has to be tested with further user studies. Different modalities discussed above as well as other approaches have to be investigated more in detail. There is also great potential to combine modalities. The resulting gestures have to be intensively user-tested and refined to fulfill users' needs.

References

1. Biedert, R., Buscher, G., Dengel, A.: The eye book. Informatik-Spektrum. **33**(3), 272–281 (2009)
2. Buxton, W.: Multi-touch systems that I have known and loved. http://www.billbuxton.com/multitouchOverview.html. Accessed Oct 2010
3. Buxton, W., Myers, B.: A study in two-handed input. In: Proceedings of the SIGCHI Conference on Human Factors in Computing Systems, pp. 321–326. ACM, New York (1986)
4. Han, J.Y.: Low-cost multi-touch sensing through frustrated total internal reflection. In: UIST '05: Proceedings of the 18th Annual ACM Symposium on User Interface Software and Technology, pp. 115–118. ACM, New York (2005)
5. Hinckley, K., Pausch, R., Proffitt, D., Kassell, N.F.: Two-handed virtual manipulation. ACM Trans. Comput. Hum. Interact. **5**(3), 260–302 (1998)
6. Holman, D.: Gazetop: Interaction techniques for gaze-aware tabletops. In: CHI '07: CHI '07 Extended Abstracts on Human Factors in Computing Systems, pp. 1657–1660. ACM, New York (2007)
7. Hornecker, E.: "I don't understand it either, but it is cool" – visitor interactions with a multi-touch table in a museum. In: Horizontal Interactive Human Computer Systems, 2008. TABLETOP 2008. 3rd IEEE International Workshop on, pp. 113–120. IEEE, New York (2008)
8. Jacob, R.J.K.: What you look at is what you get: eye movement-based interaction techniques. In: CHI '90: Proceedings of the SIGCHI Conference on Human Factors in Computing Systems, pp. 11–18. ACM, New York (1990)
9. Kaltenbrunner, M., Bovermann, T., Bencina, R., Costanza, E.: Tuio: A protocol for table-top tangible user interfaces. In: Proceedings of the 6th International Workshop on Gesture in Human-Computer Interaction and Simulation, 1 May 2006. Springer, Berlin (2005)
10. Kumar, M., Winograd, T.: Gaze-enhanced scrolling techniques. In: UIST '07: Proceedings of the 20th Annual ACM Symposium on User Interface Software and Technology, pp. 213–216. ACM, New York (2007)
11. Maceachren, A., Brewer, I.: Developing a conceptual framework for visually-enabled geocollaboration. Int. J. Geogr. Inf. Sci. **18**(1), 1–34 (2004)
12. MultitouchJava. http://www.mt4j.org/mediawiki/index.php/Main_Page. Accessed Oct 2010

13. Pakkanen, T., Raisamo, R.: Appropriateness of foot interaction for non-accurate spatial tasks. In: Conference on Human Factors in Computing Systems, pp. 1123–1126. ACM, New York (2004)
14. Pearson, G., Weiser, M.: Of moles and men: the design of foot controls for workstations. ACM SIGCHI Bull. **17**(4), 333–339 (1986).
15. Pearson, G., Weiser, M.: Exploratory evaluation of a planar foot-operated cursor-positioning device. In: CHI '88: Proceedings of the SIGCHI Conference on Human Factors in Computing Systems, pp. 13–18. ACM, New York (1988)
16. Ryall, K., Forlines, C., Shen, C., Morris, M.R., Everitt, K.: Experiences with and observations of direct-touch tabletops. In: TABLETOP '06: Proceedings of the First IEEE International Workshop on Horizontal Interactive Human–Computer Systems, pp. 89–96. IEEE Computer Society, Washington, DC (2006)
17. Schöning, J., Hecht, B., Raubal, M., Krüger, A., Marsh, M., Rohs, M.: Improving interaction with virtual globes through spatial thinking: Helping users ask "Why?". In: IUI '08: Proceedings of the 13th Annual ACM Conference on Intelligent User Interfaces. ACM, New York (2008)
18. Schöning, J., Daiber, F., Rohs, M., Krüger, A.: Using hands and feet to navigate and manipulate spatial data. In: CHI '09: CHI '09 Extended Abstracts on Human Factors in Computing Systems. ACM, New York (2009)
19. Sibert, L.E., Jacob, R.J.K.: Evaluation of eye gaze interaction. In: CHI '00: Proceedings of the SIGCHI Conference on Human Factors in Computing Systems, pp. 281–288. ACM, New York, NY, USA (2000)
20. Smith, J.D., Graham, T.C.N.: Use of eye movements for video game control. In: ACE '06: Proceedings of the 2006 ACM SIGCHI International Conference on Advances in Computer Entertainment Technology, p. 20. ACM, New York (2006)
21. Tanriverdi, V., Jacob, R.J.K.: Interacting with eye movements in virtual environments. In: CHI '00: Proceedings of the SIGCHI Conference on Human Factors in Computing Systems, pp. 265–272. ACM, New York (2000)
22. tobii X60 Eye Tracker. http://www.tobii.com/market_research_usability/products_services/eye_tr%acking_hardware/tobii_x120_eye_tracker.aspx. Accessed Oct 2010
23. UNIGIS. Guidelines for Best Practice in User Interface for GIS: ESPRIT/ESSI project no. 21580. (1998)
24. Wasinger, R., Stahl, C., Krüger, A.: M3I in a pedestrian navigation & exploration system. In: Human–Computer Interaction with Mobile Devices and Services: 5th International Symposium, Mobile Hci 2003, Udine, Italy, 8–11 September 2003: Proceedings (2003)
25. Wii Ballance Board. e3nin.nintendo.com/wii_fit.html. Accessed Oct 2010
26. Wilson, A.D., Izadi, S., Hilliges, O., Garcia-Mendoza, A., Kirk, D.: Bringing physics to the surface. In: UIST '08: Proceedings of the 21st Annual ACM Symposium on User Interface Software and Technology, pp. 67–76. ACM, New York (2008)
27. Wobbrock, J.O., Morris, M.R., Wilson, A.D.: User-defined gestures for surface computing. In: CHI '09: Proceedings of the 27th International Conference on Human Factors in Computing Systems, pp. 1083–1092. ACM, New York (2009)
28. World Wind Java SDK. http://worldwind.arc.nasa.gov/java/. Accessed Oct 2010
29. Wu, M., Balakrishnan, R.: Multi-finger and whole hand gestural interaction techniques for multi-user tabletop displays. In: Proceedings of the 16th Annual ACM Symposium on User Interface Software and Technology, pp. 193–202. ACM, New York (2003)
30. Wu, M., Shen, C., Ryall, K., Forlines, C., Balakrishnan, R.: Gesture registration, relaxation, and reuse for multi-point direct-touch surfaces. In: TABLETOP '06: Proceedings of the First IEEE International Workshop on Horizontal Interactive Human-Computer Systems, pp. 185–192. IEEE Computer Society, Washington, DC (2006)
31. Zhai, S.: Human performance in six degree of freedom input control. Ph.D. thesis, University of Toronto, Toronto (1995)

Index

D. England (ed.), *Whole Body Interaction*, Human-Computer Interaction Series,
DOI 10.1007/978-0-85729-433-3, © Springer-Verlag London Limited 2011